MARKETING CASES

1850

MARKETING CASES

Second Edition

CHARLES W. LAMB, JR.

Texas Christian University

O. C. FERRELL

Texas A & M University

WILLIAM M. PRIDE

Texas A & M University

Houghton Mifflin Company   **Boston**

Dallas   Geneva, Illinois   Hopewell, New Jersey   Palo Alto

To
Christine and Jennifer Lamb
Mary and Jim Ferrell
Jack and Grace Burkett

Printed in the U.S.A.

Library of Congress Catalog Card Number: 84-82502

ISBN: 0-395-36289-X

ABCDEFGHI-H-8987654

CONTENTS

PREFACE

The application of marketing concepts and techniques is often described as a combination of art and science. Decision making in marketing is a skill that is developed over time through practice. The purpose of *Marketing Cases* is to provide students with an opportunity to develop marketing skills by applying marketing concepts and techniques to real business problems. It is intended to be used as a learning tool to bridge the gap between academic analysis and practical application of information. Cases provide students with an opportunity to use their knowledge and skills in identifying problems, analyzing alternatives, and developing strategies to deal with a wide range of opportunities and problems faced by marketing decision makers.

Marketing Cases illustrates a broad range of situations in many different industries. Students are exposed to problems and opportunities faced by marketers of consumer and industrial products, domestic and multinational companies, manufacturers and distributors, firms marketing goods and services, profit and nonprofit organizations, and both large and small firms. The cases are organized into nine parts that generally reflect the organization of marketing textbooks. The first part, "The Analysis of Marketing Opportunities," includes cases addressing fundamental marketing management issues, forecasting, consumer behavior, and marketing research. Parts Two through Five include cases dealing with a variety of problems and opportunities regarding product, distribution, promotion, and pricing decisions. The sixth part gives students the opportunity to wrestle with some difficult environmental issues that affect marketing decisions. Part Seven provides cases in marketing management and strategy. Cases in Part Eight reflect unique problems faced by industrial, international, nonprofit, and service marketers. The final section includes three comprehensive cases.

The cases included in this book range from short to medium in length and vary somewhat in difficulty. Some are best suited for emphasizing and reinforcing basic marketing concepts whereas others will challenge students to analyze situations and develop creative solutions based on sound fundamental marketing knowledge.

This casebook is an appropriate ancillary for a variety of courses. Many adopters of the first edition found it useful in illustrating practical business applications of marketing knowledge in introductory marketing courses. Others found it particularly helpful in the second level marketing management course. Another group of colleagues reported that they used *Marketing Cases* in conjunction with other texts in capstone undergraduate or MBA core courses.

Users of the first edition of *Marketing Cases* will find similarities and changes in this edition. The book is again organized into parts that generally reflect the organization of many marketing textbooks. Each case is still followed by an analysis form that presents a series of structural questions with ample space for students to respond. These forms are perforated and can easily be removed. This feature encourages and facilitates grading of written analyses, enabling even those instructors with large sections to expose students to case analysis. However, the structural forms should not inhibit instructors from using the traditional approach to case analysis. In small sections or advanced courses instructors may wish to require students to identify the case problem, propose and evaluate alternatives, and recommend and defend solutions. Blank analysis forms are included in the back of the book for this purpose as well as for students to use when they require additional space to respond to the questions following each case.

Based on suggestions from users of the first edition of *Marketing Cases*, we have made several changes. We increased the total number of cases from 32 to 37 to provide more choices and variety. Over half of the cases in the text are new to this edition. A new part, "Comprehensive Cases," addresses the full range of decisions that must be addressed by marketing decision makers. We have added more of the longer, somewhat more rigorous cases with quantitative or financial data to this edition. Also, because most textbook examples focus on large well-known corporations, we have included more cases depicting marketing problems or decisions facing smaller organizations.

Several people were particularly helpful in the development of this edition of *Marketing Cases*. These include the case authors who are acknowledged on the following page, many users of the first edition who offered suggestions and guidance, our colleagues at Texas Christian University, Texas A&M University, and elsewhere, and Bill Setten and others at Houghton Mifflin Company. Special thanks to Patricia Townsend, Edna Beatty, Sharon Lamb, and Kathy Rubin for typing, proofreading, editing, and helping out as needed in the development of this book.

We invite comments, questions, or criticisms from instructors and students. We want to do our best to provide the best teaching/learning vehicle possible. Your input will be sincerely appreciated.

C. W. L.
O. C. F.
W. M. P.

CONTRIBUTORS

We are indebted to many friends and colleagues for permitting us to include their work in this collection. It is with much appreciation that these individuals are acknowledged for their contributions to this book.

ROY D. ADLER
JANELLE C. ASHLEY
DANNY BELLENGER
RICHARD F. BELTRAMINI
KENNETH BERNHARDT
JAMES D. BLASER
JACK BRITNEY
EDWARD C. BURSK
JAN E. CARLSON
STEPHEN B. CASTLEBERRY
MAURICE G. CLABAUGH
THOMAS J. COSSÉ
HAZEL S. EZELL
RON FRANZMEIER
DANIEL FREEMAN
JANE G. FUNK
THOMAS F. FUNK
O. HOYT GIBSON
THOMAS D. GIESE
GEORGE B. GLISAN
ALLAN GOWAN
STEPHEN A. GREYSER
THOMAS INGRAM
A. H. KIZILBASH

DONNA LEGG
DAVID LOUDON
DEBRA LOW
MAURICE I. MANDELL
J. BARRY MASON
MORRIS L. MAYER
DAVID MCCONAUGHY
MARTIN MEYERS
FRED L. MILLER
PATRICK E. MURPHY
PHILLIP B. NIFFENEGGER
CHARLES H. PATTI
LARRY M. ROBINSON
LARRY J. ROSENBERG
DON E. SCHULTZ
DENISE SMART
ROBERT H. SOLOMON
NANCY STEPHENS
IAN STEWART
JAMES L. TAYLOR
JOE THOMAS
MARK TRAXLER
TERRY TRUDEAU
BERT VALENCIA

MARKETING CASES

PART ONE

THE ANALYSIS OF MARKETING STRATEGIES

CASE 1

THE ELECTRIC FEATHER PIROGUE

The Fin and Feather Products Company of Marshall, Texas, produces a line of small, versatile, lightweight boats called the Electric Feather Pirogue (pronounced pē rō). The term *feather* was chosen to emphasize the light weight of the boat and *electric* because it is propelled by an electric trolling motor. The name Pirogue refers to the historic small riverboats used on the Louisiana bayous. The kayak-shaped boat is 12 feet long, 38 inches wide, and 12 inches deep. It comes complete with motor and has a load capacity of about 540 pounds. Power is provided by a standard 12-volt automotive-type storage battery. The built-in Shakespeare motor is available with 18-pound or 24-pound thrust. The hull is handcrafted fiberglass, sturdily constructed by a hand-layup process.

The stable, flat-bottomed Pirogue can operate in very shallow water, so it is ideally suited for fishing, duck hunting, bird watching, or just leisurely stream cruising. The propeller is protected from submerged objects by specially engineered motor guards on each side of the exposed drive unit. A 1½-inch sheet of polyurethane foam is built into the bottom to provide flotation. The boat is extremely simple to operate. A panel just below the wraparound gunwale contains two control switches—a forward–off–reverse switch and a low–medium–high speed switch. A horizontal lever just above the panel provides steering control. There is only one moving part in the entire control system. The three-speed, 18-pound thrust motor has a maximum speed of 10 miles an hour, and the four-speed, 24-pound thrust motor

This case was prepared by Robert H. Solomon and Janelle C. Ashley of Stephen F. Austin State University as a basis for class discussion.

Courtesy of Fin and Feather Products, Inc.

can attain a speed of 14 miles an hour. The company furnishes a one-year unlimited warranty on the boat, and the Shakespeare Company provides a similar warranty on the motor.

The company produced only one basic model of the boat but offered optional equipment that provided some variation within the product line. Retail prices ranged from approximately $490 to $650 depending on motor size and optional equipment. Although designed to accommodate two people, the standard model has only one molded plastic seat. The second seat, deluxe swivel seats, marine carpeting, and tonneau cover are the major optional items. No trailer is required because the boat fits nicely on the roof of even the smallest car or in the back of a station wagon or pickup truck. Without battery, the Pirogue weighs only about 80 pounds and can easily be handled by one person.

In year 1 (the base year), Mr. Bill Wadlington purchased controlling interest in, and assumed managerial control of, the seven-year-old Fin and Feather Products Company. One of Mr. Wadlington's first moves was to adopt a strict cash-and-carry policy; supplies and equipment were paid for at the time of purchase, and all sales were for cash prior to shipment whether shipment was to a dealer or directly to a customer. All shipments were F.O.B. the factory in Marshall, Texas. As a result of this policy, the firm had no accounts receivable and virtually no accounts payable. Mr. Wadlington anticipated sales of between 800 and 1000 units in year 1. This volume would approach plant capacity and produce a wholesale dollar volume of approximately $350,000 to $400,000. After only six months of operation Mr. Wadlington would not predict an exact annual net profit figure, but he was very optimistic about the first year's profit prospect. It was also difficult to predict exactly what future volume would be, but sales had shown a steady increase throughout the first half of the year. The flow of inquiries from around the United States and from several foreign countries made the future look bright.

The company hired no outside salespeople, and Mr. Wadlington was the only in-house salesman. There were 15 independent dealers around the country who bought at wholesale and assume a standard markup. There was no formal agreement or contract between the company and the dealers, but to qualify as a dealer, an individual or firm's initial order had to be for at least five boats. Subsequent orders could be for any quantity desired. Dealers' orders had to be accompanied by a check for the entire amount of the purchase.

In addition to the dealers, the company had 20 agents who were authorized to take orders in areas outside the dealer territories. These agents accepted orders for direct shipment to customers and were paid a commission for the boats they sold. Agents were not assigned a specific territory but could not sell in the areas assigned to dealers. As with all sales, agent orders had to be prepaid. Direct orders from individuals were accepted at the factory when the customer lived outside a dealer territory. Most direct sales were the result of the company's advertisements in such magazines as *Ducks Unlimited, Outdoor Life, Argosy, Field and Stream,* and *Better Homes and Gardens.*

Mr. Wadlington had not established a systematic promotional program. The services of an out-of-state advertising agency were used to develop and place ads and to help with brochures and other promotional materials. Almost all negotiations with the agency were handled by phone or mail. The amount of advertising done at any time depended on existing sales volume. As sales declined, advertising was increased; when orders approached plant capacity, advertising was curtailed. Magazines were the primary advertising medium used. The dealers and agents were provided with attractive, professionally prepared brochures. The company had exhibited, or had plans to exhibit, at boat shows in Texas, Ohio, and Illinois. Arrangements had been completed for Pirogues to be used as prizes on one of the more popular network game shows.

A detailed analysis of sales, in terms of who was buying the boats and for what purpose, had not been made. However, Mr. Wadlington did know that one of the most successful ads was in *Better Homes and Gardens*. An examination of orders produced by the ad indicated that they were primarily from women who were buying the boat for family use. There had been reports of the boats being used as utility boats for large houseboats and yachts, but the extent of such use was unknown. Although orders had been coming in from all parts of the country, the best sales areas in 1979 were in the eastern and southeastern parts of the United States. Mr. Wadlington attributed this, at least in part, to the fact that the company's past sales efforts had been concentrated almost exclusively in the southern and southwestern areas of the country. After the company began using national media, totally new markets were tapped. The Pirogue had virtually no direct competition, particularly outside the Texas-Louisiana area.

CASE ANALYSIS

CASE 1

The Electric Feather Pirogue

1. In your opinion, who are the most likely customer target groups for boats like the Pirogue?

_____

_____

_____

_____

_____

_____

_____

_____

_____

_____

_____

2. Analyze the firm's current distribution system. Can you suggest ways in which it might be improved?

_____

_____

_____

_____

_____

_____

_____

_____

_____

_____

_____

_____

_____

_____

_____

_____

_____

_____

_____

_____

_____

_____

_____

_____

_____

_____

_____

_____

_____

_____

3.   Suggest other types of promotion that Mr. Wadlington might find profitable. Do you think the heavy dependence on magazine advertising is wise? Why or why not?

_____

_____

_____

_____

_____

_____

_____

4.   Do you agree with the practice of scheduling advertising only when sales volume is below plant capacity? Defend your answer.

_____

_____

_____

_____

_____

_____

_____

5.   Do you agree with Mr. Wadlington's policy of requiring that all or-
     ders, even from dealers or agents, be fully paid for before shipment?
     What changes, if any, would you suggest?

_____

_____

_____

_____

_____

_____

_____

_____

_____

6.   What data would Mr. Wadlington find useful for analyzing the effec-
     tiveness of his marketing program? How might he obtain these data?

_____

_____

7.   Mr. Wadlington is opposed to changing his present marketing system. He contends that the plan is working because sales are strong and profit is satisfactory, and he asks, "Why change a winner?" How would you respond to his question?

CASE 2

PANTRY MARKETS

Pantry Markets is a medium-sized southeastern grocery chain head-quartered in Tampa, Florida. Sales for the chain have been growing at an average rate of 20% per annum; the chain opened four new stores last year. Although Mr. Carl Royal, president of Pantry Markets, is modest about his achievements, the grocery chain has been increasingly recognized as a strong competitor in several markets.

"In a nutshell," Mr. Royal says, "our marketing strategy over the years has been to give our customers value for their money and known quality products. We are not like these modern discount supermarkets or warehouse grocers. We provide a nice self-service supermarket atmosphere. Being a small chain is not easy. We have to strive for a concentrated strategy among segments of the market where Pantry Markets can satisfy customer needs better than anybody else. We're looking for markets where we have a competitive advantage. So far we have found our market segment among the 'middles'; middle class, middle aged, and the middle stages of the family life cycle."

A "new" market awakening

Five months ago, Mr. Royal attended a Latin Market Seminar in Miami which generated some serious thinking. In his own words: "The seminar was an awakening event. I knew these Spanish people were out there in many of my markets, but never realized how important they were. I guess I had Spanish market myopia."

This case was prepared by Bert Valencia and Danny Bellenger, Texas Tech University.

17

Courtesy of Peter Menzel/Stock, Boston

Some of the key facts that made Mr. Royal reappraise Pantry Markets' marketing strategy toward Hispanics were as follows:

1. Latin households in Dade County, Miami, spent 30% more per week on groceries than Anglos. In 1980 the median weekly grocery expenditures among Latins was $87.23, whereas the same figure for Anglos was $66.99.[1]
2. In 1980 about one-fourth of all Latin households spent more than $100 on groceries per week, whereas only 15% of Anglo households did.[1]
3. Six out of seven Latin households had patronized, at least once, an American chain supermarket during the past month.[1]

[1] Strategy Research Corporation, *The Dade Latin Market 1980*. Miami: Strategy Research Corporation, 1980.

4. The Miami area had 767,000 Latins. The Tampa–St. Petersburg area itself had 133,200 Latins.[2]

Altogether there are nearly one half million Latin households or 1.5 million Latin people in the Southeast.

In the past, Pantry Markets had in a sense neglected the Latin market. Top executives, including Mr. Royal, perceived that Latins were not an essential part of their customer base. They thought that Latins tended to buy their groceries from the Cuban *bodegas* (small mom-and-pop neighborhood stores) that cater to their ethnic taste. Any efforts to reach Latins had come from store managers who had to deal with the Latin presence in their stores. Managers of stores located in Latin enclaves typically tried to recruit Spanish-speaking clerks and cashiers, and they bought some ethnic products (i.e., black beans and Cuban coffee) from local Cuban wholesalers.

Over the five months following the Latin Market Seminar several things took place. First, a top management meeting was called by Mr. Royal to discuss the key facts about the Latin market and to plan a strategy for taking advantage of this market opportunity. In the meeting it was decided that the Latin market was definitely worth exploring and that Ms. Linda Guzman should develop an action plan. Ms. Guzman suggested that she should interview store managers in the affected areas and that a secondary data search be undertaken. If things looked good after these two steps, a study would be commissioned to fill in the information gaps and provide a basis for a formal strategy. Top management was supportive of this action plan.

The store managers' input

Store managers from the locations with heavy Latin traffic were interviewed by Ms. Guzman. They were all very pleased to see that top management was willing to research the Latin market, a market that they had been dealing with in their own ways. Each store manager volunteered to do a Latin traffic count to find out how many Latins shopped in their stores. However, they were all in agreement that they knew very little about the way Latins shopped for groceries. They could not answer such questions as, What are the general shopping orientations of Latins? Are they brand-name shoppers? Are they impulsive shoppers? Are they quality conscious shoppers?

[2]Marc Watanabe, "Hispanic Marketing: A Profile Grows to New Heights," *Advertising Age* (April 6, 1981), Section 2, pp. 5, 22–24.

Secondary research input

The secondary data search had two purposes. The first was to produce a demographic profile of the Latin market. The second was to find examples of how other supermarkets had been successful in reaching this ethnic market.

Demographic profile

The most relevant characteristic of Latins in the Southeast is that they are Cuban. Roughly seven out of eight Latins in this area are of Cuban origin. The rest are from Spain, Puerto Rico, Mexico, and other Central and South American countries. They are geographically clustered particularly in Miami, and to a lesser extent in Tampa–St. Petersburg, Atlanta, Orlando, and Jacksonville.

The Cuban influence in Miami is so pervasive that a section of the downtown is called "Little Havana." Local shops in this part of "Cuba in exile" often have signs in the front entrance reading "We speak English." Thus, it is not unusual for tourists in Miami to feel that they are in a foreign country, though on American soil.

The summary profile for Latins compared to Anglos in Miami for 1980 is presented below.

	Latins	Anglos
Average household size	3.6 persons	2.6 persons
Median age	34.7 years	36.1 years
HOH occupation		
Blue collar	37%	43%
White collar	44%	35%
Other	18%	22%
Median education	11.4 years	11.8 years
Household income per year	$22,356	$26,928

Source: Strategy Research Corporation, *The Dade Latin Market 1980.* Miami: Strategy Research Corporation, 1980.

Strategic examples

Two examples are relevant: A&P's promotional strategy and E&B supermarkets in New York.

A&P is known to many Hispanics as *Amigo del Pueblo* (friend of the people). The promotional campaign stressed friendliness, backed by community involvement in ethnic events and minority scholarships.

E&B supermarkets in New York had grown from a small grocery store to an eight-store chain by targeting Hispanics. They accomplished this success by meeting the demand for Spanish ethnic products and staffing stores with Spanish-speaking personnel. The manager or assistant manager in each store had to be fluent in Spanish. E&B was also supportive of the Latin community.

In summary, the secondary research indicated to Ms. Guzman that the Latin market fits in well with Pantry Markets' original market segment, the "middles" (middle class, middle aged, and middle stages of the family life cycle). It also indicated the need for Spanish-language promotion, Spanish-speaking personnel, and Spanish-oriented community involvement. Perhaps even a Spanish term to stand for Pantry Markets could be developed.

Ms. Guzman was not satisfied. She felt a market research study of Latin shopping orientations was needed. Such a study was conducted and the details are provided below.

The Latin shopping orientations study

From a practical standpoint, shopping orientations help the retailer in several ways. Shopping orientations can be used by retailers as a basis for retail planning. The merchandise mix, retail service mix, pricing mix, promotional mix, and other retail decisions can be used on the shopping orientations.

Research methodology

A total of 220 mall intercept interviews were conducted with an equal number of Latins and Anglos. To ensure adequate representation of working women, interviews were conducted after 4 P.M. on weekdays and on Saturdays. The Latin sample was interviewed in either Spanish or English according to the interviewees' wishes. Overall, the researchers felt that the sample demographics were in general agreement with the population demographics.

The shopping styles were measured on twenty different orientation dimensions using a five-point Likert scale. Respondents were asked to indicate whether they strongly agree, agree, are indifferent or don't know, disagree, or strongly disagree with each of the statements read to them. Responses were coded from 1 to 5, respectively, and an average was computed for each ethnic group. Details are provided in Exhibit 2–1.

Developing a strategy

Ms. Guzman is now faced with the task of developing a strategy for Pantry Markets to capture the Latin market. A top-level management meeting is set for next week where she has been asked to present her recommendation.

Exhibit 2–1
Latin versus Anglo shopping orientations

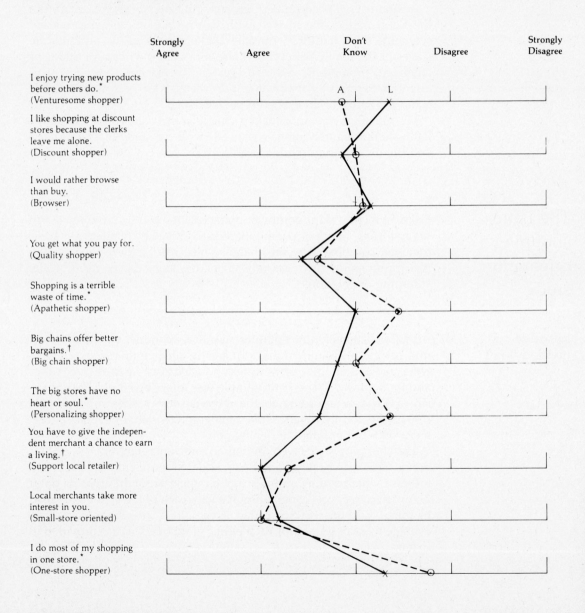

L = Latins; A = Anglos

*F-statistic is significant at the .05 level or lower.
†F-statistic is significant at the .10 level or lower.

Exhibit 2–1 *(cont.)*

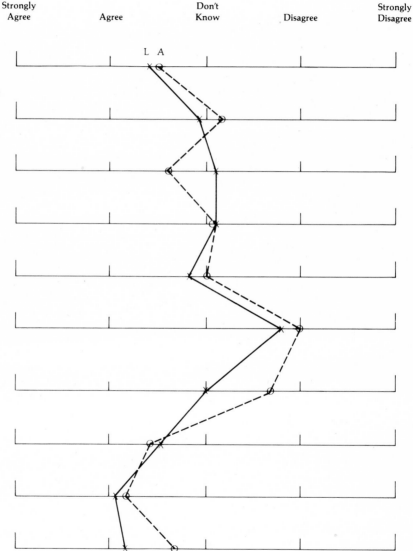

L=Latins; A=Anglos

*F-statistic is significant at the .05 level or lower.
†F-statistic is significant at the .10 level or lower.

CASE ANALYSIS

CASE 2

Pantry
Markets

1. On the basis of the available data, what are the primary differences
    between Hispanics and Anglos?

    _____

    _____

    _____

    _____

    _____

    _____

    _____

2. What similarities can be presumed from the research data?

    _____

    _____

    _____

    _____

    _____

    _____

    _____

3.   What retail strategy alterations are suggested by the research findings?

_____

_____

_____

_____

_____

_____

_____

_____

_____

_____

_____

_____

_____

_____

_____

_____

_____

_____

_____

_____

_____

_____

_____

_____

_____

4. Is it reasonable to segment the market by ethnic origin?

_____

_____

_____

_____

_____

_____

_____

_____

_____

_____

5.   What steps should be taken to remedy the Spanish market myopia?

_____

_____

_____

_____

_____

_____

_____

CASE 3

MODERN PLASTICS

Institutional Sales Manager Jim Clayton had spent most of Monday morning planning for the rest of the month. It was early July and Jim knew that an extremely busy time was coming with the preparation of the following year's sales plan.

Since starting his current job less than a month ago, Jim had been involved in learning the requirements of the job and making his initial territory visits. Now that he was getting settled, Jim was trying to plan his activities according to priorities. The need for planning had been instilled in him during his college days. As a result of his three years of field sales experience and development of time management skills, he felt prepared for the challenge of the sales manager's job.

While sitting at his desk, Jim recalled a conversation that he had a week ago with Bill Hanson, the former manager, who had been promoted to another division. Bill told him that the sales forecast (annual and monthly) for plastic trash bags in the Southeast region would be due soon as an initial step toward developing the sales plan for next year. Bill had laughed as he told him, "Boy, you ought to have a ball doing the forecast being a rookie sales manager!"

When Jim had asked what Bill meant, he explained by saying that the forecast was often "winged" because the headquarters in Chicago already knew what they wanted and would change the forecast to meet their figures, particularly if the forecast was for an increase of

This case was prepared by Thomas Ingram, Danny Bellenger, and Kenneth Bernhardt, Georgia State University, as a basis for class discussion rather than to illustrate either effective or ineffective handling of an administrative situation. All publication rights reserved. Copyright © 1977 by Danny N. Bellenger and Kenneth L. Bernhardt.

less than 10%. The experienced sales manager could throw numbers together in a short time that would pass as a serious forecast and ultimately be adjusted to fit the plans of headquarters. However, he felt an inexperienced manager would have a difficult time "winging" a credible forecast.

Bill had also told Jim that the other alternative meant gathering mountains of data and putting together a forecast that could be sold to the various levels of Modern Plastics management. This alternative would prove to be time-consuming and could still be changed anywhere along the chain of command before final approval.

Clayton started reviewing pricing and sales volume history (see Exhibit 3–1). He also looked at the key account performance for the past two and a half years (see Exhibit 3–2). During the past month Clayton had visited many of the key accounts, and on the average they had indicated that their purchases from Modern would probably increase about 15–20% in the coming year.

Schedule for preparing the forecast

Jim had received a memo recently from Robert Baxter, the Regional Marketing Manager, detailing the plans for completing the 1978 forecast. The key dates in the memo began in only three weeks:

August 1	—Presentation of forecast to Regional Marketing Manager
August 10	—Joint presentation with Marketing Manager to Regional General Manager
September 1	—Regional General Manager presents forecast to Division Vice-President
September 1–30	—Review of forecast by staff of Division Vice-President
October 1	—Review forecast with corporate staff
October 1–15	—Revision as necessary
October 15	—Final forecast forwarded to Division Vice-President from Regional General Manager

Company background

The Plastics Division of Modern Chemical Company was founded in 1965 when Modern Chemical purchased Cordco, a small plastics manufacturer with national sales of $15 million. At that time, the key products of the Plastics Division were sandwich bags, plastic table-cloths, trash cans and plastic-coated clothesline.

Exhibit 3–1
Plastic trash bags
Sales and pricing history, 1975–1977

	Pricing: Dollars per case THIS SUCKS!			Sales volume in cases			Sales volume in dollars		
	1975	1976	1977	1975	1976	1977	1975	1976	1977
January	$6.88	$ 7.70	$15.40	33,000	46,500	36,500	$ 227,000	$ 358,000	$ 562,000
February	6.82	7.70	14.30	32,500	52,500	23,000	221,500	404,000	329,000
March	6.90	8.39	13.48	32,000	42,000	22,000	221,000	353,000	296,500
April	6.88	10.18	12.24	45,500	42,500	46,500	313,000	432,500	569,000
May	6.85	12.38	11.58	49,000	41,500	45,500	335,500	514,000	527,000
June	6.85	12.65	10.31	47,500	47,000	42,000	325,500	594,500	433,000
July	7.42	13.48	9.90[E]	40,000	43,500	47,500[E]	297,000	586,500	470,000[E]
August	6.90	13.48	10.18[E]	48,500	63,500	43,500[E]	334,500	856,000	443,000[E]
September	7.70	14.30	10.31[E]	43,000	49,000	47,500[E]	331,000	700,500	489,500[E]
October	7.56	15.12	10.31[E]	52,500	50,000	51,000[E]	397,000	756,000	526,000[E]
November	7.15	15.68	10.72[E]	62,000	61,500	47,500[E]	443,500	964,500	509,000[E]
December	7.42	15.43	10.59[E]	49,000	29,000	51,000[E]	363,500	447,500	540,000[E]
Average	$7.11	$12.21	$11.61						
Total				534,500	568,500	503,500	$3,810,000	$6,967,000	$5,694,000

[E]July–December 1977 figures are forecasts of Sales Manager J. A. Clayton and other data come from historical sales information.

Exhibit 3–2
1977 Key account sales history (in cases)

Customer	1975	1976	1st 6 months 1977	1975 monthly avg.	1976 monthly avg.	1st half 1977 monthly avg.	1st qtr. 1977 monthly avg.
Transco Paper Company	125,774	134,217	44,970	10,481	11,185	7,495	5,823
Callaway Paper	44,509	46,049	12,114	3,709	3,837	2,019	472
Florida Janitorial Supply	34,746	36,609	20,076	2,896	3,051	3,346	2,359
Jefferson	30,698	34,692	25,044	2,558	2,891	4,174	1,919
Cobb Paper	13,259	23,343	6,414	1,105	1,945	1,069	611
Miami Paper	10,779	22,287	10,938	900	1,857	1,823	745
Milne Surgical Company	23,399	21,930	—	1,950	1,828	—	—
Graham	8,792	15,331	1,691	733	1,278	281	267
Crawford Paper	7,776	14,132	6,102	648	1,178	1,017	1,322
John Steele	8,634	13,277	6,663	720	1,106	1,110	1,517
Henderson Paper	9,185	8,850	2,574	765	738	429	275
Durant Surgical	—	7,766	4,356	—	647	726	953
Master Paper	4,221	5,634	600	352	470	100	—
D.T.A.	—	—	2,895	—	—	482	—
Crane Paper	4,520	5,524	3,400	377	460	566	565
Janitorial Service	3,292	5,361	2,722	274	447	453	117
Georgia Paper	5,466	5,053	2,917	456	421	486	297
Paper Supplies, Inc.	5,117	5,119	1,509	426	427	251	97
Southern Supply	1,649	3,932	531	137	328	88	78
Horizon Hospital Supply	4,181	4,101	618	348	342	103	206
Total cases	346,007	413,217	156,134	28,835	34,436	26,018	17,623

Since 1965, the Plastics Division has grown to a sales level exceeding $200 million with five regional profit centers covering the United States. Each regional center has manufacturing facilities and a regional sales force. There are three product groups in each region:

(1) Food Packaging —PVC meat film, plastic bags for various food products
(2) Institutional —Plastic trash bags and disposable tableware (plates, bowls, etc.)
(3) Industrial —Case overwrap film, heavy duty fertilizer packaging bags, plastic film for use in pallet overwrap systems

Each product group is supervised jointly by a product manager and a district sales manager, both of whom report to the regional marketing manager. The sales representatives report directly to the district sales manager but also work closely with the product manager on matters concerning pricing and product specifications.

The five regional general managers report to Mr. J. R. Hughes, Vice-President of the Plastics Division. Mr. Hughes is located in Chicago. Although Modern Chemical is owned by a multi-national paper company, the Plastics Division has been able to operate in a virtually independent manner since its establishment in 1965. The reasons for this include:

(1) Limited knowledge of the plastic industry on the part of the paper company management.
(2) Excellent growth by the Plastics Division has been possible without management supervision from the paper company.
(3) Profitability of the Plastics Division has consistently been higher than that of other divisions of the chemical company.

The institutional trash bag market

The institutional trash bag is a polyethylene bag used to collect and transfer refuse to its final disposition point. There are different sizes and colors available to fit the various uses of the bag. For example, a small bag for desk wastebaskets is available as well as a heavier bag for large containers such as a fifty-five gallon drum. There are twenty-five sizes in the Modern line with thirteen of those sizes being available in three colors—white, buff, and clear. Customers typically buy several different items on an order to cover all their needs.

The institutional trash bag is a separate product from the consumer grade trash bag which is typically sold to homeowners through retail outlets. The institutional trash bag is sold primarily through paper wholesalers, hospital supply companies and janitorial supply companies to a variety of end users. Since trash bags are used on such a wide scale, the list of end users could include almost any business or institution. The segments include hospitals, hotels, schools, office buildings, transportation facilities and restaurants.

Based on historical data and a current survey of key wholesalers and end users in the Southeast, the annual market of institutional trash bags in the region was estimated to be fifty-five million pounds. Translated into cases, the market potential was close to two million cases. During the past five years, the market for trash bags has grown at an average rate of 89% per year. Now a mature product, future market growth is expected to parallel overall growth in the economy. The 1978 real growth in GNP is forecast to be 4.5%.

General market conditions

The current market is characterized by a distressing trend. The market is in a position of oversupply with approximately twenty manufacturers competing for the business in the Southeast. Prices have been on the decline for several months, but are expected to level out during the last six months of the year.

This problem arose after a record year in 1976 for Modern Plastics. During 1976, supply was very tight due to raw material shortages. Unlike many of its competitors, Modern had only minor problems securing adequate raw material supplies. As a result, the competitors were few in 1976 and all who remained in business were prosperous. By early 1977 raw materials were plentiful and prices began to drop as new competitors tried to buy their way into the market. During the first quarter of 1977 Modern Plastics learned the hard way that a competitive price was a necessity in the current market. Volume fell off drastically in February and March as customers shifted orders to new suppliers when Modern chose to maintain a slightly higher than market price on trash bags.

With the market becoming extremely price competitive and profits declining, the overall quality has dropped to a point of minimum standard. Most suppliers now make a bag "barely good enough to get the job done." It was believed that this quality level is acceptable to most buyers who do not demand high quality for this type of product.

Modern Plastics vs. competition

A recent study of Modern versus competition had been conducted by an outside consultant to see how well Modern measured up in several key areas. Each area was weighted according to its importance in the purchase decision and Modern was compared to its key competitors in each area and on an overall basis. The key factors and their weights are shown below:

	Weight
(1) Pricing	0.50
(2) Quality	0.15
(3) Breadth of line	0.10
(4) Sales coverage	0.10
(5) Packaging	0.05
(6) Service	0.10
Total	1.00

As shown in Exhibit 3–3, Modern compared favorably with its key competitors on an overall basis. None of the other suppliers were as strong as Modern in breadth of line nor did any competitor offer as good sales coverage as that provided by Modern. Clayton knew that sales coverage would be even better next year since the Florida and North Carolina territories had grown enough to add two salespeople to the current eight in the institutional group by January 1, 1978.

Pricing, quality, and packaging seemed to be neither an advantage nor a disadvantage. However, service was a problem area. The main cause for this, Clayton was told, was temporary out of stock situations which occurred occasionally primarily due to the wide variety of trash bags offered by Modern.

During the past two years, Modern Plastics had maintained its market share at approximately 27% of the market. Some new competitors had entered the market since 1975 while others had left the market (see Exhibit 3–4). The previous district sales manager, Bill Hanson, had left Clayton some comments regarding the major competitors. These are reproduced in Exhibit 3–5.

Developing the sales forecast

After a careful study of trade journals, government statistics and surveys conducted by Modern marketing research personnel, projections for growth potential were formulated by segment and are shown in Exhibit 3–6. These data were compiled by Bill Hanson just before he was promoted.

Exhibit 3–3
Competitive factors ratings by competitor*

Weight	Factor	Modern	National Film	Bonanza	Southeastern	PBI	BAGCO	Southwest Bag	Florida Plastics	East Coast Bag Co.
.50	Price	2	3	2	2	2	2	2	2	3
.15	Quality	3	2	3	4	3	2	3	3	4
.10	Breadth	1	2	2	3	3	3	3	3	3
.10	Sales coverage	1	3	3	3	4	3	3	4	3
.05	Packaging	3	3	2	3	3	1	3	3	3
.10	Service	4	3	3	2	2	2	3	4	3

Overall weighted ranking**

(1) BAGCO	2.15		(6) Southeastern	2.55
(2) Modern	2.20		(7) Florida Plastics	2.60
(3) Bonanza	2.25		(8) National Film	2.65
(4) Southwest Bag (Tie)	2.50		(9) East Coast Bag	3.15
(5) PBI (Tie)	2.50			

*Ratings on a 1 to 5 scale with 1 being the best rating and 5 the worst.
**The weighted ranking is the sum of each rank times its weight. The lower the number, the better the overall rating.

Jim looked back at Baxter's memo giving the time schedule for the forecast and knew he had to get started. As he left the office at 7:15 he wrote himself a large note and pinned it on his wall—"Get Started on the Sales Forecast!"

Exhibit 3–4
Market share by supplier 1975 and 1976

Supplier	% of market 1975	% of market 1976
National Film	11	12
Bertram	16	0*
Bonanza	11	12
Southeastern	5	6
Bay	9	0*
Johnson Graham	8	0*
PBI	2	5
Lewis	2	0*
BAGCO	—	6
Southwest Bag	—	2
Florida Plastics	—	4
East Coast Bag Co.	—	4
Miscellaneous & unknown	8	22
Modern	28	27
Total	100	100

*Out of business in 1976.
Source: This information was developed from a field survey conducted by Modern Plastics.

**Exhibit 3–5
Characteristics of
competitors**

National Film	Broadest product line in the industry. Quality a definite advantage. Good service. Sales coverage adequate, but not an advantage. Not as aggressive as most suppliers on price. Strong competitor.
Bonanza	Well established tough competitor. Very aggressive on pricing. Good packaging, quality okay.
Southeastern	Extremely price competitive in Southern Florida. Dominates Miami market. Limited product line. Not a threat outside of Florida.
PBI	Extremely aggressive on price. Have made inroads into Transco Paper Company during 1977. Good service but poor sales coverage.
BAGCO	New competitor in 1977. Very impressive with a high quality product, excellent service, and strong sales coverage. A real threat, particularly in Florida.
Southwest Bag	A factor in Louisiana and Mississippi. Their strategy is simple—an acceptable product at a rock bottom price.
Florida Plastics	Active when market is at a profitable level with price cutting. When market declines to a low profit range, Florida manufactures other types of plastic packaging and stays out of the trash bag market. Poor reputation as a reliable supplier, but can still "spot-sell" at low prices.
East Coast Bag	Most of their business is from a state bid which began in January 1976 for a two-year period. Not much of a threat to Modern's business in the Southeast, as most of their volume is north of Washington, D. C.

Exhibit 3–6
1978 Real growth projections by segment

Total industry	+5.0%
Commercial	+5.4%
Restaurant	+6.8%
Hotel/Motel	+2.0%
Transportation	+1.9%
Office users	+5.0%
Other	+4.2%
Non-commercial	+4.1%
Hospitals	+3.9%
Nursing Homes	+4.8%
Colleges/Universities	+2.4%
Schools	+7.8%
Employee feeding	+4.3%
Other	+3.9%

Source: Developed from several trade journals.

CASE ANALYSIS

CASE 3

Modern Plastics

1. Should Mr. Clayton use past average sales increases to prepare his 1978 forecast? Why?

_____

_____

_____

_____

_____

_____

_____

_____

_____

2. What are the advantages and disadvantages in using a survey of the sales force in this case?

_____

_____

_____

_____

_____

_____

_____

_____

_____

3.   Evaluate the "intentions to buy" data provided.

_____

_____

_____

_____

_____

_____

_____

_____

_____

4.   Is trend and cycle analysis appropriate? Why?

_____

_____

_____

_____

_____

_____

_____

_____

_____

_____

5. Would correlation analysis be an appropriate technique for Mr. Clayton to consider? Why?

_____

_____

_____

_____

_____

_____

_____

6. What do we know about the industry outlook and Modern's likely market share?

_____

_____

_____

_____

_____

_____

_____

_____

_____

_____

7.   Advise Mr. Clayton on the approach or approaches to be used.

_____

_____

_____

_____

_____

_____

_____

_____

CASE 4

JOHNSONS BUY A FOOD PROCESSOR

At 4:52 P.M. on Friday, January 19, 1983, Brock and Alisha Johnson bought a food processor. There was no doubt about it. Any observer would agree that the purchase took place at precisely that time. Or did it?

When questioned after the transaction, neither Brock nor Alisha could remember which of them at first noticed or suggested the idea of getting a food processor. They do recall that in the summer of 1981 they attended a dinner party given by a friend who specialized in French and Chinese cooking. The meal was scrumptious, and their friend Brad was very proud of the Cuisinart food processor he had used to make many of the dishes. The item was quite expensive, however, at about $200.

The following summer, Alisha noticed a comparison study of food processors in *Better Homes and Gardens.* Four different brands were compared across a number of dimensions. At about the same time, Brock noticed that *Consumer Reports* also compared a number of brands of food processors. In both instances, the Cuisinart brand came out on top. Brock had even run his own weighting schemes on some of the results, using additive, conjunctive, and disjunctive weightings on the reports of the study to confirm the Cuisinart as the top-rated brand.

Later that fall, new models of the Cuisinart were introduced and the old standard model went on sale in department stores at $140.

DO YOU NEED A FOOD PROCESSOR THIS GOOD? OUR COMPETITORS CERTAINLY DON'T THINK SO.

Not everyone thinks you need a food processor with a feed tube* so large it can accept foods as big as many whole tomatoes, onions, oranges, even Idaho potatoes—a large feed tube that lets you process food faster than ever.

Not everyone thinks you need a food processor that has an exceptionally efficient, powerful motor. A bigger bowl that lets you do more at one time. And superior blades and discs as standard equipment, including a blade for kneading dough (plus optional accessory discs that enable you to prepare dishes that appear to come from the hands of a professional chef).

Simply, not everyone thinks you need a food processor as good as the Cuisinart® DLC-7E, the finest food processor available for home use.

WHAT IF YOU REALLY DON'T NEED ONE THIS GOOD?

If you need less or want to spend less, then we suggest the second finest food processor: The Cuisinart DLC-8E. It costs less, but has the same large feed tube, a larger than standard workbowl and motor power to match. And is still perfectly worthy of the Cuisinart name.

FOR MORE INFORMATION.

We haven't compromised. If you don't want to either, write Cuisinarts, Inc., 411(H) West Putnam Avenue, Greenwich, CT 06830 for more on our food processors. We'll also be pleased to send you information on our magazine, "The Pleasures of Cooking" (for those to whom cooking is a joy, a means of expression).

*The revolutionary Cuisinart Large Feed Tube, formerly available only as part of the Large Feed Tube Accessory Kit, is now standard equipment on DLC-7E and DLC-8E models.

Cuisinart®
Food Processor

Courtesy of Dick Tarlow of Kurtz & Tarlow in collaboration with Carl Sontheimer of Cuisinarts, Inc.

The Johnsons searched occasionally for Cuisinarts in discount houses or in "wholesale showroom" catalogs, hoping to find an even lower price for the product. They were simply not offered there.

For Christmas 1982, the Johnsons traveled from Atlanta to the family home in Michigan. While there, the Johnsons received a gift of a Sunbeam Deluxe Mixer from a grandmother. While the mixer was beautiful, Alisha immediately thought how much more versatile a food processor would be. One private sentence to that effect brought immediate agreement from Brock. The box was (discretely) not opened, although many thanks were expressed. The box remained unopened the entire time the Johnsons kept the item.

Back home in Atlanta in January, Alisha again saw the $140 Cuisinart advertised by Rich's, one of the two major full-service department stores in Atlanta. Brock and Alisha visited a branch location on a Saturday afternoon, and saw the item. The salesperson, however, was not knowledgeable of its features and not very helpful in explaining its attributes. The Johnsons left, disappointed.

Two days later, Alisha called the downtown location, where she talked to Mrs. Evans, a seemingly knowledgeable salesperson who claimed to own and love exactly the model that the Johnsons had in mind. Furthermore, Mrs. Evans said that they did carry Sunbeam mixers and would make an exchange of the mixer which had been received as a gift and for which no receipt was available.

On the following Friday morning, Brock put the mixer in his car trunk when he left for work downtown. That afternoon, Alisha and six-month-old Brock, Jr., rode the bus downtown to meet her husband and to make the transaction. After meeting downtown, they drove through heavy, rainy-day traffic to Rich's to meet Mrs. Evans, who they liked as much in person as they did through telephone contact. After a brief "dry run" demonstration of the use and operation of the attachments for all of the models, the Johnsons confirmed their initial decision to take the $140 basic item. They then asked about exchanging the Sunbeam mixer that they had brought with them. "No problem," said Mrs. Evans.

After making a quick phone call, Mrs. Evans returned with bad news. Rich's had not carried that particular model of mixer. This model mixer (i.e., I-73) was a single-color model that is usually carried at discount houses, catalog sales houses, and jewelry stores. The one carried by the better department stores, such as Rich's, was a two-tone model which allowed a two-tiered pricing structure through two different channels of distribution. Mrs. Evans was sorry she could not make the exchange, but suggested that other stores such as Davison's, Richway Discount, or American Jewelers might carry the item. She even offered to allow the Johnsons to use her phone to verify the availability of the item. The Johnsons did exactly that.

Alisha dialed several of the suggested stores, looking for a retailer who carried both the Cuisinart and the Sunbeam model I-73, but she quickly learned that they were distributed through mutually exclusive distribution channels. The young man who answered the phone at American Jewelers, however, seemed friendly and helpful, and Alisha was able to obtain his agreement to take the item as a return if she could get there that afternoon.

American Jewelers was about one-half mile away. Brock volunteered to baby-sit for Brock, Jr., at Rich's while Alisha returned the mixer. She took the downtown shopper bus to American Jewelers with the still unopened mixer box under her arm.

About an hour later, Alisha returned, cold and wet, with a $57 refund. Brock, having run out of ways to entertain a six-month old, was very happy to see her. Together they bought the Cuisinart at 4:52 P.M., and proudly took it home.

CASE
ANALYSIS

CASE 4

Johnsons
Buy a Food
Processor

1. Which of the Johnsons decided to buy a food processor? The Cuisinart? Defend your answer.

_____

_____

_____

_____

_____

_____

2. When was the decision to buy made? Discuss.

_____

_____

_____

_____

_____

_____

3. What, in your opinion, was the deciding factor in purchasing the item? The particular brand?

_____

_____

_____

_____

_____

_____

4. Would you consider this purchase process to be careful and deliber-
    ate? Was it an inefficient use of time? Is it a good model to follow?

_____

_____

_____

_____

_____

_____

5. Would your answer to question 4 change if you learned that on Feb-
    ruary 19, 1983, discount stores began to sell the same model Cuisinart
    for $99.98?

_____

_____

_____

_____

_____

_____

6. You are suddenly granted perfect hindsight and are thrust into the role of Brock or Alisha (your choice) at the 1981 dinner party. How would your subsequent behavior differ from that reported here? Note: the events described in question 5 may or may not happen.

_____

_____

_____

_____

_____

_____

_____

_____

_____

CASE 5

FAMILY SERVICE, INC.

Introduction

Family Service was established in 1941 as a private nonprofit organization. In 1942, the agency obtained United Way funding for the addition of a school lunch program. Since that time the agency has undergone a series of name changes in an attempt to reflect changes in service offerings. In 1983 the agency once again operated under the name of Family Service, Inc., and its services included counseling, family life education, and home health care.

During 1983, Ann Marek, director of Community Affairs, became concerned about the community's lack of knowledge regarding available services. Before embarking on an awareness campaign, however, she felt it necessary first to assess the community's attitudes and perceptions toward Family Service as well as attitudes and perceptions toward other agencies offering similar services.

Ann arranged for a local graduate student in marketing to assist with the project. It was determined that the project would involve a market research survey of the general public with emphasis on home health services since the home health market was extremely competitive. Ann felt it was important also to survey physicians because many of Family Service's home health clients were referred by their doctors.

General public survey

Telephone interviewing yielded 184 completed interviews from a random sample of 400 names, drawn from the residence pages of the telephone directory. Respondents were first asked how they would

This case was prepared by Donna Legg, Texas A&M University.

55

rate the services provided by voluntary organizations in general. Ratings were on a scale of 1 to 5, where 5 was high and 1 was low. The results are shown in Table 5–1.

Table 5–1
Overall rating of voluntary organizations

Excellent (5)	38
Good (4)	87
Fair (3)	14
Poor (2)	1
Very poor (1)	1
No rating	43
Mean = 4.13	
Standard deviation = .781	

Respondents were then asked if they were aware of several specific organizations. Awareness did not mean knowledge of services, only that they were aware of the organizations' existence. Respondents were then asked to rate (on a scale of 1 to 5) the overall performance of all organizations of which they were aware. The results are shown in Table 5–2.

Table 5–2
Awareness and ratings of specific organizations

Organization	No. aware	No. rated	Mean rating
United Way	160	128	3.70
North Texas Home Health Services	36	23	4.00
Crisis Intervention	118	79	3.84
Family Service	75	48	3.90
Meals on Wheels	170	138	4.59
Parenting Guidance Center	100	69	4.12
Visiting Nurses Association	107	72	4.31
Mental Health/ Mental Retardation	154	108	4.11
Home Health Services of Tarrant County	69	41	3.93

The 75 respondents who were aware of Family Service were also asked what they considered to be the most important criteria in selecting a provider of counseling, home health, and educational services. The results are shown in Table 5–3.

Table 5–3
Criteria for selecting provider of services

Criteria	No. of responses
Quality	5
Accreditation	3
Cost	5
Recommendations*	23
Image/reputation	8
Credentials/knowledge of staff	9
Supportive staff	1
Success rate	2
Needs/benefits	2
Tradition	1
Confidentiality	1
Communication	1
Christian organization	1
Don't know	13

*Many respondents specified recommendations from doctors, ministers, school counselors, friends, and relatives.

Physician survey

Telephone interviewing produced 102 completed interviews from a random list of 350 physicians (M.D.s and D.O.s). Each doctor was asked first to rate the efforts of home health organizations in general (scale of 1 to 5). The mean response was 3.8250 with a standard deviation of .612 and 80 no responses.

Physicians were then asked if they were aware of several specific organizations. If aware of an organization, he or she was also asked to rate the performance of that organization. The results are shown in Table 5–4.

The interviewer noted that several doctors had heard of an organization but did not know enough about it to rate it. Others, however, said they knew of an organization and had actually referred patients to it but were unable to give a rating because they did not know how well the organization had served the patient.

Doctors were also asked to which home health organizations they refer their patients. Of the 102 interviewed physicians, 15 reported that they never refer to home health agencies. Of the remaining 87, 25 could not name any specific agency. Several of these 25 stated that they do not make the actual referral—they prescribe the needed services but the nurse or the hospital discharge planner actually selects the provider.

Table 5–4
Awareness and ratings of specific organizations

Organization	No. aware	No. rated	Mean rating
United Way	94	75	3.68
North Texas Home Health Services	52	35	3.86
Crisis Intervention	65	35	4.03
Family Service	50	38	3.71
Meals on Wheels	89	68	4.25
Parenting Guidance Center	50	28	4.00
Visiting Nurses Association	78	61	3.95
Mental Health/ Mental Retardation	91	64	3.63
Home Health Services of Tarrant County	57	41	3.76

CASE ANALYSIS

CASE 5

Family Service, Inc.

1. How does the general public view Family Service and the other agencies?

   _____

   _____

   _____

   _____

   _____

   _____

   _____

   _____

2. What are the marketing implications of Table 5–3?

   _____

   _____

   _____

   _____

   _____

_____

_____

3. How do physicians view Family Service and the other agencies?

_____

_____

_____

_____

_____

_____

_____

_____

_____

_____

4. What is the importance of the discrepancy between the number of physicians who were aware of an organization and the number who rated the organization?

_____

_____

_____

_____

_____

_____

_____

_____

_____

5.   What are the marketing implications of the 25 doctors who could not
     name the agency or agencies to which their patients were referred?

_____

_____

_____

_____

_____

_____

_____

6.   What recommendations would you make to Family Service?

_____

_____

_____

PART TWO

PRODUCT DECISIONS

CASE 6

HENRIETTA'S BURGER CASTLE

Background

Henrietta's Burger Castle is a restaurant located in a Midwestern town with a population approaching 17,000 people. Henrietta's has been in the same location since 1957, when Henrietta opened the business shortly after her husband's sudden death. The restaurant is situated on the corners of Main and Washington, in the heart of the town's business and shopping district. It specializes in hot dogs and hamburgers. Other items on the menu include fried chicken, french fries, potato chips, cole slaw, and soft drinks. Customers wait in line to place their orders. They have the option of having their food packaged to go or eating in the restaurant. Henrietta's comfortably seats 100 people.

Henrietta's enjoys an excellent reputation for its food, cleanliness, reasonable prices, and courteous service. Of the restaurants in the area, none has a more loyal clientele than Henrietta's. Many have been regular customers since the business began.

Target market

Henrietta's has always appealed to consumers in the over-40 age bracket. One possible explanation is a classier image than the other fast-food restaurants. Another reason could be the more personalized service.

Shoppers have always been attracted to Henrietta's. In addition to quality food at reasonable prices, the relaxed atmosphere appeals to shoppers.

This case was prepared by Professor Martin Meyers, MacMurray College, Jacksonville, Illinois.

Courtesy of Michael Weisbrot and Family/Stock, Boston

Another segment of the population that patronizes Henrietta's is workers in the area. Most of the workers are secretaries, sales clerks, and a few lower level managers. Laborers rarely patronize the restaurant.

Compared to the other fast-food restaurants in the area, Henrietta's attracts very few families.

Sales

Henrietta's experienced a tremendous increase in sales during the late 1960s and early 1970s. During the mid-1970s sales increased, but at a slower rate. The first year sales fell was 1980, and they have continued to fall. In the autumn of 1983 Henrietta's concern reached the level where she pursued the issue. She wondered whether it was only her sales that were falling or the sales of all the local fast-food restaurants. She was especially interested in the sales figures of the two newest restaurants, Tio Pedro and Nature's Delight. Table 6–1 outlines Henrietta's sales figures. Table 6–2 outlines the sales figures for all the local fast-food restaurants. Table 6–3 outlines the sales figures for the newest restaurants. Tio Pedro specializes in Mexican food, and Nature's Delight specializes in natural and health foods.

Table 6–1
Sales and profits for Henrietta's Burger Castle

Year	Sales	Profits
1957	25,000	2,000
1958	26,250	2,100
1959	27,563	2,480
1960	29,216	2,630
1961	30,970	3,407
1962	33,447	3,679
1963	36,791	4,415
1964	40,470	5,666
1965	46,541	6,516
1966	53,522	8,564
1967	63,156	10,737
1968	73,892	11,823
1969	84,977	13,596
1970	97,723	15,636
1971	112,382	16,858
1972	126,992	17,779
1973	143,500	18,665
1974	162,156	19,458
1975	178,371	19,620
1976	196,208	19,700
1977	207,980	18,718
1978	218,380	17,470
1979	222,743	16,705
1980	220,516	16,418
1981	216,105	16,207
1982	211,783	16,190
1983	207,543*	15,540*

*Estimated.

Year	Sales	Profits
1957	500,000	35,000
1958	530,000	38,150
1959	561,800	41,965
1960	601,126	47,000
1961	655,227	52,640
1962	727,302	60,010
1963	821,851	69,012
1964	986,222	79,364
1965	1,193,329	94,443
1966	1,503,594	113,331
1967	1,909,564	137,131
1968	2,463,337	164,557
1969	3,202,339	194,178
1970	4,034,947	229,130
1971	5,043,684	268,082
1972	6,102,857	313,656
1973	7,323,429	360,704
1974	7,714,880	414,810
1975	10,109,261	477,032
1976	11,625,650	543,816
1977	13,253,241	609,724
1978	15,108,694	699,981
1979	16,921,737	716,080
1980	18,613,910	752,724
1981	20,475,301	790,360
1982	22,113,325	805,410
1983	23,882,311*	821,975*

Table 6–2
Sales and profits for
all local fast-food
restaurants

*Estimated.

Table 6–3
Sales and profits for
Tio Pedro and
Nature's Delight

Year	Sales	Profits
	Tio Pedro	
1980	80,000	12,000
1981	96,000	14,280
1982	120,000	18,136
1983	159,670*	24,120*
	Nature's Delight	
1980	60,000	9,000
1981	73,200	10,000
1982	92,232	13,824
1983	122,669*	18,662*

*Estimated.

Promotion

Henrietta advertises in the local newspaper, the *Greenville Press*. It is a daily publication read by most of the town's permanent residents. Henrietta generally places a quarter-page advertisement the first Sunday of every month. This costs her $165 per month. She has changed the advertisement on a few occasions, but the theme has remained the same. The name of the restaurant is printed in large type. Many of the items, along with their prices, are listed in smaller type. Exhibit 6–1 shows a typical advertisement.

**Exhibit 6–1
A typical newspaper
advertisement for
Henrietta's Burger
Castle**

Henrietta's Burger Castle

not just another hamburger joint

Hamburger	$1.69	with fries or coleslaw	$2.09
Hot Dog	$1.09	with fries or coleslaw	$1.59
Basket of Chicken	$2.19	with fries or coleslaw	$2.69

**Eat in or take away!
Phone ahead, we'll have
your order ready!
359-1900**

**41 Washington
Greenville**

Hours: Mon–Thurs   11 a.m.–9 p.m.
              Fri–Sun   11 a.m.–10 p.m.

Henrietta also uses radio advertising. She places seven commercials each week. Each commercial costs $7.00 for a 20-second spot. Exhibit 6–2 shows the commercial she has recently been using.

Exhibit 6–2
A typical radio commercial for Henrietta's Burger Castle

Enjoy lunch or dinner in the relaxed atmosphere of Henrietta's Burger Castle, located on the intersection of Main and Washington. Phone ahead, we'll have your order ready. Items on the menu include hot dogs, hamburgers, and fried chicken to please everyone in the family.

CASE
ANALYSIS

CASE 6

Henrietta's
Burger Castle

1. During what years was Henrietta's Burger Castle in the introduction, growth, maturity, and decline stages of its life cycle? Illustrate your answer by plotting sales and profits graphically.

2. Plot the fast-food industry on another graph and identify the various stages.

3. Plot the life cycles of Tio Pedro and Nature's Delight on another graph. Are they in a different stage from **Henrietta**'s Burger Castle? Explain your answer.

4. Should Henrietta expand her product line? Explain your answer and suggest possible products if you recommend expansion.

_____

_____

_____

_____

_____

_____

_____

_____

_____

_____

_____

_____

_____

5.   What advice would you offer Henrietta regarding promotion?

_____

_____

_____

_____

_____

_____

_____

_____

_____

_____

_____

CASE 7

APEX CHEMICAL COMPANY

(The executive committee of Apex Chemical Company—a medium-size chemical manufacturer with annual sales of $60,000,000—is trying to determine which of two new compounds the company should market. The two products were expected to have the same gross margin percentage. The following conversation takes place among the vice-president for research, Ralph Rogovin; the vice-president for marketing, Miles Mumford; and the president, Paul Prendigast.)

VP-Research. Compound A-115, a new electrolysis agent, is the one; there just isn't any doubt about it. Why, for precipitating a synergistic reaction in silver electrolysis, it has a distinct advantage over anything now on the market.

President. That makes sense, Ralph. Apex has always tried to avoid "me too" products and if this one is that much better . . . what do you think, Miles?

VP-Marketing. Well, I favor the idea of Compound B-227, the plastic oxidizer. We have some reputation in that field; we're already known for our plastic oxidizers.

VP-Research. Yes, Miles, but this one isn't really better than the ones we already have. It belongs to the beta-prednigone group, and they just aren't as good as the stigones are. We *do* have the best stigone in the field.

President. Just the same, Ralph, the beta-prednigones are cutting

Edward C. Bursk/Stephen A. Greyser, *Cases in Marketing Management*, 2nd ed., © 1975, pp. 204–206. Reprinted by permission of Prentice-Hall, Inc., Englewood Cliffs, N.J.

into our stigone sales. The board of directors has been giving me a going over on that one.

VP-Marketing. Yes, Ralph, maybe they're not as good scientists as we are—or think we are—but the buyers in the market seem to insist on buying beta-prednigones. How do you explain that? The betas have 60 percent of the market now.

VP-Research. That's your job, not mine, Miles. If we can't sell the best product—and I can prove it *is* the best, as you've seen from my data and computations—then there's something wrong with Apex's marketing effort.

President. What do you say to that, Miles? What *is* the explanation?

VP-Marketing. Well, it's a very tricky field—the process in which these compounds are used is always touch-and-go; everyone is always trying something new.

VP-Research. All the more reason to put our effort behind Compound A-115, in the electrolysis field. Here we know that we have a real technical breakthrough. I agree with Paul that that's our strength.

President. What about that, Miles? Why not stay out of the dogfight represented by Compound B-227, if the plastic oxidizer market is as tricky as you say?

VP-Marketing. I don't feel just right about it, Paul. I understand that the electrolysis market is pretty satisfied with the present products. We did a survey and 95 percent said they were satisfied with the Hamfield Company's product.

President. It's a big market, too, isn't it, Miles?

VP-Marketing. Yes, about $10 million a year total.

President. And only one strongly entrenched company—Hamfield?

VP-Marketing. Yes, I must admit it's not like the plastic oxidizer situation—where there are three strong competitors, and about a half-dozen who are selling off-brands. On the other hand, oxidizers are a $40 million market—four times as big.

President. That's true, Ralph. Furthermore, our oxidizer sales represent 25 percent of our total sales.

VP-Research. But we've been losing ground the past year. Our oxidizer sales dropped 10 percent, didn't they, Ralph? While the total oxidizer market was growing, didn't you say?

VP-Marketing. Well, the electrolysis field is certainly more stable. Total sales are holding level, and, as I said before, Hamfield's share is pretty constant, too.

President. What about the technical requirements in the electrolysis field? With a really improved product we ought to be able . . .

VP-Marketing. Well, to tell you the truth, I don't know very much about the kind of people who use it, and how they . . . You see, it's really a different industry.

President. What about it, Ralph?

VP-Research. It's almost a different branch of chemistry, too. But I have plenty of confidence in our laboratory men. I can't see any reason why we should run into trouble. . . . It really does have a plus three point superiority on a scale of 100—here, the chart shows it crystal clear, Miles.

VP-Marketing. But aren't we spreading ourselves pretty thin—instead of concentrating where our greatest know-how . . . You've always said, Paul, that . . .

President. Yes, I know, but maybe we ought to diversify, too. You know, all our eggs in one basket . . .

VP-Marketing. But if it's a good basket. . . .

VP-Research. Nonsense, Miles, it's the kind of eggs you've got in the basket that counts—and Compound A-115, the electrolysis agent, is scientifically the better one.

VP-Marketing. Yes, but what about taking the eggs to the market? . . . Maybe people don't want to buy that particular egg from us, but they would buy Compound B-227—the plastic oxidizer.

President. Eggs, eggs, eggs—I'm saying to both of you, let's just be sure we don't lay any!

CASE ANALYSIS

CASE 7

Apex Chemical Company

1. Which product, A-115 or B-227, has the larger total market?

   _____

   _____

   _____

   _____

   _____

2. Potentially, which product has the most lucrative market for Apex? Why?

   _____

   _____

   _____

   _____

   _____

   _____

   _____

   _____

   _____

3.   Discuss the pros and cons associated with selecting A-115.

_____

_____

_____

_____

_____

_____

_____

_____

4.   Discuss the pros and cons associated with selecting B-227.

_____

_____

_____

_____

_____

_____

_____

5. If you had to choose one of these two products, which would it be? Why?

_____

_____

_____

_____

_____

_____

_____

_____

_____

_____

_____

_____

_____

_____

_____

_____

CASE 8

NATIONAL TOBACCO COMPANY

National Tobacco Company, a Virginia-based cigarette manufacturer, had witnessed a declining market share over the past five years, and management had become concerned about how this trend might be reversed. In a meeting of key executives three facts emerged. First, a review of the four major markets served by the industry revealed that none of the leading brands was produced by National.

A second fact confronting management was the changing smoking habits of Americans. Currently the ultra-low-tar market accounts for only 8.3% of total industry volume. Projections, however, show that by 1985 this market will account for 22% of all sales. Thus, the ultra-low-tar market has become the fastest growing segment of the tobacco industry. Indeed, cigarette producers are planning to spend $300 million, out of a total advertising expenditure of $800 million, on their ultra-low-tar brands.

A third area of concern was the nature of the competition. Though demand for the industry as a whole had been relatively flat for the last several years, competition had become very aggressive. Philip Morris, in particular, had grown especially competitive. Its market share in the last 10 years had climbed from 18% to nearly 31%. Management was concerned that Reynolds and Philip Morris, in their fight to become number one in the industry, were taking shares of the market away from the competition (including National) rather than each other. One consequence of this was that National was no longer in a position to match the marketing expenditures of its big rivals.

Copyright © 1982 by Dr. George B. Glisan.

Courtesy of Marjorie Nichols/The Picture Cube

Management had concluded that the best strategy for National to pursue was to focus on the fast-growing ultra-low-tar segment, where National currently lacked a viable brand. Their goal was to produce a product which could capture a 1.5% share of the market within 18 months (a 0.5% share is regarded in the industry as the minimum benchmark for success). Each 1% of market share translates into $125 million worth of sales, therefore a 1.5% share should be equivalent to $200 million in revenue to National. Senior management had appointed Jackie Tulasne and Scott Ellison to determine what branding strategy alternatives were available to enter the ultra-low-tar segment and to make a recommendation.

After examining the strategies of other tobacco companies, Tulasne and Ellison concluded that three approaches had potential. One strategy, successfully employed by Lorillard Tobacco, was to use brand extension. Lorillard had taken a successful existing brand—Kent—

and entered the low-tar segment with a new brand named Kent Golden Lights, thus capitalizing on the established name. The new brand had captured in excess of 1.5% of the market. After the brand became established, Lorillard dropped the Kent name and offered the brand as simply Golden Lights. Tulasne and Ellison had noted, however, that Lorillard's effort to enter the ultra-low-tar segment with another extended brand, Kent III, had not been as successful. They were also concerned about the extent to which extended brands, such as those offered by Lorillard, might take sales away from the original brand.

A second strategy alternative was to employ a family-branding approach. Philip Morris had used the strategy with its Merit family. Merit, appearing in similar package designs, was offered in four different versions: low-tar, low-tar menthol, ultra-low-tar, and ultra-low-tar menthol. The Merit low-tar version had achieved a 4.25% market share, but the other versions had not achieved anything near this level of success. Tulasne and Ellison wondered whether such an approach might not lead to confusion on the part of the consumer and thus limit the potential for some versions of the family brand. In addition, they feared that any one version might lose some of its identity as a unique product in the minds of consumers.

A final strategy Tulasne and Ellison felt had potential was to simply bring out a new individual brand name. American and Lorillard had used this approach to enter the ultra-low-tar segment and now had the top two brands—Carlton and True. Recently Brown & Williamson had used this strategy for their new ultra-low-tar entry—Barclay. After less than a year on the market, it had achieved a market share of 1.2%, fourth place in the ultra-low-tar segment. It was noted, however, that other Brown & Williamson new brand entries in this segment—Arctic Lights and Fact—had not been nearly as successful. Even the industry heavyweights, Reynolds and Philip Morris, had had less-than-successful new brand entries in this segment with their Real and Cambridge offerings. Furthermore, Tulasne and Ellison had received reports indicating that Brown & Williamson had spent upwards of $150 million to launch their new brand—Barclay. By comparison, Reynolds had spent $40 million to bring out Real. Tulasne and Ellison concluded that in a marketplace populated by nearly 100 brands, to offer an entirely new brand to the market was an expensive proposition, and one filled with a high amount of risk.

Tulasne and Ellison had two days to finalize their report and make a recommendation. At this point each alternative had pluses and minuses. As a result, the team was uncertain which alternative they should recommend.

CASE ANALYSIS

CASE 8

National Tobacco Company

1. What are the brand strategy alternatives available to National, and what are the strengths and weaknesses of each alternative?

_____

_____

_____

_____

_____

_____

_____

_____

_____

_____

_____

_____

_____

_____

_____

_____

_____

_____

_____

2.   Which brand strategy carries the most risk for National?

_____

_____

_____

_____

_____

_____

_____

_____

_____

_____

3.   Which brand strategy should Tulasne and Ellison recommend to management?

_____

_____

_____

_____

_____

_____

_____

_____

_____

_____

_____

4. Are there any viable alternatives that management has not considered? Discuss.

_____

_____

_____

_____

_____

_____

CASE 9

POTTY POSIES

New England Mop Company, Inc., has for the past several months been engaged in the development of a new product to be known as "Potty Posies," a new style of toilet bowl deodorizer. Mr. Ronald Felici, president of the company, must soon make a decision as to the market feasibility of the product and whether to launch it in the marketplace or abandon the idea.

Company background

New England Mop is a small 28-year-old firm located in Pawtucket, Rhode Island, that manufactures wool dust mops. The company was taken over two years ago by new management, which changed several marketing policies and boosted sales of the mops. Peak sales under the old management were $220,000, whereas under Mr. Felici's leadership the company has grown to over $400,000 in sales.

In addition to Mr. Felici, the company's management consists of a plant manager (who was a minority partner in the previous company before it was purchased) and a sales manager. The plant manager has developed machinery and techniques for manufacturing and has helped in the design of packaging for the mops. He has a staff of 9 to 17, depending on business at any time. The sales manager is responsible for generating and supervising the company's sales programs. Mr. Felici has assisted most heavily in this area of the company's activities. He describes the company as being undercapitalized. Although the firm was purchased at a price greater than the value of its assets, the

This case was prepared by Dr. David Loudon of Northeast Louisiana University.

new owners thought that with young, aggressive management this premium could be overcome by higher volumes. The president describes the company's current situation as being cash poor. "We are keeping our heads above water, with minimal profits being made," he said. "We don't have the physical manpower to really run the company the way it should be," he commented, adding that "any small company has the disadvantage of manpower and good follow-through to really capitalize on all phases of its business."

Current marketing activities

New England Mop manufactures what it considers to be the "Cadillac" or "Bayer aspirin" of the dust mop market. The product is made of wool and has the brand name Magnetic Mop, so named because wool creates static electricity as it is rubbed across a floor and thus captures and holds dust particles. The company estimates its market share to be 75% of the wool mop sales made to the retail trade.

Product

Most dust mops produced in the United States are made of acrylic fiber and are sold at low prices. Most acrylics retail at $2.00 to $3.00, while the "Magnetic Mop" sells for $4.98. Some wool mops are even more expensive; for example, some companies sell wool mops door to door for approximately $9.00. Even compared to these higher priced products, however, New England Mop considers the quality of their own product to be superior.

Channels of distribution

As of the late 1950s distribution of the mop was largely through hardware and department stores. This pattern has changed over time, especially under the new management, away from the traditional hardware-houseware field toward large mass merchandisers and supermarkets. The company does no private branding.

The process of shifting its emphasis from one channel to another has not been an easy one. Some resistance has been met on two fronts: (1) store buyers who never thought that top-quality (i.e., high-priced) mops would sell in mass outlets such as supermarkets; and (2) consumers who were not used to buying high-quality dust mops, especially in mass outlets. These resistances are being overcome and the company's penetration has been very successful.

New England Mop's sales force consists of 43 manufacturer's representatives who cover the United States. The representatives are paid commissions based on a percentage of sales and carry complementary (i.e., noncompeting) lines of other manufacturers.

Promotion

New England Mop offers an advertising allowance to its department store customers. The stores then advertise to final consumers. This program has been abused in the past, however—a fact which led to the shift to supermarkets and other mass merchandisers. The problem was that some stores exceeded their advertising allowance, which then had to be made up by New England Mop. For example, a store that ordered 100 mops would receive a $50 advertising allowance (at 50¢ per mop). But this store's advertising for the mop might total $125. New England Mop would then have to pay the additional $75 expenditure. The difficulty in controlling these expenditures led the company to intentionally forgo much of the potentially profitable department store business for other outlets. In spite of this lost business, however, overall sales have still risen substantially.

Pricing

Magnetic Mop presently retails for $4.98 and wholesales for $2.36. Previous management raised prices five years ago from $3.95 to $4.49. As a result, sales to retailers dropped 33%. Two years ago, present management again raised prices, but by only 10%. Over the same two-year period, however, costs of materials have gone up much more than 10%. For example, prices of corrugated cardboard for packaging have risen 50% in 1½ years. As a result of this particular increase, the company is designing a package to fit over only the mop's head, whereas previously the entire mop was placed in a box. In spite of large and rapid cost increases, management did not think it could raise prices as fast as costs because of its desired penetration into new retail outlets. It was feared that such price increases might alienate new customers. Management decided instead to concentrate on higher volume to offset the lower prices.

In retrospect, management thinks this decision was unwise. "We probably should have gone immediately to higher prices when increases were rampant, generally. Buyers would definitely have accepted the increases," Felici stated.

Price is determined by adding the cost of raw materials, labor, and manufacturing burden (directly related to fixed expenses of the business; expressed as a percentage of labor cost), together with allowance for poor products or rejects to yield total manufacturing costs. Variable costs consisting of general and administrative expenses, selling commissions, cash discounts, freight, and other selling costs (e.g., advertising) are added to yield total costs. A profit margin is then applied to determine selling price.

New product development activities

With the increases in costs during the new management's first year of operation, it was determined that greater diversification was necessary in order to generate additional profits. It was also thought that the company had a good channel of distribution that was not being capitalized on with only one product. As Felici stated, however, "Getting into a new business without being experienced in this type of venture, and feeling as though we were amateurs in it, was not to be undertaken lightly."

The company decided to hire the services of an industrial designer who had worked for some of the largest manufacturers in the country. The designer was given only one criterion in his work: to develop a product that would fit New England Mop's channel of distribution.

The designer returned to the firm with the idea of a toilet bowl deodorizer made of colored cakes of paradichlorobenzene (a petroleum derivative, which is better known as the material comprising mothballs), molded into the shape of flowers, which would hang in the toilet bowl and emit a pleasant flower scent. He designed the product's shape, color, packaging, merchandising display, and so on. Exhibit 9–1 shows the proposed merchandising display.

The coloring of the chemical is actually not new. It was tried many years ago; however, it apparently created no great interest among consumers. The idea was discarded at that time because it also created manufacturing problems, such as shorter production runs, downtime to clean machines, and other problems.

Other minor changes that have been made in toilet bowl deodorizers in the past primarily involve improved packaging, such as more beautiful cellophane and boxing of the product. However, there is currently no product on the market like that suggested by the designer. All toilet bowl deodorizers presently on the market are simply round white cakes with rather antiseptic scents—basically the same form as that in which the product first appeared.

The industrial designer did not explicitly consider the market potential for the product in his development of the idea. He looked mainly for a way to glamorize a product already on the market. Realizing that little had been done to merchandise toilet bowl deodorizers more effectively, he suggested this product to New England Mop.

Mr. Felici therefore tried to estimate the market size for this item.

Exhibit 9–1
Merchandising display for Potty Posies

Provided by Ron Felici

He was not able to determine precise sales figures for toilet bowl deodorizers but did estimate that the market for all paradichloroben-zene products (including such items as mothballs, closet fresheners, and toilet bowl deodorizers) is between $10 million and $15 million annually in the United States, based on estimated sales of some of the largest companies in the industry. Felici suspected that toilet bowl deodorizers account for approximately one-third of this total market. He determined that over a dozen large firms are active in the paradichlorobenzene market.

Although not able to obtain a precise quantitative estimate of the size of the toilet bowl deodorizer market, he had read that, according to two large associations of service merchandisers, such products are the second largest selling item (behind panty hose) in the nonfood assortment in supermarkets. His impression was that well over one-half of all toilet bowl deodorizers sold are marketed through super-markets. The only other important channel appears to be through mass merchandisers such as discount houses and variety chains.

Although the market potential looked sizable, Felici was somewhat uneasy over the fact that the item seemed rather obscure to the aver-age consumer. In talking with friends and acquaintances he found that practically none of them uses this item. For this reason he sus-pected that the product was used mainly by lower income families who live in crowded housing and require deodorizing of the bath-room.

Based on the normal channels for this product, it appeared that New England Mop would not be able to capitalize on one major por-tion of their distribution, that of the houseware–hardware field, since they generally do not carry this item. Felici was optimistic, however, that they might be enticed to carry it because of the product's glamorization.

New England Mop has no facilities for production of a product like this. It would therefore have to find a company to produce it. Mr. Felici knew that his company, not being the primary manufacturer, could not be competitive on price with other companies in the busi-ness. He thought that the company could, however, opt for a larger size cake with all its glamour and hit a price line not comparable with similar products yet still in a price range the average consumer could afford. Felici therefore decided that a reasonable retail price would be 69¢ for 5-ounce Potty Posies. This compares favorably with the stan-dard, white 3-ounce cakes produced by other manufacturers, which generally sell for 39¢. Potty Posies would probably not be advertised. Such products are advertised very little, and when they are it is strictly price oriented; for example, a discount house may advertise a 39¢ toilet bowl deodorizer for 19¢.

Mr. Felici saw no reason why sales of this item could not capture at least 5% of the toilet bowl deodorizer market, assuming it to be $5 million. He thus determined that a realistic sales potential for this product would be $250,000 the first year. He estimated that the gross profit on the item should be 30%, with an expected return of 12% net profit on sales ($30,000 on sales of $250,000). This seemed to be quite an adequate return for not even touching the product.

No marketing research on sales or market shares of other deodorizers (e.g., Tidy Bowl, Glade, etc.) was considered by Felici, not only because of its cost, but, more important, because of his greater concern with head-to-head competition from other paradichlorobenzene cakes. Felici thought that this product would reach a much different consumer than that reached by competitive toilet bowl deodorizers. He expected it would not only attract roughly 5% of present buyers but also appeal because of its glamorization to those who do not normally buy toilet bowl deodorizers. Those who buy aerosols should also be attracted because of the increased fear of danger associated with inhaling such products. Penetration in the market might also be increased by offering it in new outlets such as hardware stores.

At this point the product's prospects looked sufficiently promising for Mr. Felici to have product mockups made. The company spent $600 on handmade plaster of Paris toilet bowl deodorizers and a working model of a display merchandiser to be used in stores. These were then taken to a large trade show in Chicago to test buyer reaction to the product. The display merchandiser and Potty Posies were presented to two national groups of service merchandisers and the reception by buyers was described by Felici as "great elation and enthusiasm."

Buyer reaction at the show was translated by Felici into an estimate of initial orders for the product. He determined that from the initial orders that would be generated, even if the product turned out to be a flop at the consumer level, it would not lose the company any money. He felt that $150,000 of the product could be sold "as easily as falling off a log."

In order to take advantage of the initial enthusiasm generated at the trade show, Mr. Felici felt that if he were to market this product, he should immediately find a manufacturer and get it into production. He recognized, however, that there were still some unanswered questions, and he therefore wondered what steps to take next.

CASE ANALYSIS

CASE 9

Potty Posies

1. Evaluate the product development process of New England Mop Co., Inc., for Potty Posies.

    _____

    _____

    _____

    _____

    _____

    _____

    _____

    _____

    _____

    _____

2. What would you have done differently? Keep in mind that New England Mop is a fairly small company.

    _____

    _____

    _____

    _____

    _____

_____

_____

_____

_____

_____

3. Should Potty Posies be marketed? What additional information is needed or desired?

_____

_____

_____

_____

_____

_____

_____

_____

_____

_____

_____

_____

_____

_____

_____

_____

_____

_____

_____

_____

_____

_____

_____

4.   Are the product design and name appropriate?

_____

_____

_____

_____

_____

_____

5.   What price do you recommend and why?

_____

_____

_____

_____

_____

6.   What channel of distribution do you recommend?

_____

_____

_____

_____

_____

_____

_____

_____

_____

7.   How should Potty Posies be promoted?

_____

_____

_____

_____

_____

_____

_____

_____

CASE 10

THE SONY COMPACT DISK PLAYER

In June 1980 Sony Corporation of Japan and the Dutch firm N. V. Phillips began codevelopment of the compact disk (CD) player. The design of the player was to feature two advanced technologies, the laser optical scanner and computer-based digital audio. The objective of the firms was to do away with the limitations of the conventional 12-inch long-playing (LP) record player/turntable and raise the state of the art in audio reproduction to a standard never before thought possible—near perfection. Toward the end of 1982 Sony realized the fruits of its labor and introduced its version of the player in the Japanese market. Within the first month 100,000 units were sold, and production had to be doubled to catch up with demand. Given that the price of the new player was $1000, Sony was pleased with its new entry into the marketplace.

The early success of the CD player was also observed by competitors. More than two dozen firms began offering their version of the player by licensing the technology from Sony/Phillips. John C. Koss, chairman of a firm that manufactures headphones and loudspeakers, states that this new technology represents "the next generation of improvement."[1]

There are several benefits the CD player offers, but it is the player's audio performance that stands out. The dynamic range (the difference between the quietest and loudest passages of music) of the new format approaches 90+ decibels. This compares with a range of approxi-

Copyright © 1984 by Dr. George B. Glisan.

[1] "Digital Sound Gets Set to Shake Up the Market," *Business Week*, September 13, 1982, p. 40.

Courtesy of Sony Corporation of America

mately 50+ decibels for conventional 12-inch LP records and turn-tables. The decibel system of measuring sound is a logarithmic function. In other words, for every 3-decibel increase in sound level, there is a doubling of sound volume. Thus, the CD player is not merely 50% better than conventional records in sound intensity but many times better. The result is a range that comes close to matching that of an actual concert performance.

The CD player also offers other performance benefits. Because the disks are turning at such high speeds in the player (200–500 revolutions per minute versus 33⅓ for conventional records) speed variations, known as "wow and flutter," are simply nonexistent. Another benefit of this new technology is that it generates better transient response than conventional players. That is, the transition from, say, a high musical note to a low one occurs so instantaneously that it duplicates the original musical performance. Additionally, the CD format is capable of reproducing an extended frequency response. Conventional records have great difficulty in reproducing frequencies below 45 Hz (the low bass notes found in music). Although such low bass notes are not encountered often in music, the CD player is capable of reproducing them. Thus, the full impact of a low C on a pipe organ is thunderously reproduced.

A final performance benefit is the absence of noise when playing CDs. When playing conventional LP records the listener frequently encounters pops, ticks, and other surface noises. Also heard is a background hiss that emanates from the master tape (the recording format) used to produce the record. All of these annoyances are missing from the CD format. This performance benefit is partly a result of how the music is recorded. The music information on a CD is stored on the disk as pits, or spots, etched onto the surface. These pits are then "read" by the optical scanning laser in the player. The result is an uncanny silence between musical passages, and a lack of noise intrusion during the music.

At the heart of this superb music reproduction system is the digital audio technology. When the music is recorded at the studio, recording technicians dispense with the conventional analog method (sequential recording onto a reel-to-reel tape recorder), and use machines that incorporate digital technology. With this method the music information is converted to binary code (0 or 1), and is then stored/recorded. Each sample of music is converted into a 16-bit "word." About 4.3 million (yes, million) bits are scanned each second by the digital processor. The precision of this system is a virtual one-for-one recording of the original performance. To take advantage of this recorded performance necessitates a digital playback device. The CD player is this device.

Although performance is the principal strength of this new technology, there are additional latent benefits. The disks themselves represent a series of advantages over conventional records. Their smaller size (4.7 inches in diameter) makes them easier to handle and store. Furthermore, the CDs are not susceptible to the kinds of warpage common to conventional vinyl records. This is because the disks are made of aluminum and sheathed in hard plastic. Additionally, such things as dust, fingerprints, even scratches in the plastic will not diminish playback quality as they do on conventional records.

Sony, and most of the other manufacturers, have incorporated additional features into their players. For instance, many of the machines are programmable. If you desired to listen to selections 3, 7, and 1 on a disk (and, in that out-of-sequence order) you could program the player to play only those selections. Some of the manufacturers have such features as seek-and-scan, memory, and remote control devices added to their players.

Without question, the state-of-the-art in home music reproduction has been significantly raised by the advent of the CD player. After Sony's successful fall 1982 introduction in Japan, they set their sights on the U.S. market in the spring of 1983. With their record in consumer electronics innovation Sony was hopeful for another success. Past successes include the pocket transistorized radio, high-performance color television (the Trinitron), videocassette recorders (Betamax and Betamax HiFi), and portable stereo (the Walkman). On its introduction, U.S. consumer stereo publications (*Audio, Stereo Review*, and *High Fidelity*) heralded the format as the greatest innovation since the transition from high fidelity to stereophonic playback in the 1950s.

Unfortunately, Sony's player has not come anywhere near the level of sales success in the United States that it has in Japan. The problem is not specific to Sony, however, as none of the other manufacturers have achieved any hint of sales success. Several reasons have been offered for the lack of widespread acceptance of the CD player. Retailers have cited resistance to price as one difficulty. They point out that consumers view the player as an alternative to the conventional turntable, which has an average price with cartridge of $350 and generates very respectable sound. The $650 difference, buyers point out, can be used to buy a lot of albums, or better amplifier and speakers if a whole system is being purchased.

Another dilemma is software—that is, the disks themselves. Although all the major record companies have offered CDs, their number is relatively small compared to conventional records, and buyers are reluctant to buy a player if they have little to play on it. Sony established a joint venture with CBS to bring out several hundred titles by the end of 1983, as had Toshiba and EMI. Poly Gram, one of the largest record companies in the world, had hoped to have about 600 titles in its catalog by the end of the year. Unfortunately, the record companies' hopes were not met. Even though more titles are being released each month, many record retailers have shown reluctance to carry many of the disks. They cite two difficulties. First, they retail for about $18 each, which is double the price of conventional record albums. Second, the retailers are reluctant to stock the disks until more of the players have been sold.

Consumer electronics analysts point out that even more fundamental difficulties exist for the acceptance of compact disk players in this country. First, they point out that to fully realize the benefits of the technology all components in the stereo system need to be of a high level of quality. If, for example, the user's amplifier puts out 25 watts per channel, they may discover rather quickly that it has difficulty keeping up with demands of the digital audio signals. It is not uncommon for instantaneous peaks of 200 watts to be reached. Some manufacturers and retailers, however, cite this as an opportunity to upgrade the buyer's amplifiers and speakers as "digital ready" to take advantage of this opportunity. Needless to say, these new components are frequently more costly.

Another dilemma offered by the analysts is the listening habits of Americans. The majority of stereo owners listen to rock music. However, the full audio potential of compact disks is not realized in this type of music. It is classical music that possesses the greater frequency

Table 10–1
Compact disk players available in the United States

Manufacturer	Model	Frequency response (Hz)	Dynamic range (dB)	Harmonic distortion (%)	Price ($)
Aiwa	DX-1000	0–20,000	90	0.003	1000.00
Akai	CD-D1	20–20,000	90	0.005	1000.00
Denon	DCD-2000	5–20,000	90	0.03	995.00
	DN-3000F	20–20,000	90	0.007	8500.00
Dual	CD120	5–20,000	90	0.003	899.95
Fisher	AD850	20–20,000	90	0.006	999.95
Hitachi	DA1000	20–20,000	93	0.003	1000.00
	DA800	20–20,000	93	0.003	1000.00
JVC	XL-V1	5–20,000	90		1000.00
Kyocera	DA-01	20–20,000	90	0.005	1050.00
Luxman	DX-104	5–20,000	90	0.004	1199.95
Magnavox	FD1000SL	20–20,000	90	0.004	800.00
	FD2000SL	20–20,000	90	0.004	800.00
	FD2020SL	20–20,000	90	0.004	850.00
	FD3030SL	20–20,000	90	0.004	950.00
Marantz	CD 73	20–20,000	90	0.005	999.00
Micro Seiki	CD-M1	20–20,000	90	0.005	1100.00
Mitsubishi	DP-101	5–20,000	96	0.004	1050.00
NEC	CD-803E	5–20,000	90	0.01	1300.00
Phase Linear	9500	20–20,000	92	0.005	995.00
Sansui	PC-V1000	5–20,000	90	0.004	1000.00
Sanyo	DAD8	5–20,000	90	0.006	999.95
Sears Roebuck	57 E 9750C	6–20,000	90	0.003	589.99
Sharp	DX-3	5–20,000	90	0.01	950.00
Sony	CDP-701ES	5–20,000	90	0.004	900.00
Sony ES	DEP-701ES	5–20,000	95	0.003	1500.00
Sylvania	FDC303SL	20–20,000	90	0.004	950.00
Technics	SL-P10	4–20,000	96	0.003	1000.00
	SL-P8	4–20,000	96	0.003	800.00
	SL-P7	4–20,000	96	0.003	700.00
Toshiba	XR-Z90	4–20,000	90	0.004	1000.00
Yamaha	CD-1	10–20,000	90	0.004	1395.00

response and dynamic range. Although there are many who listen to classical music, their numbers are not as great as those who listen to popular music.

A final point emphasized by analysts is that unlike in the past, electronics consumers today are faced with a number of competing choices for their dollar. One can choose from videocassette recorders, computers, satellite receiving dishes, and even such new phenomena as cordless telephones. Indeed, some retailers are repositioning themselves as consumer electronics stores so that they can sell buyers something, even if it is not CD players.

All of the foregoing concerns face Sony as it attempts to generate greater acceptance of its new product. As if all of these troubles were not enough, there has been the emergence of many competing firms offering their own version of the CD player. Table 10–1 lists those firms and their respective models. The table also points up another dilemma—the specifications for all of these players reveal relatively little differences. They are all capable of outstanding audio performance. This requires manufacturers to seek other means of differentiation, such as cosmetics, features, or price.

As Sony managers ponder the situation, they are looking for a marketing strategy that will facilitate greater acceptance of the CD player in the United States. Given the difficulties, they wonder if their player will be a replay of the four-channel stereo that debuted in the early seventies, and is now but a memory. Four-channel offered sonic improvement and faced some of the same challenges as the compact disk player, yet it still failed. Needless to say, Sony does not want a replay of the four-channel fiasco.

CASE ANALYSIS

CASE 10

The Sony Compact Disk Player

1. Discuss the relative advantage of the CD player over conventional turntables.

_____

_____

_____

_____

_____

_____

_____

_____

_____

2. How compatible is the CD player with potential buyers' past experiences?

_____

_____

_____

_____

_____

_____

_____

3.   Discuss the complexity of the CD player.

_____

_____

_____

_____

_____

_____

_____

_____

_____

4.   How "trialable" is the CD player?

_____

_____

_____

_____

_____

_____

_____

_____

_____

5. Assess the "observability" of the CD player's performance.

_____

_____

_____

_____

_____

_____

_____

_____

6. Advise Sony.

_____

_____

_____

_____

PART THREE

DISTRIBUTION DECISIONS

QUESTION/ACT DECISIONS

CASE 11

THE TOUCH OF NATURE COMPANY

Background

The Touch of Nature Company was started by Linda Miller and Debbie Johnson in 1971. They started the company to capitalize on the growing natural foods industry.

The Touch of Nature Company has experienced tremendous success in the short period it has been in existence. Sales volume has increased each year. In fact, last year's sales volume exceeded $6 million. Sales are projected to double within three years.

Product line

Initially, Touch of Nature depended on a line of candy bars. The candy bars were given the brand name of Nature's Finest. They were made from ingredients to appeal to the health-minded consumer. For example, honey was substituted for sugar, and carob was used instead of chocolate. A variety of candy bars were produced. The different types included plain carob, carob and almond, carob and peanuts, and carob and coconut.

Distribution

Initially, the sole channel of distribution consisted of utilizing wholesalers to reach health food stores. It would not have been feasible for Touch of Nature to distribute directly to the health food stores

This case was prepared by Professor Martin Meyers, MacMurray College, Jacksonville, Illinois.

119

Courtesy of Peter Vandermark/Stock, Boston

because the sales made in each store would not be large enough to cover the expenses of a sales representative.

In 1980 Touch of Nature expanded their distribution channels. They began marketing their product lines in grocery stores. They used wholesalers for the smaller grocery stores, but used sales representatives for the larger grocery stores. By 1982 there were eleven sales representatives, each assigned to a designated territory.

In 1983 Linda Miller analyzed recent sales figures to determine if their products were doing well in the grocery stores. She was satisfied when she discovered that 10 percent of the company's sales were to grocery stores.

Channel conflict

The health food store operators were becoming increasingly unhappy about Touch of Nature's natural candies and cookies being sold in supermarkets. They felt that Touch of Nature was being disloyal to them. The following letter from a health food store owner reflects many of their feelings.

Dear Ms. Miller and Ms. Johnson:

I have been carrying your products since 1971. When the public had not even heard of Nature's Finest, I prominently displayed your entire product line on my shelves and personally recommended them to my customers.

How do you think I felt when I saw your products in a grocery store? (At a lower price yet!) After everything I've done for your products, I feel that I deserve better treatment.

At a recent convention for health store owners, I discussed this situation with other store operators. They shared my sentiments.

In conclusion, I am considering dropping the Nature's Finest product line from my product mix.

Very truly yours,

Margaret Hein

CASE 12

SONAID, INC.

For the first 50 years of its history, the hearing-aid industry was relatively stable. The eight top manufacturers controlled approximately 80 percent of the market. They maintained this control through exclusive franchises, by which dealers were limited to a single brand. For a dealer, to lose a franchise meant going out of business, since no other franchise was usually available.

In the mid-1960s, the industry entered a new era. Then, a group of franchisers sued their respective manufacturers for restraint of trade. They won the suit, and the Federal Trade Commission (FTC) used the precedent to get other companies to sign consent decrees releasing their franchises. The result was a rapid shift of power from the manufacturer to the retailer. Instead of being locked into a single brand for better or worse, the retailer could select those brands that offered the best profit potential. Companies that could not keep their dealers happy simply could not get their products on the market. Two of the top eight manufacturers went bankrupt, and the market share of the remaining six slipped to a total of 32 percent as smaller companies began to gain.

Enter Sonaid

This transition of power provided a perfect opportunity for Sonaid to gain a foothold in the hearing-aid market. Tanja Larson, Sonaid's cofounder, had followed developments in the hearing-aid industry

M. I. Mandell/L. J. Rosenberg, *Marketing*, 2nd ed., © 1981, pp. 441–443. Reprinted by permission of Prentice-Hall, Inc., Englewood Cliffs, N.J.

for several years. She had previously been convinced that under the exclusive franchise system product development was being stifled because there was no incentive to innovate. Sensing that the FTC would rule against the franchise system, she astutely teamed up with George Richards, an electrical engineer and sometime inventor, to develop a better hearing aid.

Sonaid was organized in December 1965. Its prototype model was finished in late 1966, just as the franchise system had begun to crumble. Larson negotiated distribution agreements with several key hearing-aid dealers in southern California. Richards arranged for funding from a consortium of private investors, and he subcontracted production to a small electronics firm in Santa Barbara.

Sonaid's first hearing aids reached dealers in early 1967. By late 1968 the company was able to move into its own production facilities. By this time, the company had begun to attract attention in the industry and its growth was beginning to accelerate rapidly.

More changes in the market

The growth of Sonaid coincided with other changes in the hearing-aid market. The aggressive sales tactics of the hearing-aid dealers had drawn the attention of consumer groups, inspiring Ralph Nader to issue his report, "Paying through the Ear." At the same time, the industry saw a dramatic increase in third-party payments—hearing aids funded by Medicaid and various state departments of vocational rehabilitation. The funding agencies were reluctant to leave hearing-aid selection in the hands of relatively uninformed consumers and self-interested sales personnel. As a safeguard, they brought in professional audiologists to test hearing and make purchase recommendations.

The effect on retailers was dramatic. Previously, they only had to carry one or two of the most profitable lines. Now they had to carry seven or eight lines to meet the demands of the audiologists. They could no longer buy in volume from any one manufacturer. While this did not affect sales volume, it eliminated quantity discounts in many cases, and thus resulted in a decline of $100 in the average dealer's profit margin per bulk purchase.

Sonaid responded to this situation in two ways. First, it offered discounts to regular dealers, even if they did not purchase in large enough quantities to merit them. Given the large number of lines the dealers needed to stock, Larson was afraid that they would be tempted to drop Sonaid in favor of more commonly ordered brands.

Courtesy of George Bellerose/Stock, Boston

Second, Richards organized a publicity campaign, supported by direct-mail advertising, directed at audiologists. Convinced that their importance would continue to increase, he reasoned that in the long run, their acceptance of Sonaid's products would be even more important to the survival of the company than that of the dealers.

Looking to the future

Once again Sonaid's strategy proved to be right on target. Like the manufacturers before them, the retailers failed to react to the changing environment, and as a result, health professionals began to take a more dominant role in hearing-aid distribution. In 1978, the FTC charged the American Speech and Hearing Association (ASHA), whose members were retailers, with restraint of trade, because its code forbade audiologists to sell hearing aids for profit. ASHA amended its code and, in a short time, over 300 audiologists had begun to sell hearing aids. Hospitals and medical groups also began to sell them.

All of these developments worked in Sonaid's favor. By the end of 1979, it had established itself as a major producer of quality hearing aids and as the fastest growing firm in the industry. Despite the company's success, however, both Larson and Richards were worried. It was apparent to both of them that Sonaid had been quite fortunate during the decade and a half of its existence. The two partners had made some good decisions, but their competitors had aided their cause by making some bad ones. This was not as likely to happen in the future. A number of highly sophisticated foreign manufacturers had recently entered the market, and the American firms that remained had learned a lot from the turmoil of the past 15 years.

Of even greater concern to the partners was the increased emphasis consumers were putting on price and the potential for accelerated price competition. Sonaid had built its business on high quality, high-priced hearing aids. The brand's high price had supported the generous margins allowed to dealers and a vigorous research and development program. Recently, several mass merchandisers had taken advantage of these high margins by engaging in a high-volume, low-price form of competition. For instance, Sears, Roebuck had recently purchased 200 soundproof rooms for testing and dispensing operations in a number of stores around the country.

On the manufacturer's side, a number of high-technology electronics companies had begun investigating the hearing-aid market. Were they to enter the market, Sonaid would not be able to compete in both price and quality. The larger companies had lower costs because of economies of scale in research and development.

Larson and Richard saw several strategic alternatives open to them:

1. Sonaid could maintain its present policy of offering high-priced top-quality hearing aids by continuing to support its dealers with high margins and promotions aimed at audiologists.
2. Sonaid could lower prices and seek mass distribution using high volume to offset lower unit margins.
3. Sonaid could seek greater economies of scale through horizontal integration—perhaps by merging with a high technology electronics firm.
4. Sonaid could seek greater distribution efficiency through vertical integration—perhaps by acquiring wholesale or retail operations.

CASE
ANALYSIS

CASE 12

Sonaid, Inc.

1. Why did channel leadership shift from manufacturers to retailers during the mid-1960s?

_____

_____

_____

_____

_____

_____

_____

_____

2. What might manufacturers have done to maintain leadership?

_____

_____

_____

_____

_____

_____

_____

_____

_____

3.   Why did channel leadership shift from the retailers in the early 1970s?

_____

_____

_____

_____

_____

_____

_____

_____

4.   What might the retailers have done to maintain leadership?

_____

_____

_____

_____

_____

_____

_____

_____

_____

5. Who assumed channel leadership after the retailers lost it in the early 1970s?

_____

_____

_____

_____

_____

_____

_____

_____

6. Who is likely to assume channel leadership in the 1980s?

_____

_____

_____

_____

_____

_____

_____

_____

_____

_____

7.   Evaluate the four strategies proposed by Larson and Richards.

_____

_____

_____

_____

_____

_____

_____

_____

_____

8.   Can you think of any other strategies that Larson and Richards might consider?

_____

_____

_____

_____

_____

_____

_____

_____

_____

_____

CASE 13

THE SAN ANTONIO HOBBY CENTER

Bill Mason was transferred to Randolph Air Force Base near San Antonio, Texas, in October 1977. Bill anticipated that this would be his last military assignment.

He had completed three years of college before enlisting in the service in 1961 and was not unhappy with his progress in the military. He had been commissioned from the ranks in 1973 and presently held the rank of captain. After 19 years in the service he was seriously considering early retirement to avoid possible subsequent separation from his family. He also felt that civilian job opportunities would be distinctly better at age 41 than after 30 years' service at age 51.

Bill's principal hobbies were wood carving, painting, and model airplane building. Shortly after his arrival in San Antonio he became a frequent visitor to the San Antonio Hobby Center located near his home.

The Hobby Center was owned and operated by Mr. Gus Velasco, a retired Air Force officer. It was in a suburban shopping center located at the junction of two of the main traffic arteries on the northeast side of the city. The center was composed of 34 diversified retail stores including a supermarket, drugstore, two small department stores, a restaurant, a bank, and several fashion and other specialty stores. The Hobby Center was the only retail store of its kind on the north side of the city.

Because of their common interests in the military and in hobbies, Bill and Mr. Velasco came to know each other quite well. On several

This case has been prepared by O. Hoyt Gibson, M. J. Neeley School of Business, Texas Christian University. Names of the company and persons have been disguised.

occasions, Mr. Velasco complained about the demanding responsibilities of owning and operating a retail store. Specifically, he felt
that he was required to spend too many hours in the store. Several
times he mentioned that he would like to find someone to take over
some of the managerial responsibilities.

Bill had told Mr. Velasco he was seriously considering retirement,
and Mr. Velasco suggested that Bill work part time in the store to see
how he might like retailing. Then, if he liked the work and if satisfactory conditions of employment could be agreed on, Bill could become
manager of the store when he retired.

Despite the fact that Bill had no experience in retailing, Mr. Velasco
considered him to be an excellent prospect for store manager. His
service record indicated that he was an achiever. It was a simple
matter to check among some of the officers who knew Bill at Randolph
Field. They all expressed genuine respect for Bill's ability as an administrative officer. He had a keen interest in hobbies, a quick mind, and
could learn what was needed to be manager of the San Antonio
Hobby Center.

Bill accepted Mr. Velasco's offer and began working part time in
August 1980. His schedule at the base was such that he could work 10
to 15 hours each week at the store and he could do some paper and
administrative work in the evenings and on weekends.

In January 1981 Bill retired from the service and became manager of
the Hobby Center. For the next few months, Mr. Velasco continued to
come to the store each day. By September 1981, he had turned over to
Bill responsibility for all aspects of store operation except the financial
considerations. Bill did the hiring, firing, buying, pricing, and merchandising. His responsibility, however, did not extend to record
keeping beyond these functions.

In January 1982 Mr. Velasco told Bill that he would like to sell the
store and suggested that Bill buy it. He indicated also that he would
do anything he could to help Bill.

Bill and his wife talked at length about how they could buy the store
from Mr. Velasco. They had bought a home in San Antonio, making a
minimum down payment, when he came to Randolph Field. They
owned two automobiles, one a 1976 Ford, which was paid for, and the
other a 1981 Buick, on which they still owed almost $2500. They
owned all their household furniture and fixtures. They also had a
savings account of $1900 and a checking account of approximately
$900.

Bill felt that his assets were inadequate to request a bank loan to
purchase the Hobby Center. He explained his financial position to Mr.

Velasco and told him that, while he would like to buy the store, he felt that there was no possible way to do this. Mr. Velasco encouraged him to make some reasonable offer, saying he was tired and wanted to retire.

In February 1982 Bill decided to make Mr. Velasco an offer for the store. He estimated the value of existing inventory to be $110,000 at cost. Based on his own experience in the store and information from one of the women who had worked in the store for three years, he estimated that approximately 30 percent of the inventory was more than 12 months old. Fixtures and equipment were valued at $12,500.

Unfortunately, Mr. Velasco had never kept accurate inventory control records. Also, the only permanent records of sales and expenses available to Bill were portions of Mr. Velasco's income tax return for the previous year. In that year, Mr. Velasco had paid income tax on store net income of $23,450.

Based on this information, Bill entered into further negotiations with Mr. Velasco. In March 1982 they reached an agreement. Bill signed a personal note to Mr. Velasco for $65,000 at 12 percent interest in monthly payments of $1000 plus interest. He also assumed $18,600 outstanding store indebtedness. Of the indebtedness, $2400 was the balance due on a store-owned 1981 station wagon, $4400 was for a note payable to a vendor due August 31, 1982, at no interest, and the balance was for merchandise. Approximately one-third of the balance was in current accounts payable. The rest was due immediately or past due. Bill took possession of the San Antonio Hobby Center on April 1, 1982.

A physical inventory was made on March 31, 1982. Based on this inventory and allowing a 50 percent reduction on $49,500 in merchandise that was more than 12 months old, inventory for April 1, 1982, was valued at $136,850. The inventory was divided among five classifications of merchandise as follows:

Toys and games	65%
Hobbies and crafts	20%
Art supplies	10%
Picture frames	3%
Miscellaneous	2%

Of the merchandise over 12 months old, 90 percent was estimated to be toys and games.

During the time Bill had worked at the Hobby Center, he had observed an imbalance in inventory. He felt demand for toys had declined substantially, as reflected by the amount of old inventory. In

Table 13–1
Net sales for the San
Antonio Hobby
Center, 1982 and 1983

	1982	1983
January	na*	$ 10,138
February	na	9,460
March	na	9,926
April	$ 9,358	10,166
May	12,656	9,828
June	12,248	8,090
July	12,956	10,148
August	12,356	12,000
September	14,626	10,750
October	12,076	9,620
November	16,344	14,626
December	33,010	26,352
	$135,630	$141,104

*Not available.

large part, he felt this was mostly due to the opening of two new discount stores in North San Antonio. He also sensed an increase in the demand for art supplies and picture frames.

As a result of this, Bill held a month-long clearance sale in May 1982, followed by a two-week sidewalk sale in June. He regarded both sales as successful in that a great deal of the old merchandise was removed from inventory. However, much of this merchandise was priced at cost or lower.

During the rest of the year, Bill continued to concentrate on getting rid of the remaining old inventory and improving his stock balance. He even purchased some new merchandise to improve the attractiveness of his month-end clearance sales. Merchandise purchased, however, was sold at a reasonable retail markup.

At the end of the year, Bill was pleased with the progress he had made in the store. Year-end accounting statements revealed sales of $135,630 and before-tax profit of $17,591 for the nine months of operation (see Table 13–1 and Exhibit 13–1).

Bill thought the inventory balance was much improved although still overbalanced in toys and games. Year-end inventory figures revealed the following balance of stock:

Toys and games	45%
Hobbies and crafts	20%
Art supplies	25%
Picture frames	10%

Analysis of sales for the nine-month period revealed sales in the same categories to be as follows:

Toys and games	26%
Hobbies and crafts	25%
Art supplies	38%
Picture frames	11%

Exhibit 13–1
Statement of profit or loss, April 1982–December 1982

Sales			
Gross sales		$135,852	
Returns and allowances		222	
Net sales			$135,630
Cost of goods sold			
Beginning inventory, January 1, 1982		$ 54,000	
Add: Purchases	$69,330		
Freight in	1,278	70,608	
Merchandise available		$124,608	
Less: Ending inventory, December 31, 1982		41,170	
Cost of goods sold			83,438
Gross profit			$ 52,192
Business deductions			
Depreciation (truck, equipment, and fixtures)		$ 2,416	
Rent		7,344	
Repairs (truck and equipment)		906	
Salaries and wages		12,466	
Insurance		1,658	
Legal and professional fees		162	
Interest on business indebtedness		1,247*	
Bad checks		254	
Advertising expense		2,224	
Utilities		1,764	
Materials and supplies		1,036	
Taxes (state and city sales and FICA)		1,550	
Other miscellaneous expense		1,574	
Total business deductions			34,601
Net operating profit before tax			$ 17,591

*Interest on the Velasco note was regarded as a personal expense rather than a business expense.

During the nine-month period, Bill had taken little money out of the business for himself. He had paid $900 on the station wagon note and met each payment on the note to Mr. Velasco. He had realized in April that he could not meet the $4400 vendor's note due in August. The vendor agreed to extend the note and Bill paid half the amount due.

By negotiating with vendors and careful control of cash, Bill had managed to bring all payables to current status but had not been able to reduce them appreciably. Meeting his obligations had placed a heavy drain on the store and Bill was unable to take cash discounts on any but the smallest purchases.

In June 1982 Bill borrowed $4000 at 14 percent to buy "back-to-school" art supplies and in October he borrowed another $15,000 at 14 percent to buy Christmas merchandise. Both notes were negotiated with his bank. The first note came due and was paid in December. The second note was not due until April 1983.

All in all, Bill felt the operation had been successful. He had reduced the indebtedness substantially, relationships with vendors were much better now that all payables were current, inventory balance was not what he wanted but it was improved, and the store had shown what he considered to be a healthy profit. Bill was looking forward to a good year in 1983.

Sales for the first three months of 1983 were better than expected. Bill was reducing prices of toys to bring inventory into balance and this was reflected in the sales figures (see Table 13–1). In May he repeated the clearance sale he had held the previous year. He also repeated the sidewalk sale. Through April Bill was very optimistic. The note due in April was met although it severely reduced cash on hand.

Beginning in May, sales fell below Bill's expectations for the first time. By August, the situation had become critical. All note payments except the note to Mr. Velasco were being met on time, but many purchases were being negotiated on a 30–60–90–day basis. He had to borrow another $6000 in August to purchase "back-to-school" art supplies.

In May a discount store had opened in the northern part of San Antonio. For the next three months, the new store conducted an intensive introductory promotional campaign. This was accompanied by an equally intensive counterpromotional campaign by two other discount stores on the east and west sides of town. Many of the items that appeared in the ads were the same items Bill carried, particularly in toys and games. They were often sold at or below Bill's cost.

In November, the White's Auto Store in the same shopping center

Exhibit 13–2
Statement of profit or loss for the San Antonio Hobby Center, 1983

Sales			
Gross sales		$142,914	
Returns and allowances		1,810	
Net sales			$141,104
Cost of goods sold			
Beginning inventory, January 1, 1983		$ 41,170	
Add: Purchases	$71,250		
Freight in	1,618	72,868	
Merchandise available		$114,038	
Less: Ending inventory, December 31, 1983		35,946	
Cost of goods sold			78,092
Gross profit			$ 63,012
Business deductions			
Depreciation (truck, equipment, and fixtures)		$ 3,216	
Rent		9,790	
Repairs (truck and equipment)		630	
Salaries and wages		14,308	
Insurance		1,752	
Legal and professional fees		126	
Interest on business indebtedness		1510	
Bad checks		726	
Advertising expense		3,814	
Utilities		1,958	
Materials and supplies		2,012	
Taxes (state and city sales and FICA)		1,726	
Other miscellaneous expense		2,804	
Total business deductions			44,372
Net operating profit before tax			$ 18,640

with Bill brought in $30,000 in toys and games and $7500 in pictures and ready-made frames for the Christmas season. This store had not carried any of these items the previous year.

During the year, Bill had noticed a marked decline in sales in toys and games. He felt this was due to competition from the discount house and the White's Auto Store Christmas offerings plus the decrease in toys and games inventory in his own store. He had also noticed a substantial increase in sales of art supplies and picture frames. This, he felt, was because of increased inventory in his own store and the relative lack of competition.

During 1983 he had paid the oldest bills first. He had retired the note on the station wagon and the balance of $2700 on the note he had assumed for Mr. Velasco at the time he purchased the store. In December he also paid $6000 he had borrowed in August. However, he had paid Mr. Velasco the $1617 due on his note only through April. No payment had been made to Mr. Velasco after the April 30 payment.

Mr. Velasco had been very understanding about the note payment and had assured Bill he was willing to work the problem out with him. Some of the vendors, however, were pressing for their payment as due.

When all the figures were in for the year 1983, they were very disappointing. Profit for the year was only $18,640 on sales of $141,104 (see Exhibit 13–2). On January 16, 1984, there was a cash balance of $1836, accounts payable of $21,429, of which $7038 was past due, and a balance due Mr. Velasco of $60,150 including accumulated interest.

CASE
ANALYSIS

CASE 13

The San
Antonio
Hobby Center

1. What other financial and operating data would have aided Bill in his decision whether or not to buy the Hobby Center?

_____

_____

_____

_____

_____

_____

_____

_____

_____

2. Did Bill's experience adequately prepare him for the task of operating the business? Discuss.

_____

_____

_____

_____

_____

_____

_____

3. In view of prospective earnings, evaluate Bill's decision to sign a six-year note for $65,000 at 12 percent interest as well as assume an $18,000 debt to acquire the store.

    _____

    _____

    _____

    _____

    _____

    _____

    _____

4. Is the purchase of new merchandise "to improve the attractiveness" of distressed merchandise a sound merchandising practice? Discuss.

    _____

    _____

    _____

    _____

    _____

5. To what extent did Bill achieve his objective of bringing the stock into better balance during the first nine months of operation? What were the alternatives available to achieve this goal when he took over the store?

_____

_____

_____

_____

_____

_____

_____

_____

_____

_____

_____

_____

_____

_____

_____

_____

_____

6. Bill has an urgent need for capital to operate the San Antonio Hobby
    Center. What are the alternatives? Which do you recommend?

_____

_____

_____

_____

_____

_____

7. What are the implications of personal bankruptcy in this case?

_____

_____

_____

_____

_____

CASE 14

SPEEDYBIND

Since the beginning of carpet manufacturing, producers have made carpets several hundred feet long in 12- or 15-foot-wide reels. Therefore, before 1960 most rugs were available in such standardized sizes as 9 × 12, 12 × 12, and 15 × 21. Standardization allowed carpet manufacturers to maximize their production efforts by minimizing the number of sizes obtainable from each reel of carpet and by minimizing the size of roll ends (i.e., nonstandardized pieces). Each standard-sized rug was bound by the manufacturer on all four sides using an industrial sewing machine. The binding of the carpet prevented fraying caused by wear.

During the decades of the 60s and 70s more and more requests for nonstandard-sized rugs were received by carpet manufacturers. The demand for wall-to-wall carpeting grew rapidly, completely reshaping the industry's operations. In 1981, 95 percent of all the carpeting sold was installed on a wall-to-wall basis. The rug-binding function was thus shifted from the manufacturer to the retail carpet dealer. Manufacturers will only bind carpets on a custom order basis, which requires a four- to eight-week delivery time.

Although the vast majority of carpeting is permanently installed wall-to-wall, there is still a sizable market for bound rugs. In general, this market can be segmented as follows: (1) people who do not like wall-to-wall carpeting and prefer to have area rugs; (2) people who move their furnishings from place to place and wish to move their

This case was prepared by Maurice G. Clabaugh, University of Montevallo. Reprinted from J. Barry Mason, Morris L. Mayer, and Hazel F. Ezell, *Cases and Problems in Contemporary Retailing*, copyright © Business Publications, Inc., 1982, by permission of the author and publisher.

carpet investment with them; and (3) people who wish to use the excess waste from their wall-to-wall installations as area rugs in heavily trafficked areas (e.g., in front of doorways or frequently used sofas and chairs).

To cater to the shift in consumers' tastes, a new retail service industry—carpet laying—evolved. Most carpet laying operations are locally owned and operated firms which provide services for retail carpet stores and for consumers who wish to have one of several functions performed. These service retailers may install, repair, restretch, and bind carpeting.

Carpet laying as well as carpet binding is a labor-intensive business which takes a minimum of capital. Typically, a carpet-laying crew consists of three people—a skilled carpet layer and two semiskilled helpers. A carpet laying firm may have one crew or several dozen crews. Installing wall-to-wall carpeting incorporates 95 percent of the firm's time and income; approximately 5 percent of the firm's time is spent repairing, restretching, and binding carpeting. Carpet binding is an auxiliary service having minimal impact on the carpet profits; therefore, according to trade sources, those who provide carpet binding services do not promise their customers a definite delivery date. Carpet binding performed by carpet layers takes from one week to as long as four months because it is performed at the whim of carpet layers and only done after hours.

Business conceptualization

Bob Roberts and Tom Clay, salesmen at a locally owned furniture store in Champaign, Illinois, found the carpet binding situation intolerable. They were receiving many complaints from their customers concerning the amount of time needed to obtain bound carpets. After calling other furniture and carpet retailers in the area, Roberts and Clay found the problem to be universal. In fact, many of the dealers asked to be informed if a way were found to solve the problem. Several of the dealers contacted were disturbed by the undependability of their current supplier of carpet binding materials and work as well as by slow delivery.

Further investigation of the carpet-binding business showed it to be a rather simple operation. Little machinery is needed, and new technology concentrates on hand-stapled binding rather than the sewed binding of the past. Thus, the business is labor intensive. It requires at least two people to handle the carpet material, which is either 12 or 15 feet wide, is usually at least 9 feet long, and weighs 100 to 200 or more pounds. These standard widths of carpeting require a shop at least 10 feet by 32 feet to perform the binding operation. A station wagon or truck is needed to transport the carpets.

After investigating the potential as well as the problems of this business, Roberts and Clay established a partnership called Speedybind. They told friends that they lacked only one business prerequisite—financing. Clay provided his 2½-car garage for the shop location, while Roberts provided his station wagon for the hauling. Clay and Roberts agreed to work an equal amount of time after the furniture store closed each day. Since a major customer complaint was uncertain, lengthy delivery time, Speedybind's motto was "24-hour service and guaranteed satisfaction."

Because Speedybind was located in a residential subdivision which customers might find hard to locate, it contacted all of the retail outlets which carried carpeting and offered its services to them. The retail outlets would be expected to do their own collection from customers not only for the carpets and installation but for the binding as well. In return, Speedybind would guarantee 24-hour service and customer satisfaction, or there would be no charge to the retail dealers. A majority of the retailers agreed to be subcontractors for Speedybind just to have the promise of customer satisfaction. Speedybind also expected a number of walk-in and/or call-in customers—people who preferred to deal directly with it.

After the concept and the accompanying marketing strategy had been developed, financing had to be arranged. Roberts and Clay submitted pro forma financial statements to a bank to support their application for a $2500 loan. The loan was obtained on the signatures of the partners only. Less than two weeks after the idea of Speedybind was conceived, the retail service firm was in operation, and the partners were enthusiastic about its growth potentials.

Operations

Roberts and Clay agreed formally to critically analyze the performance of Speedybind every six months to uncover real or potential problems and to develop new strategies. During the first six months of business, Speedybind averaged three to four carpet jobs of varying sizes a day. The business, which was operating on a part-time basis, was showing a monthly income of $700 on a $1500 sales volume. Cash flow was excellent, as Speedybind had no accounts receivable. The "bottom line" of the income statement was pleasing to the partners. Speedybind was financially sound (see Exhibit 14–1).

Exhibit 14–1
Speedybind monthly
income statement

Sales		$1,500
Expenses		
Auto expenses	$100	
Loan expenses	55	
Depreciation	45	
Building rent	100	
Supplies	100	
Wages	400	800
Profit before taxes		$ 700

Problems, however, began to arise with Roberts' and Clay's hours. Since they currently worked a 60-hour week at the furniture store, including an 8 A.M. to 9 P.M. day on Mondays and Fridays, the additional work of binding carpets on these days was beginning to cause problems. Although each planned to work three to four hours a night, Speedybind's 24-hour service caused complications. For example, if eight carpets were picked up on Friday at 5 P.M., they were promised by Speedybind for Saturday at 5 P.M., which meant that they had to be bound after the 9 P.M. closing of the furniture store. These carpets would then have to be delivered by Roberts on his Saturday lunch hour. This made both Clay and Roberts irritable, and their furniture sales were beginning to be affected.

Expansion

Still Roberts and Clay saw that business was growing and they believed that many more carpet retailers would use Speedybind after it was apparent that it was not a fly-by-night outfit. The partners also projected that they could expand without jeopardizing their cash flow; thus, they agreed to expand their operation. They rented a store, hired one full-time employee and one part-time employee, and purchased a panel truck. Their idea was essentially to be the financial backers for Speedybind, which the full-time employee would run as a manager. This expansion would increase the monthly expenses by only $500. However, business was expected to increase, because a full-time person would not only bind carpets but would also be expected to solicit new customers from the local retail carpet outlets. Even if business did not increase rapidly, the return on investment for Speedybind would be around 10 percent without the partners' investing "sweat capital." With the adoption of this new strategy, Speedybind was a full-fledged service retail store with such assets as a permanent location, employees, a truck, and equipment.

After the 12th month, the partners carefully analyzed the operations of Speedybind. The business had good months and bad months. However, neither partner was happy with the progress of the business. It had not increased as planned but had decreased to average gross sales of $800 a month. Investigation indicated that a lack of supervision by the partners had allowed inefficiencies to creep into the operation.

The partners were shocked, during several spot checks, to find Claude Hay, the manager, asleep at his desk. After lengthy interrogation they found that while Hay claimed that "the sickness of my wife keeps me up nights," it was something else. He was working additionally in the evenings at a local animal feed manufacturing firm which was demanding of his time and energy and paid him well. Hay offered to quit his night job if Speedybind would increase his salary 50 percent.

Financially, Speedybind was solvent. But the business needed to increase to a minimum volume of $1000 in gross sales a month to be a good investment for both partners. Both partners agreed that their objective was to have a sound investment in Speedybind.

Several conflicting alternatives were proposed by each partner. Roberts proposed that they diversify the business to include carpet laying. He reported that most carpet businesses laid carpets as well as bound them and that Speedybind was the only one which just bound carpets. "The money is in laying wall-to-wall," said Roberts.

Roberts' investigations of carpet selling organizations showed a demand for additional carpet layers. Five stores said that they felt they could guarantee Speedybind $1000 a month should Speedybind decide to enter the carpet laying business. Also, Roberts had contacted Frank Gibbs, who was an experienced carpet layer in the region. Gibbs had owned a carpet laying business which had recently gone bankrupt. He agreed to work for Speedybind for the same salary Hay was receiving for the binding operation plus 50 percent, with a guaranteed raise if sales reached $5000 per month. Gibbs had experience, carpet tools, and a fine reputation as a good carpet layer. With Gibbs on board, Roberts knew Speedybind could easily enter the carpet laying business, and he strongly supported this move.

Clay was vehemently opposed to expanding into carpet laying. In fact, he wanted to retreat to the old garage setup that they had begun with. "We just tried to run before we knew how to walk," said Clay, who pointed out that laying carpet violated the partnership mission and would make Speedybind just like any other carpet laying business.

Clay's "retreat" proposal centered on reducing expenses, increasing the partners' sweat capital through having them do the binding themselves, and increasing promotional activities. Promotional activities in the past had been confined to word-of-mouth contacts to retail carpet outlets and a Yellow Pages advertisement. Although consumer promotional campaigns via mass media would be possible, Clay felt that promotional efforts should focus on encouraging employees of carpet outlets to specify Speedybind rather than their usual carpet binding outlet. Several promotional ideas were discussed in the conversation between Roberts and Clay.

In the heated discussion that ensued, Roberts insisted that Gibbs' expertise was sufficient and that Gibbs could hire the crew he needed, so that the partners did not need to know how to lay carpet. Roberts also argued that there would be a guaranteed income from the five stores already solicited. Clay was equally adamant, and in trying to settle the dispute, he offered to sell out to Roberts for $1000 if Roberts would take over Speedybind's debts.

CASE ANALYSIS

CASE 14

Speedybind

1. It appears that demand for carpet binding is diminishing. Is it reasonable for a carpet-binding company like Speedybind to expect growth? Discuss.

_____

_____

_____

_____

_____

_____

_____

_____

_____

2. How well is Speedybind being managed?

_____

_____

_____

_____

3.   Assess Mr. Roberts' diversification proposal.

4.   Assess Mr. Clay's retreat proposal.

_____

_____

_____

_____

_____

5. Identify and assess at least two other options available to Speedybind.

_____

_____

_____

_____

_____

_____

_____

_____

_____

_____

_____

_____

_____

6.   Advise the Speedybind organization.

_____

_____

_____

_____

_____

_____

CASE 15

THE AJAX PUMP COMPANY

The Ajax Pump Company is the number two supplier of small pumps and valves to industrial replacement markets.

The Company's early (1940s and 1950s) success was built on the basis of local availability of virtually all replacement pumps and valves. In response to that market need, Ajax developed a strong distributor network, backed up by twenty-three small Company owned field warehouses under the direct control of the local marketing managers.

Two plants, one in New York and one in Chicago, ship to the field warehouses directly through small plant warehouses. Warehouse replenishment orders are generated by warehouse clerks who maintain a manual Kardex system, utilizing a minimum/maximum order point approach. Forecasted demand is based on a review of historic monthly usage at each field warehouse.

Order entry is accomplished in the field, utilizing a manual system. Manual order records are mailed to headquarters, for billing and accumulation of sales statistics.

Several important market trends developed in the 1960s:

1. Ajax's distributors, since being caught in the first modern credit crunch (1966), have become much less willing to hold adequate inventory. They carry most of the line but now rely more heavily on the Ajax field warehouse for backup stock and all fringe items.
2. The Company's marketing department has successfully developed

This case was prepared by James D. Blaser, Cleveland Consulting Associates. Reprinted by permission.

national service contracts with major industrial concerns to be administered on a direct basis. These accounts are served from the regional warehouses and their demand is more difficult to predict than the demand generated through the local distributors.

3. The product line has proliferated: in 1960 the line amounted to 1575 SKUs; today's product offering amounts to 5320 SKUs.

4. Manufacturing completed a three year program to reconfigure the production facilities and integrate foundry and aluminum die casting capabilities. While costs are lower, economic run sizes are now substantially larger and flexibility has been reduced from before when most components were purchased outside.

During the chaotic 1973–1975 economic period, Ajax was thrown into a loss position for the first time in thirty-six years. Inventories skyrocketed and, coupled with funding requirements associated with the manufacturing program, forced the Company to borrow funds up to the limit of its financial ability. Market conditions have stabilized but inventory remains too high by traditional standards. In spite of high inventories, Ajax's customer service level is below customer expectations and industry standards. In fact, Marketing has gone on record that Ajax has lost market share because of poor service.

A new Distribution Manager has been hired and been given responsibility for the warehouses, finished goods inventory control, order processing, and traffic. His first job is to develop a plan to restore Ajax's distribution position for presentation to top management for approval within the next three months.

The new Distribution Manager has been through an improvement effort like the one required at Ajax before and, after becoming thoroughly familiar with the situation, has developed a shopping list of major projects and programs he would like to evaluate and hopefully implement:

1. Evaluate a consolidated distribution network with five to seven new modern DC's to take the place of the present twenty-three warehouses.

2. Design a new order entry/inventory control/billing system that would automatically update inventory records and have extensive order and stock inquiry capabilities.

3. Develop a shipment consolidation program to accumulate a greater share of outbound shipments into truckloads.

4. Evaluate the possibility of pulling back the fringe items into a master warehouse and provide rapid-response national service for those items using premium transportation.

Over lunch one day, the Distribution Manager bounced these ideas off the President and Vice President-Marketing. The President was very interested but reminded the Distribution Manager that these appeared to all be major long-term projects, requiring considerable analysis and capital to implement. He reiterated his wish that the distribution improvement plan include detailed financial evaluations and justification.

In view of his objective to restore a sound financial position, the President asked that less capital intense improvements be looked at first. The Vice President-Marketing added that Ajax's major competitors were delivering orders within a three day turnaround time and achieving a reported 92% initial order fill level. As a result, the Company was losing sales and market share every day.

With those facts in mind, the Distribution Manager set about developing an approach to evaluating his options and developing the improvement plan.

Your assignment is to develop an approach, together with conceptual exhibits if possible, that shows how to evaluate alternatives and express the distribution plan in financial terms.

**Exhibit 15–1
Ajax Pump Company,
Summary financial
statements, 1976**

Profit and loss statement

	Thousands
Sales	$75,000
Cost of goods	42,220
Gross profit	$32,780
Distribution costs	$12,760
Selling and administrative	5,750
Depreciation	9,000
Interest	2,520
Income taxes	1,250
Net income	$ 1,500

Balance sheet

Assets		Liabilities and capital	
Cash	$ 400	Current liabilities	$ 5,600
Receivables	8,000	Long term debt	26,500
Inventories	20,000		
Manufacturing facilities[1]	38,200	Total debt	$32,100
Distribution facilities[1]	12,900		
Other	500	Shareholder equity	$47,900
Total	$80,000	Total	$80,000

Note: [1] Net of accumulated depreciation

**Exhibit 15–2
Ajax Pump Company,
Key financial relation-
ships and ratios**
(Dollars in thousands)

Incremental pretax profit contribution

				Per cent of sales
Reported gross margin (sales less cost of goods)				43.7%

Other variable costs	*Total % of sales*		*Variable portion of cost*		
Distribution	17%	×	38%	=	−6.5%
Selling and administrative	8	×	15	=	−1.2
Contribution margin					36.0%

Finished goods inventory turns

Cost of goods	$42,220	
		2.6
Average F.G. inventory	16,000	

Exhibit 15–3
Key distribution data

Analysis of distribution costs

	Thousands	Per cent of sales
Freight costs		
Outbound	$ 3,150	4.2
Warehouse replenishment	2,100	2.8
Warehouse operating costs		
Fixed	3,345	4.5
Variable	1,380	1.8
Order entry/billing system	1,100	1.5
Packaging	535	0.7
Logistics administration	100	0.1
Traffic, receiving & shipping	600	0.8
Taxes, obsolescence & insurances	450	0.6
Total	$12,760	17.0

Shipment profile

	Truckload	LTL	Other
Inbound replenishment	73%	27%	0%
Outbound	3	96	1

Exhibit 15–4
Key distribution data

Average shipment size	$700	800 pounds

Order cycle time

	Average	95% confidence
Order mail in	2	4
Internal processing	4	10
Outbound shipment	1	3
Total	7	17

Customer service level
Per cent of items filled   83%

CASE
ANALYSIS

CASE 15

The Ajax Pump Company

1. What must Ajax do to reverse the present trend?

   _____

   _____

   _____

   _____

   _____

2. What has caused physical distribution costs to rise? Identify several contributing factors.

   _____

   _____

   _____

   _____

   _____

   _____

   _____

   _____

3. How is it possible that inventories increased while customer service declined?

_____

_____

_____

_____

_____

_____

_____

_____

4. Compare Ajax's order processing time and initial order fill level with that of its major competitors.

_____

_____

_____

_____

_____

5. Evaluate the new Distribution Manager's four-step improvement plan.

_____

_____

_____

_____

_____

_____

_____

_____

_____

6.   What immediate steps would you recommend?

_____

_____

_____

_____

_____

_____

_____

_____

_____

_____

_____

_____

_____

_____

_____

_____

_____

_____

_____

7.   What inventory control techniques should Ajax adopt?

_____

_____

_____

_____

_____

PART FOUR

PROMOTION DECISIONS

CASE 16

COMPUTER BOUTIQUE

Introduction

George Johnson first became interested in home computers in his role as a math teacher at a Centerville high school. After reading a number of reports in business magazines, George became convinced that the market for home/personal computers was worth looking into. Even the least optimistic predictions seemed to indicate a very good potential for growth. Discussions with other faculty members, as well as local businessmen, convinced George further that sufficient demand potential existed in his local market area, which was situated in a medium-sized town in the western part of Kentucky, to support a dealership for one of the major home computer brands. He also felt that his own past experience in teaching business courses would prepare him, to some degree, to be a part-time salesperson.

His wife, Brenda, was also enthusiastic about the proposed business venture. After some evaluation of the various brands available, George became convinced that the Apple computer offered the best value and best growth prospects for the near future. The two of them decided to open a dealership to sell Apple computer products.

Brenda had been employed with large accounting firms in Chicago and New York and, more recently, with a local company as a systems analyst. She was quite familiar with the design and installation of computers in the business environment. Brenda was anxious to strike out on her own and felt that by leaving her present job with the firm and entering into a partnership with her husband she could gain some freedom to do the type of work she really enjoyed. She also felt that the long-term profit prospects were much better in this industry

This case was prepared by Phillip B. Niffenegger and Fred L. Miller, Murray State University.

for the independent dealer than for the career programmer/analyst. Thus in the summer of 1981, George and Brenda entered into a partnership to distribute the Apple computer in their market area which covered about 100 square miles of western Kentucky. They named their new business "The Computer Boutique."

Under the terms of the new agreement, Brenda was to manage the organization, and act as a primary sales and technical resource person. George was to serve as a consultant to the firm, concentrating on educational and individual small business clients. Additional salespeople would be hired as business grew. They would be paid by a combination of salary and commission.

Present situation

The Apple Computer Company was founded in 1976 by two college dropouts named Steve Jobs and Steve Wozniak. The two had worked as design engineers in California's Silicon Valley where they became intimately familiar with the technology required to build a microcomputer. After building a number of models for their friends, they decided to enter the commercial market. By mid 1977, they had introduced the Apple II computer, which sold for as little as $1,500, and was aimed at the home hobbyist market. The Apple II was extremely successful, and by 1979 the incorporated firm had attained a total sales of $60 million, up both from total revenues of under $2 million its first year of operation. Success continued for the company with the introduction of the Apple III computer in May of 1980, leading to total 1980 sales of $165 million—up 175 percent.

During this high-growth period, Apple also had undergone several changes in their distribution structure. In early 1980, Apple terminated independent distributors and established company-owned regional support centers for its dealers. This was aimed at providing better support to Apple's 850 domestic dealers.

The Johnsons had applied to Apple and had been accepted as a dealer for Centerville, which had a population of about 50,000. It was located in a rural area of the state, and the Johnsons believed that in addition to local businessmen, professionals and home hobbyists, the large-scale farm operators would also provide potential customers. Furthermore, George commuted to his high school teaching job in an adjacent town, about 50 miles from Centerville, in which was located a university. The town also had a population of about 20,000 people. Under the terms of his dealership agreement, the Boutique was allowed to make sales in the nearby university town. According to their calculations, the total population of his potential market area numbered close to 100,000 people, which he felt should be adequate to support his projected sales target.

The plan was that George would sell part-time in the university town as well as in Centerville to assist Brenda, who would manage the firm and be its primary salesperson. Through his ties with the university George hoped that he could also develop a pool of potential people who could write custom programs (software) for users who needed specialized applications.

George and Brenda made arrangements with a local distributor of business machines to lease 500 square feet of floor space on the first floor of the office equipment firm. They believed this provided an ideal location both because potential business users for other business machines would pass by his display area, and because it was within a few minutes drive of most of the major businesses located in Centerville.

The Johnsons planned a sales program based around in-store equipment demonstrations as well as sales calls in the field, with and without computer equipment. They planned to use local advertising which aimed at small business users and identified the Boutique with Apple's national advertising campaigns. As manager, Brenda prepared a pro forma income statement (Exhibit 16–1) to guide the first year's operations and expenditures.

Exhibit 16–1
Pro forma income statement, first year's operation

		Dollars	% Sales
Sales: 70 systems @ $5,000		350,000.00	0.98
Consultation & instruction fees		6,000.00	0.02
Total revenues		356,000.00	1.00
Cost of sales		234,500.00	0.66
Gross margin		121,500.00	0.34
Administrative salaries	18,000.00		0.05
Allowance for advertising	48,500.00		0.14
and sales force compensation			0.00
Instructor's fees	3,000.00		0.01
Rental of office space	6,000.00		0.02
Miscellaneous	5,000.00		0.01
Total expenses	80,500.00	80,500.00	0.23
Income before taxes		41,000.00	0.12
Provision for income taxes		9,020.00	
Net income		31,980.00	0.09

Exhibit 16–2

The renaissance man is alive and well.

This once endangered species has made an astounding comeback.

Take Tom McWilliams.

He grew up with lots of skis, bicycles and microscopes.

And an Apple® II Personal Computer.

Using the latter to design a few video games, 16-year-old Tom was able to supplement his allowance.

By about $50,000. Without mowing a single lawn.

Of course, as we all know, some of the best renaissance men are women.

Like Margaret Waldmann. Who spent the first 50 years of her life becoming a world class pianist. And the last ten building one of the finest music schools in New York City—with some recent help from *her* Apple II.

After four decades of ever-narrowing specialization, more and more people are broadening their talents in more and more ways.

And more of them are using Apple IIs. Or our newest version, the Apple IIe.

It's even easier to use.

And thanks to the most sophisticated circuitry available, even more reliable.

But improvements aside, it's basically the same remarkable design that's already earned access to more software programs, accessories and peripherals than any other personal computer.

With more on the way.

So year after year, Apple IIe's will become even more valuable.

Just like the people who use them.

Soon there'll be just two kinds of people.
Those who use computers and
those who use Apples.

Brenda was quite optimistic that the long-term growth opportunities in the personal computer market were excellent. She based this assumption on a number of projections done by private industry analysts. Informed projections of yearly sales growth in the total industry through 1985 ranged from 32 percent to nearly 50 percent; and in just six years total industry revenues had grown from nothing to over 1.5 billion dollars. Personal computers were expected to approach the 5 billion dollar level by 1985 (see Exhibit 16–3).

The Johnsons felt that the area they served was relatively unsophisticated in its knowledge and use of microcomputer products, and that therefore a well established and recognizable brand was particularly important to their success. They felt that given the nature of the competitive environment in this industry and idiosyncrasies of the local environment, one of three potential growth patterns was possible. First they could remain primarily an Apple Computer dealer and expand by incorporating new lines of peripheral products for that system. Secondly, Computer Boutique could become a dealer for other computer systems, offering a breadth of choice, in place of depth of offering in the single product line for its customers. The potential introduction of new equipment by large computer companies such as Xerox and IBM, as well as the entry of Japanese firms into the market, might necessitate such a move. Third, the division could expand into other cities within the region, perhaps using a franchise arrangement to secure local capital.

Product data

The Apple product line consisted primarily of two models. The Apple II computer, which ranged in price from about $1,500 to about $3,500, depending on the size of the memory and the associated accessory equipment desired by the customer. Additional equipment included the choice of black and white or color T.V. monitor, disk drives to store additional programs and data files, and a range of output printers which could produce everything from letter-quality documents to a fairly simple printed record of the data output. The Apple III computer was priced from about $4,500 to over $6,000, depending on the options selected by the customer. Its major advantage was its larger memory and ability to handle more complicated types of data analysis.

But no matter how good the computer product (hardware) it would be of little value without the right program of instruction to make it suitable for a particular application (software). One benefit of the

**Exhibit 16–3
Total market size,
division of the market**

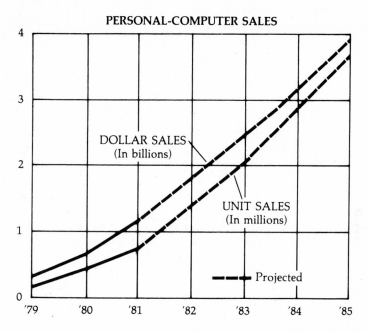

PERSONAL-COMPUTER SALES

DOLLAR SALES
(In billions)

UNIT SALES
(In millions)

━ ━ ━ Projected

'79   '80   '81   '82   '83   '84   '85

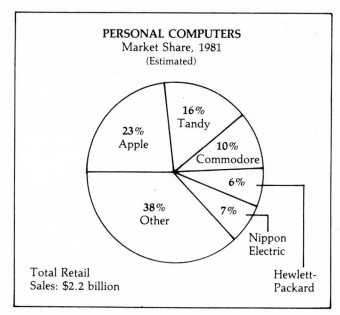

PERSONAL COMPUTERS
Market Share, 1981
(Estimated)

23%
Apple

16%
Tandy

10%
Commodore

6%

38%
Other

7%

Nippon
Electric

Hewlett-
Packard

Total Retail
Sales: $2.2 billion

Apple system was that because it was the first widely marketed personal computer, a great variety of software had been developed by interested individuals and was now marketed through a series of software houses. The price of an individual program, which might range from a video game through a complicated sales forecasting program, could range from $15 to $2000. Generally, the software was written for specific user groups such as home hobbyists or small businesses; a representative listing of the types of software available is provided in Exhibit 16–4.

The Johnsons believed that an important part of the product was the personal service necessary to acquaint the potential user with the operation of the machine, as well as guide him to standard programs which were adaptable to his particular needs. It had been their impression that the major gap or lack in the industry was a customer-centered organizational philosophy that was aimed at identifying and meeting customer needs. They felt that this type of philosophy would be even more important as the market served by the microcomputer industry changed from that of the hobbyist to the small business and professional environment. They believed this to be especially true in their sales region which had not been served by a microcomputer dealer previously. It was relatively remote, and microcomputers had not to date made a significant impact in the area. For this reason, local small businesses and professionals were rather wary of the microcomputer products. Potential buyers did recognize their need for information processing capability, but were reluctant to purchase the equipment that could supply the need without a good deal of local help, service, and support.

To respond to this opportunity, the Johnsons provided low cost training to their clients through a series of workshops which were held during evening hours at the Centerville Office Machine Store. The Johnsons thought that one competitive advantage that they could offer versus other suppliers of personal computers was their ability to sit down with a customer and show him via a one to two hour demonstration how a particular Apple equipment combination could be adapted and programmed to suit the specific needs of the customer. Stores like Radio Shack often could not provide such a personalized presentation. They believed that the provision of such a service could furnish them with a strong competitive advantage over other sellers in the area. As one industry source had put it, "There has been a missing link from day one: Nobody has started with the customer to find out what he wants in a small computer. Instead of homing in on market segments and smoothing the interface between man and ma-

Physicians
  Medical Secretary
  Medical Billing
  Medical Ed. Programs
  Data Base
  Word Processing

Lawyer
  Word Processing
  Professional Time Management
  Client Billing System
  Budgeting
  Desk Top Planner
  Speechlink 2000
  Supertalker
  Case History

Banker
  Interest and Loans
  Desk Top Plan
  Loan Analysis
  Stock Evaluator

Small Business Owner
  General Ledger
  Accounts Payable
  Accounts Receivable
  Payroll
  Inventory
  Word Processing
  Aardvark Tax Programs

Dentist
  Patient File
  Dental Management System
  Mailing List
  Case History

Sales Manager
  Desk Top Plan
  Mail List Manager
  Order/Entry Invoicing
  Information Master

Contractor
  General Ledger
  Accounts Payable
  Accounts Receivable
  Job Costing
  Payroll
  Project management

Accountant/Bookkeeper
  General Ledger
  Cost Accounting
  Mail List
  Master Tax
  Payroll

Secretary
  Word Processing
  Mail Lists
  Appointment Calendar

Manufacturing
  Warehouse/Distributor Pkg.
  A/P, A/R, Job Costing
  Machine Part Quoting
  Order Entry

Drug Store
  General Accounting System
  Patient File History

Restaurant
  Payroll
  Inventory

Real Estate
  Listings
  Financial Pkg.
  Income Property Analysis
  Lease Management
  Data Base

Retailer
  Accounting
  Cash Register
  Inventory

Plant Manager
  Records Employee
  Budgeting By Department
  Cash Flow Analysis

Agricultural
  Crop and Herd Planning
  Farm Accounting Systems
  Depreciation Records
  Linear Programming

chine, they build stuff for technical people to play with. They think they are appealing to the laymen, but they are really not."

Market analysis

Since the original introduction of the personal computer in 1976, the market had changed radically. The hobbyist market slowed down beginning around 1978. George felt that the biggest potential for sales was in the small business market, and among professionals such as doctors and lawyers. He based this belief on national trade surveys which identified the following five basic types of customers:

1. The hobbyist
2. Small business
3. Professional users
4. The agricultural community
5. The educational community

In the initial phase of growth in the microcomputer industry the home user or hobbyist provided the majority of demand for the product. Generally, they are innovators with great interest in the technical details of equipment and computer programming, but with relatively little interest in prepackaged software. Current estimates are that 6.9 percent of microcomputer sales goes to the hobbyist or home market. The hobbyist typically makes a modest initial acquisition in terms of equipment. Their needs for mass storage devices are not as great and they tend to use cassette as a storage device rather than disk. Also, the hobbyist is very price conscious and low cost is often the dominant benefit sought. For this reason, they may be lost by the retail computer dealer to mail-order houses who offer substantial discounts which the retailer is not able to meet.

Moreover, the hobbyist is generally not impressed with the offsetting advantages which the retailer can offer, such as fast local service, since time is not a big problem when equipment problems arise. The home user is more willing to consult manuals and to spend time working to solve his or her own problems than either the business or professional user.

The second market identified by the Boutique is that of small business. This group contains a number of small, local businessmen in the area who have information and managerial information needs which are not adequately handled by their present manual systems and who may benefit from computerization of their business. The average system purchased by this group ranges in the neighborhood of $8,000 to

$10,000. The benefits which they seek are: 1. accuracy of information; 2. ease of obtaining accounting information; 3. automation of manual bookkeeping services so as to free up managerial time; 4. the availability and accuracy of managerial reports on a timely basis to be used for diagnostic purposes in the management of their businesses.

This group is very concerned with local service for any computer system which they buy and with help in setting up and maintaining computerized accounting systems. Thus, the retail outlet has an advantage over mail-order firms since it is able to provide the local service and support desired. Although a wide range of prepackaged software is available for this market, many small business users are unwilling or unable to mold their operations to what is available. Thus, this customer type can also be a significant source of sales for program development, seminars in accounting software, and courses in computer usage.

Included in the professional category are accountants, lawyers, doctors, dentists, veterinarians, engineers, and surveyors. At one level, the needs of this group are identical with those of the small business, since both groups need standard accounting applications to maintain their accounting records. However, the groups differ in that the professional community tend to be businessmen by chance and not by choice. They are concerned with maintaining books for government and tax record requirements. However, their primary interest is in the ability of the computer to help them perform their specialized professional tasks. For this reason, this group is very demanding in terms of the software packages that the retailer is required to locate. See examples in Exhibit 16–4.

It is not unusual for the computer retailer to be approached by a member of one of these professions who is seeking a computer system that will handle a software package that they have located elsewhere. This represents a sale for which the dealer has had to extend very little effort. Also, once the initial purchase has been made, the professional may be approached for other software applications which can result in future sales. The professional accounts for about 17 percent of the personal computer market with an average system price of just under $7,800.

Current estimates are that some 5 percent of the farm community is using microcomputers in the analysis of their business and farming needs. Estimates project that within the next 10 years that figure could rise to as high as 85 percent. Since the region in which the Computer Boutique is located is largely rural, it seems to represent good potential for development. In general, farmers are looking for specialized accounting applications like single entry accounting systems designed for use on the farm. In addition, they need budgeting and forecasting tools, as well as programs which allow them to assess the different variables that play a role as they make their day-to-day farm operating decisions. In the absence of computer systems these calculations can be very time consuming, and take the farmer away from the demands of his real job, farming operations.

Sales to farmers tend to be cyclical, running with the seasonal harvests. Farmers are not averse to making large capital investments if the benefits of those investments can be shown to be cost effective. The farmer is accustomed to investing large sums of money in implements for farm usage, based upon extensive pay out planning. Farmers generally have well-established lines of credit and therefore are able to acquire financing on their own much more easily than other types of business firms.

The educational market is composed primarily of elementary and high school teachers who anticipate using the computer in the schoolroom, either to teach computer literacy or to use as an educational aid in other subject areas. Due to recent cutbacks in federal and state budgets, this market presently does not have a great deal of investment capital available to it. Furthermore, prices which can be charged for this market are governed by state contract.

Although the Computer Boutique was not successful in its bid for the state contract, it does have the option of matching contract prices to achieve educational sales. However, the prices are low and leave it very little operating margin.

Computer Boutique would like to meet state contract prices and pursue the educator market for two reasons. First, as the economy improves making more money available to the educational community, and as the benefits of the computer in the classroom become more apparent, the number of acquisitions should increase. An increase in volume could offset the low prices, adding to profits. Second, as young people become acquainted with the capabilities of microcomputers in the classroom, they will develop into potential markets for home use. And the system which they utilize in the classroom will tend to be the one they purchase for home use.

Since price is already established, service is important to the educator market in two respects: 1) helping the teacher to master the equipment and stay ahead of the students; and 2) helping educators to locate and keep up to date on the latest software.

In terms of competition at the national level, Brenda found some marketing research data from a trade magazine which showed that currently Apple had the largest share of the market with about 23 percent of the total estimated 1981 dollar sales. They were followed by Tandy (Radio Shack) with 16 percent, and Commodore with 10 percent (see Exhibit 16–3). When they had decided to establish an Apple dealership, the Johnsons foresaw no strong competition in their market area since the only local outlets for personal computers were Radio Shack stores in Centerville and in the university town. Based on their philosophy of the importance of personalized service, they felt these outlets did not constitute serious competition in this particular product category.

However, three months after Computer Boutique set up shop, IBM Company, the nation's largest seller of large-size computers, announced their entry into the personal computer market. Although there was no local dealer for the IBM product line, IBM was planning to sell through a series of franchise computer stores (Computer Land), as well as through a chain of specialized Sears and Roebuck business product stores which were planned for large-city areas. In addition, IBM's regular sales force will sell the new personal computer line. IBM's line was roughly comparable to the Apple. The lowest-priced system cost $1,565 but offered no visual display screen. The most elaborate, offering a capacity to display data in graphic form in 16 colors and a memory system that could store more than 250 typewritten pages of information, would cost more than $6,000.

Industry observers felt that the major strength IBM brought to the market was their strong reputation for reliability and service, even though their new microcomputer line did not offer any real technical breakthroughs. IBM planned to offer its own software, as well as software packages similar to those available for the Apple. Some industry analysts felt that the entry of IBM into the personal computer market would be good for all of the large producers since they would validate the importance of this particular market segment. Certain analysts also predicted that the large infusion of advertising and merchandising dollars by IBM would stimulate the growth of the entire market, much as the entry of Kodak into the instant-picture market helped to increase the sales of Polaroid.

Promotion

Brenda felt that the area of promotion presented both challenges and opportunities to the Boutique. She was uncertain as to how the promotional budget should be allocated to advertising and personal selling. Further she was unsure as to the maximum media allocation for advertising dollars.

The area of personal selling demanded much thought and necessitated many important decisions. How many sales people should the Boutique hire? How should they be compensated? Should they concentrate on inside or outside sales? Should they be assigned sales territories, vertical markets, or no markets at all? What sources should they use to find leads for the Boutique? What types of approaches should be used for each of the markets which the Boutique desires to reach? Brenda felt that proper decisions on these questions would be crucial in determining the success of the new business.

Finances

Based on her projected 12-month budget, Brenda felt that the Boutique could provide an acceptable end-of-year profit if it sold between four and six Apple systems per month. This would work out to a total monthly sales volume of about $29,000. Monthly sales for the first three months of operation averaged $22,000. However, the Apple organization felt that each distributor should be capable of selling between eight and ten Apple systems per month. There was some danger that if the Computer Boutique did not realize this latter sales level, Apple would not renew the franchise, but give it to a more successful dealer who was now operating in an adjacent city about 60 miles to the north.

Pricing

The policy of Apple Computer Incorporated is to formally discourage discounting from its basic margins of 30–35 percent. In theory the Boutique adheres to this practice of no discounting. However, there are significant exceptions. The first is the educational market in which the price level is set by the state contract. Another source of downward pressure on price comes from the home user market. The hobbyists tend to search the numerous publications of the microcomputer industry to locate a mail-order firm advertising exceptionally low prices for Apple equipment, then bring these prices to the attention of a local Apple dealer, and demand equivalent discounts. One of the most perplexing problems which Computer Boutique faces is how to respond to this type of downward price pressure from the hobbyist.

Bidding pressure on prices can also develop from the retail Apple dealers in adjacent regions. Thus far, the policy of Computer Boutique has been to maintain the price level suggested by Apple, in order to provide the margin necessary to support services such as consultation and repairs as well as to maintain the quality image of Apple products so painstakingly built by the manufacturer. Discounts have been considered, however, when the Johnsons felt they were justified by volume, the prospect of future business, or in competitive bidding situations.

Courtesy of Hazel Hankin/Stock, Boston

CASE ANALYSIS

CASE 16

Computer
Boutique

1. Upon which market segments should the Computer Boutique concentrate its marketing effort? Why?

_____

_____

_____

_____

_____

_____

_____

2. Should the promotional budget be concentrated on advertising, personal selling, or a combination of the two?

_____

_____

_____

_____

_____

_____

_____

_____

3. Assuming that the Johnsons' sales projections for the year are accurate, how can they estimate the number of salespersons they will need?

_____

_____

_____

_____

_____

_____

_____

_____

4. Would you recommend that the salesforce personnel specialize on different market segments, or should each of them try to sell to all segments? Why?

_____

_____

_____

_____

_____

_____

_____

_____

_____

_____

_____

5. Which type of compensation plan would work best for the sales-force—straight salary, straight commission, or a combination plan? Why?

_____

_____

_____

_____

_____

_____

_____

_____

_____

_____

6. What sources should the Computer Boutique use to locate individual sales prospects for Apple Computer equipment?

_____

_____

_____

_____

_____

_____

_____

_____

7. Describe two different customer approaches that could be used by Computer Boutique salespeople.

_____

_____

_____

_____

_____

_____

_____

_____

_____

8. What, if anything, should a salesperson do in terms of follow-up
    activities after an Apple Computer system is sold?

_____

_____

_____

_____

_____

_____

_____

_____

_____

CASE 17

MEDICAL EMERGICARE CENTER

Background

Dr. Jake Christie, an emergency physician, recently opened the Emergicare Center. Located in a newly built shopping center at a dense traffic intersection in a sunbelt community, the Emergicare Center was conceived by Christie as an emergency and ambulatory care (outpatient) center designed to serve the needs of a primarily upper-middle-income residential community in a rapidly growing suburb southeast of a booming sunbelt city. (See Exhibit 17–1 and Table 17–1.) This innovative medical concept provides emergency care delivered by a physician and a qualified medical team from 8 A.M. to 12 midnight, seven days a week, every day of the year in a convenient and accessible location. No appointment is necessary and waiting is minimized.

Description of services

The Emergicare Center is primarily an emergency care center providing competent, quality medical services. Although the center is not designed to treat many life-threatening emergencies, it is appointed with a fully equipped cardiac "crash cart"[1] to respond to cardiac emergencies. Primarily, this new concept of medical care is best matched to serving those persons requiring minor emergency care including treatment of cuts, minor burns, sprains, broken bones,

This case was prepared by Debra Low and Daniel Freeman. Reprinted with permission from Charles Patti and John Murphy, *Cases in Advertising and Promotion Management*, copyright © John Wiley and Sons, Inc., 1983.

Exhibit 17–1
Map of metropolitan area depicting location of the Emergicare Center

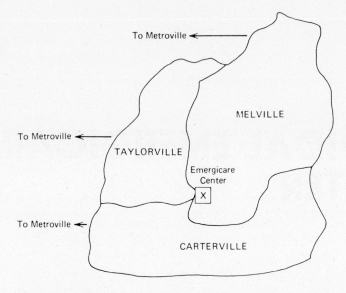

To Metroville ◄

To Metroville ◄

MELVILLE

TAYLORVILLE

Emergicare
Center

X

To Metroville ◄

CARTERVILLE

Reprinted from *Cases in Advertising and Promotion Management*, by Charles Patti and John Murphy, © 1983 John Wiley and Sons, Inc. Reprinted by permission of John Wiley and Sons, Inc.

asthma, urinary tract infections, stomach pain, and other medical problems.

In addition to emergency care, the Emergicare Center provides general medical care on a walk-in basis. This care, especially designed for episodic treatment, is an effective medical backup when the patient's regular physician is unavailable or when immediate care is required. Such procedures as preschool exams, immunizations, and premarital and insurance examinations can also be completed at the Emergicare Center.

The center also offers complete industrial medical services for local businesses. Preemployment physical examinations, emergency care, and other medical services are available. Written and telephone reports are made to the employer concerning the employee's condition.

A follow-up phone call is part of this innovative concept of care. A call is made the day after the patient's visit to check on the patient's condition. Referrals are also made, when appropriate, to the patient's personal physician or a specialist. A prescription phone-in service is also provided to the patient's personal pharmacy.

Table 17–1

Population statistics of service area

Melville (City A)	70,600
Taylorville (City B)	25,100
Carterville (City C)	29,673

Race and national origin (percent)

	White	Black	American Indian	Asian	Other	Spanish origin
City A	92.2	1.2	0.1	0.1	5.2	9.2
City B	91.5	1.8	0.1	1.5	4.4	8.2
City C	80.7	2.9	1.5	1.0	13.8	20.6
County	86.6	3.2	1.5	0.2	7.8	13.2
State	82.4	2.8	5.6	0.1	8.4	16.2

Age distribution (percent)

	Service area	County	State
Under 15	30.3	25.0	25.2
15–44	45.3	45.8	45.5
45–65	17.7	18.3	18.3
Over 65	6.8	10.8	11.0

General characteristics

	Service area	County
Median age	23.5	29.9
Median household income	$18,125	$21,933
Percent of households with children under 18	53%	44%
Percent retired heads of households	19%	28%
Median years education of head of household	12.4	19.2

The facilities and staff

The Emergicare Center is located in a 2000-square-foot site in a strip shopping mall (see Exhibit 17–2). Emergency and handicapped parking is available at a rear emergency entrance, as well as regular spaces located to provide easy access.

The Emergicare Center has four examination rooms, a fully equipped X-ray unit, a laboratory for performing routine blood, urine, and chemistry work, a minor surgery/treatment room, and a waiting room. (See Exhibit 17–3.) It is also equipped with an EKG, cardiac

**Exhibit 17–2
Plan of shopping
center**

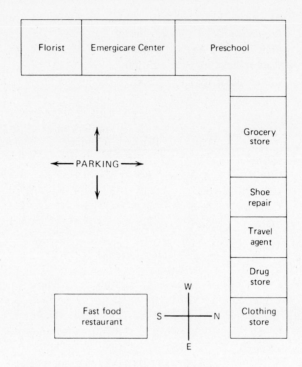

Reprinted from *Cases in Advertising and Promotion Management*, by Charles Patti and John Murphy, © 1983 John Wiley and Sons, Inc. Reprinted by permission of John Wiley and Sons, Inc.

monitor, and fully equipped "crash cart" for coronary patients, as well as all supplies for suturing, splinting, and performing other minor surgical procedures. The staff consists of Dr. Jake Christie, a physician specializing in emergency medicine, four full-time medical assistants, and four part-time medical assistants.

Price

The Emergicare Center concept is designed to provide competent medical care at prices that are substantially lower than hospital emergency rooms. Most medical insurance policies will reimburse patients for acute care, whether the care is delivered at a hospital-based emergency room or an ambulatory/emergency care center such as the Emergicare Center. Patients receiving treatment at the center with

**Exhibit 17–3
Floor plan of
Emergicare Center**

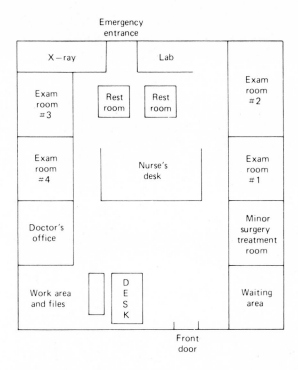

Reprinted from *Cases in Advertising and Promotion Management*, by Charles Patti and John Murphy, © 1983 John Wiley and Sons, Inc. Reprinted by permission of John Wiley and Sons, Inc.

charges of $100 or less are expected to pay at the time the services are rendered, and then may file for reimbursement with the medical insurance company. If medical charges exceed $100, or if any injury or minor surgery is involved, or if it is a work-related injury, or if hospitalization is required, the Emergicare Center will accept the patient's insurance card instead of direct payment.

Analysis of the competitive care market

Within the service area of the Emergicare Center are four existing hospitals, one proposed hospital, and two satellite facilities; all offer various levels of emergency care, in addition to the services of the Emergicare Center. (See Exhibit 17–4.) Traditionally, hospital emergency rooms have provided the majority of emergency care, presumably because they have been perceived to be best equipped to handle

**Exhibit 17–4
Proximity of
competing services**

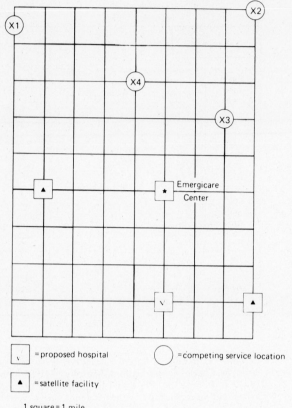

= proposed hospital   ◯ = competing service location

▲ = satellite facility

1 square = 1 mile

Reprinted from *Cases in Advertising and Promotion Management*, by Charles Patti and John Murphy, © 1983 John Wiley and Sons, Inc. Reprinted by permission of John Wiley and Sons, Inc.

emergency cases by most health care consumers. In addition, consumers have had no alternative to traditional hospital-based emergency rooms.

As an alternative to the traditional hospital emergency rooms, the Emergicare Center is in direct competition with those area hospitals that provide emergency and ambulatory care. The Emergicare Center is located within four miles of a well-known community hospital (part of an aggressive multi-institutional system) and within four miles of a small community hospital. Each hospital provides emergency care. (See Exhibit 17–4 and Tables 17–2 and 17–3.) The Emergicare Center is at a relative disadvantage to the hospital's emergency rooms because,

**Table 17–2
Emergency services
offered**

Procedure	Health care facility				
	1	2	3	4	Emergicare Center
Gastric lavage	√	√	√	√	√
Gastroscopy	√	—	√	√	—
Incision and drainage	√	—	√	—	√
Cauterization	√	—	√	—	√
Eye dilation	√	√	—	√	√
Cryotherapy	√	√	—	—	—
Wash wounds	√	√	—	√	√
Crash cart	√	√	√	—	√
Lumbar puncture	√	√	√	—	—
Sigmoidoscopy	√	√	√	√	√

√ = Services offered.
— = Not available.

**Table 17–3
Price comparisons**

Procedure	Average hospital-based emergency room[a]	Emergicare Center
Minimum fee	$37.50	$25.00
Incision and drainage	$55.80	$80.00
Cauterization	$13.55	$12.50
Eye dilation	$ 8.20	$ 7.50
Clean wounds (simple)	$ 3.83	$ 3.50
Crash cart	$58.63	$53.50

[a] This table is only for the basic Emergency Room fee. It does not include the physician's
fee, supplies, or additional procedures.

as an innovative concept, it is not yet widely known. Because it is not
affiliated with a hospital, the center has the additional problems of
low name recognition, potential misunderstanding among health care
consumers who are as yet not familiar with this concept of care, a
smaller amount of money to allocate to advertising and public relations than the hospital-sponsored emergency rooms (see Tables 17–4
and 17–5), and the potential for being poorly accepted by the hospital
community who may view the Emergicare Center as a competitive
force.

Table 17–4
Advertising and promotional budgets allocated to hospital-based
emergency rooms ($000) and Emergicare Center

Budgets	Health care facility				
	1	2	3	4	Emergicare Center
Advertising					
TV	$—	$—	$—	$10	No budget
Radio	—	2	1	4	No budget
Newspaper	1.5	1	2	6	No budget
Magazines	.5	.75	1	2.5	No budget
Billboards	—	1	—	1.5	No budget
Other	.5	1.5	—	2.1	No budget
Public relations	1.5	1	.75	3	No budget
Sales promotion					
(collateral)	2	1	1	5	No budget
Research					
Advertising	—	—	—	2	No budget
Marketing	1	2.5	2	10	No budget

Table 17–5
Estimated advertising
and promotional
expenditures of
Emergicare Center
($000) (first six months
of operation)

	Emergicare Center
Advertising	
TV	$5[a]
Radio	—
Newspaper	7.5
Magazines	1
Billboards	—
Other	1
Public relations	1.5
Sales promotion	
(collateral)	5
Research	
Advertising	—
Marketing	—

[a]Television time not yet purchased; however, this figure was being discussed as "feasible" by Dr. Christie.

The advertising and public relations plan

The center has primarily relied on publicity to generate awareness of its services in the communities it serves. A press release was sent to the newspapers, radio stations, and television stations in the metropolitan area to announce the opening of the Emergicare Center and to generate usage.

Advertising has been used in the print media, primarily in a local weekly shopping guide and in a zoned regional edition of the metropolitan daily newspaper. In addition, an informational brochure was distributed in the weekly shopping guide. It reached approximately 72,000 households one time in the local communities. Personal contact was also perceived to be important in diffusing the concept. A representative personally contacted every pharmacy in the service area.

Dr. Christie's brother-in-law, David Barnes, recently offered to shoot a 16-mm commercial at no cost; Barnes takes home movies as a hobby. Dr. Christie gladly accepted Barnes' offer. The two are presently writing the script. Dr. Christie and his staff will be the talent although none has ever appeared in commercials.

No budget has been allocated to cover advertising and promotional costs. An "all-we-can-afford" budget strategy has been implemented. Additionally, no formalized advertising/promotional objectives or plans have been specified. The target market has been identified as "women" because "they make health decisions," according to Dr. Christie.

Endnote

1. A "crash cart" contains intravenous solution, a cardiac defibrillator, a cardiac monitor, and various drugs used in resuscitation.

CASE ANALYSIS

CASE 17

Medical
Emergicare
Center

1. Identify and briefly discuss three key factors that must be addressed if the Medical Emergicare Center (MEC) is to be successful.

_____

_____

_____

_____

_____

_____

_____

_____

_____

_____

_____

_____

_____

_____

_____

_____

_____

_____

_____

_____

2.   How effective do you feel the current advertising and public relations plan has been for MEC?

_____

_____

_____

_____

_____

_____

3.   Assess MEC's definition of its target market.

_____

_____

_____

_____

_____

_____

_____

4. Based on your answer to Question 3, propose appropriate promotion
    objectives for MEC.

    _____

    _____

    _____

    _____

    _____

    _____

5. What changes, if any, do you recommend in the promotion budget
    shown in Table 17–4?

    _____

    _____

    _____

    _____

    _____

    _____

    _____

    _____

6. How would you measure the effectiveness of your promotion plan?

_____

_____

_____

_____

_____

_____

_____

_____

_____

_____

_____

_____

_____

_____

_____

_____

_____

_____

_____

_____

_____

CASE 18

MORTON SALT

George Tate strolled down Michigan Avenue on a warm spring afternoon in Chicago. He had spent the entire morning with Morton Salt's advertising agency, reviewing the company's past promotions and discussing possible plans for the upcoming fiscal year, which would begin on July 1st. As he walked, he pondered the problems facing the company, particularly with regard to table salt, traditionally Morton Salt's major product.

When it rains, it pours

In the early part of the 20th century, consumers bought salt in brown paper bags, which had been put up by a grocer from bulk salt he had purchased in barrels. The salt business was keenly competitive, and no firm had been able to gain significant consumer demand or a price advantage. Morton's product was exactly like that of its competition.

If Morton Salt could be differentiated in some way, however, they could improve consumer demand, and thus improve profit margins. By 1920, they developed an innovative way to keep salt from caking or hardening from moisture, and introduced a moisture-proof, two pound cylindrical package with an aluminum spout for easier pour-

This case was made possible by the cooperation of the Morton Salt Division of Morton Thiokol, Inc., and the author of the original Morton Salt case, Dr. Nugent Wedding. It was prepared by Nancy Stephens and Richard F. Beltramini, Assistant Professors at Arizona State University, as a basis for class discussion rather than to illustrate either effective or ineffective handling of an administrative situation. Comments, views or conclusions stated herein are not to be construed as those of the Morton Salt Division of Morton Thiokol, Inc., and the case authors are solely responsible for content.

ing. With these improvements, Morton embarked upon a modest advertising program, utilizing primarily women's magazines. "When It Rains, It Pours" was adopted as a slogan for the advertisement, and was also printed on the package (see Figure 18–1).

The idea of branding and advertising was a new one in the salt market, but it seemed to work as Morton's sales and market share grew. With this increased degree of control over consumer demand, Morton began to gradually increase prices until their packaged salt sold for double that of any competitor (10¢ per package, compared to 5¢ for unbranded bags).

No salt salts like Morton Salt salts

Since Morton's product and package improvements were unprotected by patents, competitors were quick to imitate. As a result, some consumer resistance to the price differential began to affect Morton Salt sales. At this point, therefore, Morton needed another innovation.

Because of its leadership in the salt industry, Morton was approached by health authorities and medical organizations who had discovered that an insufficient amount of iodine in the body was a cause of goiter (an enlargement of the thyroid gland, often visible as a swelling in the lower part of the front of the neck). Since salt was a universally used food product, these authorities suggested that Morton take the lead in adding iodine to their salt, in a ratio of 1 part iodine to 5,000 parts salt, for goiter prevention.

Iodized salt was introduced in the early 1920s with advertising support, and by 1926 Morton's iodized salt was outselling plain salt. It was able to continue its market leadership and brand preference for many years, maintaining a premium price.

However, in the early 1960s Morton saw its sales and market share slipping again as competitors had matched product innovations, and had engaged in price-cutting tactics. In addition, consumer lifestyles had changed to produce a declining demand for salt. More people were eating away from home, and more prepared, presalted foods were being consumed at home.

Morton expanded its advertising to focus on the 30 to 40 age group (then found to consume 75 percent of all salt sold), and reemphasized the company's early innovations in the salt market. Magazines, television, and radio carried the message "No Salt Salts Like Morton Salt Salts" to this target audience. In 1968 Morton was able to enjoy the largest market share of any year in the decade.

The next best thing to the real thing

By the late 1960s, Morton had also expanded its product offerings beyond table salt. Company divisions had been established to produce prepared foods, chemicals, and agricultural goods, partially as a result of their 1969 merger with Norwich Pharmaceutical Company.

Future growth depended upon properly defining the firm's business position. As consumers had changed, Morton was no longer just in the "salt business," it was in the "seasonings business."

In 1970 after extensive product and market research, Morton introduced a new consumer product, Salt Substitute. Morton Salt Substitute was initially available in two varieties, regular and seasoned. It was composed of potassium chloride, and had already been in limited use by people on medically supervised, low sodium diets.

The introduction of Salt Substitute as a consumer product was supported by a $242,000 advertising campaign which emphasized taste rather than the product's medical uses. "The Next Best Thing to the Real Thing" was chosen as the slogan and appeared in magazine and newspaper advertisements (see Figure 18–2). Further, a 10¢-off coupon was featured to stimulate trial purchase of the innovative product. By the end of the decade, Morton's sales achieved higher levels than all other salt brands combined.

Morton, the salt you've been passing for generations

The decade of the 1970s brought increasing attention and concern among Americans about the potential relationship between the use of salt and certain diseases. Medical researchers observed that when certain patients suffering from hypertension or high blood pressure were fed a diet severely restricted in sodium, their blood pressure decreased. Few researchers were willing to state categorically that sodium *caused* hypertension, but some troubling questions were posed.

Several years later, the U.S. Senate Select Committee on Nutrition and Human Needs responded to concerns about salt usage by including it in a set of Dietary Goals for the United States. One of the stated goals was that salt consumption be reduced to approximately five grams per day from the average of ten or twelve grams normally ingested. Such a goal might be achieved, some suggested, by eliminating most highly salted processed foods and condiments, and by eliminating salt added at the table.

Health concerns about salt intake did not escape Morton management, and in 1973 (well ahead of the U.S. Senate Committee recommendations) Morton Lite Salt was introduced to consumers. Lite Salt was the first iodized salt mixture with the taste of regular salt, but with only half the sodium. Unlike Salt Substitute which was not positioned directly against regular salt, Lite Salt was expected to cannibalize Morton's regular salt to some extent. This was not a major concern to Morton management, however, since Lite was seen as "the salt of the future."[1] A $1 million advertising campaign, largely in television, accompanied the roll-out of Lite Salt (see Figures 18–3 and 18–4).

During the 1970s Morton tested several other new seasoning products including Butter Buds, Sugar Cure, Tender Quick, and Nature's Seasons. Some of these products were reasonably successful and remained on the market, while others were withdrawn due to insufficient sales.

To supplement Morton's fluctuating advertising budgets during this period (see Tables 18–1, 18–2, and 18–3), several sales promotion programs were employed. The first attempt was a set of four porcelain mugs offered for $2 plus a spout seal from a 26 oz. table salt package. Each mug featured a different Morton girl from the four periods of the company's history (see Figure 18–5).

In 1975, another sales promotion program was developed to provide additional uses for salt. Morton introduced salt sculpture (a mixture of flour, water, and salt) for holiday decorations (see Figure 18–6). Film strips were offered to elementary schools, and a ten minute film was sent to television stations, explaining salt sculpture. Print advertising in women's magazines offered Morton's "Dough It Yourself" Handbook for $1.

The promotions for salt sculpture ran during the Christmas season, and were continued during Easter and July 4th for two years. By 1977, company executives estimated that 700,000 "Dough It Yourself" Handbooks had been sold, and distribution was expanded to craft stores as well.

Despite a series of successful consumer and trade promotions, 26 oz. table salt could not sustain the company. "It's a strong cash producer," commented Morton's president in 1977, "but not a growth market."[2] At the same time, management recognized that table salt could not be abandoned completely for although it represented only five percent of tonnage sales, it produced at least thirty-five percent of dollar sales.

Therefore, it was decided in 1977 to continue the sales promotion

[1] "Morton Lite ties into 'RD' special insert," *Advertising Age*, October 29, 1973.

[2] "Morton pours more ad dollars into image-building bid," *Advertising Age*, August 8, 1977.

for Morton 26 oz. table salt. To capitalize on Americans' increased interest in geneology, Morton sponsored a "Visit the Land of Your Ancestors" Sweepstakes. Also featured were mailed kits which contained recipes from the homelands of Americans of current and past generations. The sweepstakes was tied in with the advertising theme, "Morton, the salt you've been passing for generations" (see Figure 18–7). Morton table salt maintained its number one position among table salts in 1977 with an all-time high market share.

A third promotion (in addition to the salt sculpture and sweepstakes promotions) was begun in 1978. Special salt packages with labels from four past container designs (1914, 1921, 1933, and 1941) were featured in retail stores. Consumers were urged through media advertising to collect the entire "Keepsake Collection" (see Figure 18–8). These innovations in sales promotion were another solution to the perennial problem of maintaining brand preference for a parity product.

Summary

As George Tate opened his office door, marked Director of Communications, he realized that some important decisions now faced Morton Salt. Salt Substitute and Lite Salt were leading the market in their respective product categories, and Nature's Seasons was growing in sales as well. Regular table salt seemed to be doing well as a result of the sales promotions, although the medical concerns of the 1970s were not expected to fade.

It seemed to Tate that innovations in product development, in packaging, and in sales promotion had always solved past problems. However, he was now concerned with an advertising innovation as a remedy.

Figure 18–1

Plain or Iodized

Courtesy of the Morton Salt Division of Morton Thiokol, Inc.

Figure 18–2

If you can't have the real thing...

Now you can have the next best thing.

New Morton Salt Substitute tastes like the real thing.
After all, we've been producing the real thing for over 58 years.
We know what real salt flavor is. Now, you can know too.
When it rains, even our Salt Substitute pours.

Courtesy of the Morton Salt Division of Morton Thiokol, Inc.

Figure 18–3

Figure 18–4

Courtesy of the Morton Salt Division of Morton Thiokol, Inc.

Figure 18–5

Courtesy of the Morton Salt Division of Morton Thiokol, Inc.

Figure 18–6

Courtesy of the Morton Salt Division of Morton Thiokol, Inc.

Figure 18-7

Figure 18–8

Courtesy of the Morton Salt Division of Morton Thiokol, Inc.

Table 18–1
Blue Package, media history

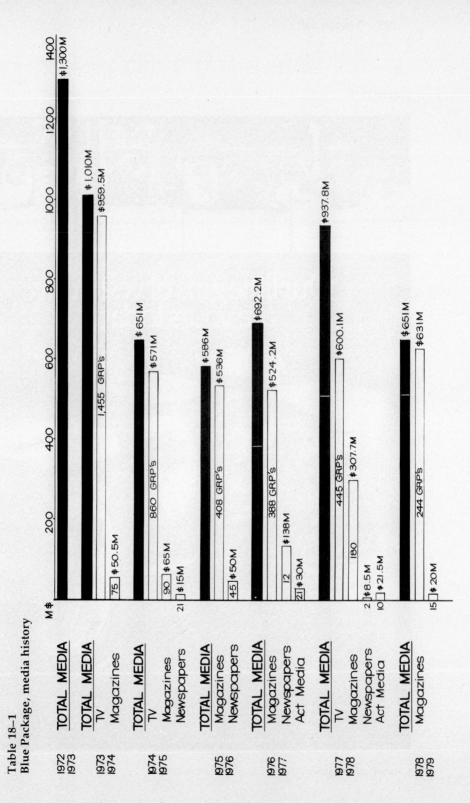

226

Table 18–2
Salt Substitute, media history

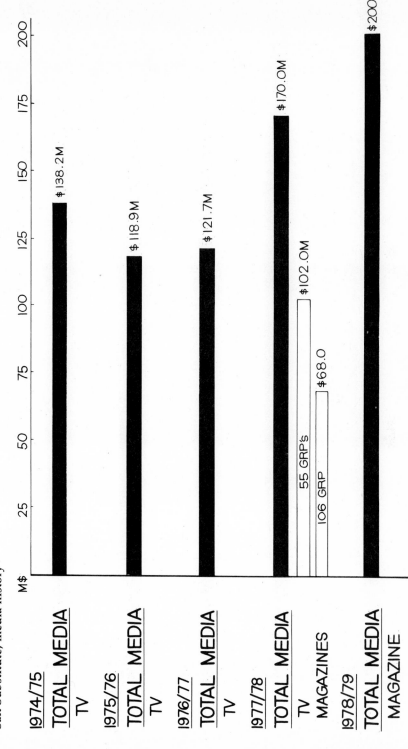

Table 18–3
Lite Salt, media history

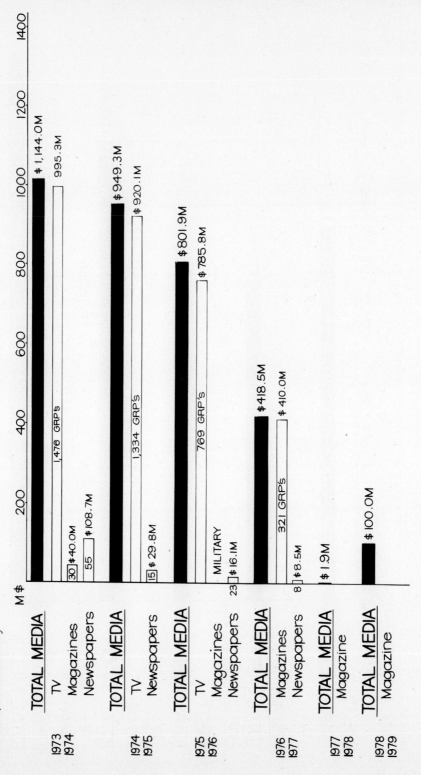

CASE ANALYSIS

CASE 18

Morton Salt

1. What basic problems face Morton Salt in marketing regular table salt?

_____

_____

_____

_____

_____

_____

_____

_____

_____

_____

2. Can consumer sales for regular table salt be substantially increased through advertising?

_____

_____

_____

_____

_____

_____

_____

_____

_____

_____

_____

3.   Should the sales promotion approach used by Morton for regular table salt in the past few years be continued?

_____

_____

_____

_____

4.   Suggest some sales promotion ideas which might help Morton increase sales of regular table salt.

_____

_____

_____

_____

_____

_____

_____

_____

5. Since no link between salt use and diseases has actually been *proved,* should Morton challenge medical and governmental authorities and counter criticisms in its advertising for regular table salt?

_____

_____

_____

_____

_____

_____

6. What is Morton's best future course for marketing regular table salt?

_____

_____

_____

_____

_____

_____

_____

_____

_____

_____

7. Is it possible to target markets other than consumers in order to expand sales?

_____

_____

_____

_____

_____

_____

_____

_____

_____

_____

8. Can Morton capitalize on the trend toward unbranded consumer package goods?

_____

_____

_____

_____

_____

_____

_____

_____

_____

_____

_____

_____

CASE 19

THE DUNN CORPORATION

Robert Head, the newly appointed sales manager for the Dunn Corporation, had completed a review of the sales force that he inherited. He knew that he had an important decision facing him regarding one of his sales representatives, John Little.

Company background

The Dunn Corporation, with headquarters in Tuscaloosa, Alabama, produced and sold asphalt roofing products and other building materials throughout the Southeastern United States. The primary market area consisted of the states of Alabama, Tennessee, Georgia, Florida, and Mississippi. There were also selected accounts in Kentucky, Indiana, and South Carolina. Five sales representatives covered the primary marketing area, with each representative having one of the states assigned as a territory. The selected accounts were assigned to the sales representatives at the sales manager's discretion.

Historically, the management of Dunn had pursued a conservative growth strategy with particular emphasis placed on achieving maximum return on investment. In order to keep costs down, capital expenditures for replacement of worn-out or obsolete equipment were given low priority. This led to a drop in production efficiency at the company's Tuscaloosa plant such that production was unable to keep pace with demand. Thus, from 1968 to 1976, company sales were

This case was developed by Professor James L. Taylor, Department of Management and Marketing, University of Alabama. The company name has been changed. From *Sales Management* by Charles Futrell. Copyright © 1981 by The Dryden Press. Reprinted by permission of James L. Taylor and The Dryden Press, CBS College Publishing.

limited by the availability of the product. However, despite these difficulties, the company had been profitable and had built an excellent reputation in the construction industry for service and quality.

The company had initiated successful capital improvement programs during 1975 and 1976; consequently, the company's production capacity had been greatly increased. No longer would Dunn's sales performance be hindered by lack of product availability. Robert Head recognized that this increase in production capacity would require some revisions in the sales representative's duties. More time would have to be spent seeking new accounts in order to fully realize this new sales potential.

One of the first tasks that Head had undertaken as sales manager was a review of the field operations and performance of each sales representative. Head traveled with the sales representatives for a week in order to obtain as much information on each representative as possible. Head also spent two days with each person compiling a territorial analysis. This analysis broke each representative's district into trade areas that were then analyzed in terms of established accounts, competitive accounts, potential of the trade territory, market position of competitive manufacturers, and selection of target accounts. Head believed that a properly prepared territorial analysis could reveal whether the sales representatives really knew and worked their districts. Some pertinent statistics uncovered by the analysis are reported in Exhibits 19–1 and 19–2.

John Little's performance

Head concluded, after reviewing the results of the territorial analysis, that John Little's sales performance could be improved. Little had been with the company for over twenty years. A tall, handsome individual with a polished, articulate manner, he appeared to be a perfect salesperson, yet his performance never seemed to equal his potential.

While evaluating Little's accounts, call reports, and expense accounts, Head uncovered a pattern of infrequent travel throughout Little's district. Little sold only thirty-four active accounts, well below the company average of approximately fifty-five. With the low number of accounts and a daily call rate of two, it appeared that Little simply was not working very hard. When Little's sales performance was compared to his district's estimated potential, it appeared that Little was realizing only about 60 percent of the potential sales of his area. When compared with the other territories, Little's district ranked last in terms of sales volume per 1000 housing starts and sales volume per 100,000 population.

Exhibit 19–1
Sales performance of the individual sales representatives: 1977–78

Sales representative	Sales volume	
	1977	1978
Peters	$2,732,464	$2,636,832
Little	1,366,232	1,315,916
Homer	1,639,420	1,879,880
Cough	2,368,136	2,443,844
Stiles	1,001,903	1,127,928
Totals	$8,748,155	$9,404,400

Exhibit 19–2
Results of territorial analysis

Sales representative	Number of accounts	New accounts in 1978	Average daily calls
Peters	63	3	4
Little	34	0	2
Homer	52	2	5
Cough	78	4	2
Stiles	47	2	3
Averages	54.8	2.2	3.2

Head had questioned Little concerning coverage in his Georgia district. Head recalled part of their conversation:

Head. John, it appears that you simply are not calling on the potential customers in the outer areas of your district. For example, last month you spent twelve out of twenty days working in Atlanta. I know you live in Atlanta, and there is a tendency to work closer to home, but I believe that we are missing a lot of business in your area simply by not calling on people.

Little. Look, I have been selling roofing for a long time, even when the plant couldn't produce and ship it. Why get upset when we have a little extra product to sell?

Head. Look, John, we have increased production by twenty percent. You will have all the product you can sell. This means extra income to you, better services to your accounts, and more profit to the company. I will be happy to assist you in working out a plan for coverage of your district.

Little. Bob, don't you ever look at the volume of our customers? If you did, you would know that the Republic Roofing Supply in

Atlanta is the second largest account of Dunn. Upchurch, the owner of Republic, is very demanding concerning my servicing Republic on ordering, delivery, and product promotion. It has taken a long time, but I have gained the trust and respect of Upchurch. That is why he looks to me to take care of the account. The reason that we have not lost the account to our competitors is that I give the type of service demanded by Upchurch.

Head. John, I agree that service to all of our accounts is extremely important. However, service does represent a cost, not only in terms of an outlay of money, but also in the potential loss of business from other accounts. I seriously question the profitability of spending approximately forty percent of your time with one account.

Little. What do you mean, profitability? My district has always made money. Just because we have new management, why does everything have to change?

Head had continued the conversation by suggesting that he and Little meet at some future date for the purpose of laying out a travel schedule. It was Head's intention to structure the schedule so that Little could make a minimum of four calls per day. Little, however, refused to even consider setting up a schedule or to increase the number of calls per day. His refusal was based on the contention that he needed at least two days a week to service Republic properly. Little further stated that if Dunn would not allow him the two days a week to service Republic, other roofing manufacturers would.

Robert Head pondered his decision regarding John Little and the Georgia territory. He felt that he had three options. First, he could simply fire Little with the possibility of losing the Republic account. Because Republic was Dunn's second largest account, Head realized that this might be a dangerous course of action. Second, Head considered rearranging Little's district by transferring some of the outer counties to other sales representatives. Finally, Head realized that he could simply accept the situation and leave things as they were now. He remembered once being told by a close friend with years of management experience that sometimes a "don't rock the boat" strategy is the best way to handle difficult situations.

CASE
ANALYSIS

CASE 19

The Dunn
Corporation

1. Identify the critical issues Mr. Head must recognize and weigh in formulating a solution to the problem with Mr. Little.

_____

_____

_____

_____

_____

_____

_____

_____

_____

_____

_____

_____

_____

_____

_____

_____

_____

_____

_____

_____

2.   Discuss the pros and cons of opening new accounts to better achieve the territory's true potential at the risk of losing the Republic account.

_____

_____

_____

_____

_____

_____

_____

_____

3.   What are the pros and cons of firing Little?

_____

_____

_____

_____

_____

_____

_____

_____

4.   What are the pros and cons of rearranging his district?

_____

_____

_____

_____

_____

_____

_____

5.   What about simply leaving things as they are?

_____

_____

_____

_____

_____

_____

_____

_____

_____

_____

_____

6. Recommend and defend a specific course of action for Mr. Head.

_____

_____

_____

_____

_____

_____

_____

_____

_____

CASE 20

THE TEXAS SERVICE COMPANY

The recently appointed district manager in Bryan, Texas, for the Texas Service Company, Joe Brown, thought he would begin his new duties by evaluating the compensation and performance evaluating system for his sales force to see where, if necessary, any changes could be made.

The company

The Texas Service Company is engaged in two basic businesses: providing oil field services and products for the domestic oil and gas industry, and providing contract drilling of oil and gas wells in offshore areas. The Bryan district is not concerned with offshore drilling, but is involved with selling a wide range of services and products domestically to the petroleum industry. The services include cementing of wells, which is placing cement between the pipe and formation of a well (the cement essentially anchors the pipe and isolates different formations); flow control, restricting fluid movement to acceptable flow rates and pressures in the well; hydraulic fracturing, the process of creating and maintaining a fracture in an oil or gas formation by pumping fluid into the formation at a pressure greater than the fracture pressure of the formation to increase the productivity of the well; and chemical treatment of oil wells, placing various chemicals in oil and gas wells to improve the flow of oil or gas to increase the life of

This case was written by Denise Smart, Texas A&M University. The company name has been changed. From *Sales Management* by Charles Futrell. Copyright © 1981 by The Dryden Press. Reprinted by permission of Denise Smart and The Dryden Press, CBS College Publishing.

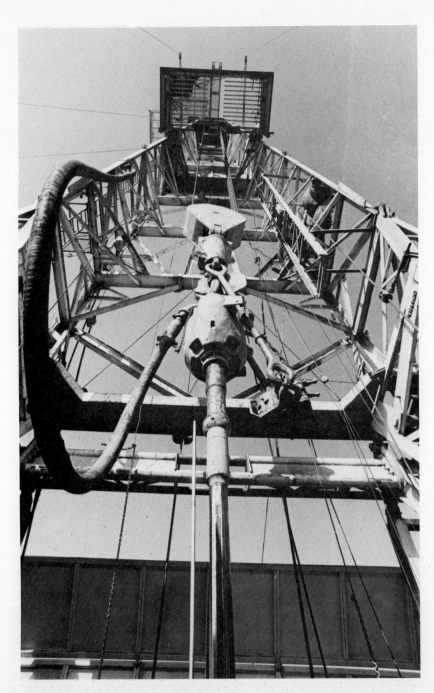

Courtesy of Peter Southwick/Stock, Boston

equipment. The company also furnishes a variety of associated products such as cement, sands of various sizes for fracturing wells, acid, and other bulk materials such as potassium chloride, corrosion inhibitors, and surfactants (a surface active agent) for new and existing wells. Primary operations are conducted in Colorado, Louisiana, Texas, New Mexico, Oklahoma, Wyoming, Montana, Kansas, and Utah.

The Bryan district started operations with a cementing division that was basically responsible for the cementing work on wells in nine surrounding counties. A stimulation division, responsible for all fracturing and chemical treatments of wells, was added and was in operation in June 1977. A typical stimulation job consists of the use of various pieces of equipment such as six fracturing pumps, one blender (chemical and sand mixer), bulk sand and chemical transport equipment, and a van for the service supervisor to monitor the progress of the job. A typical job will use 250,000 pounds of sand, 3000 pounds of gelling agent, 200 gallons of surfactant, and 8000 barrels of water. The hydraulic power necessary to perform the job would average 4,500 horsepower, and is also part of the charges to the customer. The average cost of a stimulation job is $15,000. Generally a cementing job is done with one pump and one or two pieces of bulk equipment, and can be accomplished by two or three people. The materials used on the job include cement additives and mixing water. An average job costs $6,500.

The sales organization

The company has a layered sales organization consisting of corporate, regional, and district salespeople. Because of the many organizational levels and degrees of centralization in most oil producing companies, and because of the difficulty in determining who actually makes the decision to enlist the services of TSC or those of a competitor, TSC management feels this type of an organization best provides for all contingencies. Each level is responsible for certain customer company officials, but many times there is an overlapping or combination of effort, particularly at the regional and field sales level.

At the top are five corporate salesmen located in the Dallas–Fort Worth area who are responsible for calling on the top-level executives of both major and independent oil producing companies. Next are region salespeople located at each of five regional offices. Bryan belongs to the Gulf Coast region. In this region ten salespeople are headquartered in Houston, six in Tyler, and five in Corpus Christi. These salespeople are responsible for calling on middle to upper level management in the oil-producing companies and a variety of drilling, production, engineering, and geological specialists. Of the regional salespeople, several are designated as regional technical salespeople whose main responsibilities include writing recommendations on how a particular job should be treated and calling on engineers. At the district level are six field salespeople.

The salesperson's role

The salesperson's responsibilities include calling on oil-producing company representatives (e.g., oil field supervisors) at the local level, keeping up to date on present and future drilling activity in the area, keeping abreast of what the local competition is doing, and lending technical assistance to service engineers who are in charge of completion of the contracted service. The field salespeople must complete weekly reports on activities and file a report each Friday indicating plans for the coming week. Each field salesperson has approximately twenty accounts, ranging in size from large major oil companies to small independents. These accounts include between forty and fifty people whom the salesperson must visit with varying frequency depending upon the amount of work each company is presently doing in the area. Field salespeople work an average of sixty hours each week and are paid a straight salary. In the Bryan district the sales salaries range from $18,400 to $27,600. The range represents varying amounts of experience and time with the company. In addition to the salary, salespeople have the full-time use of a company car, health insurance, and a generous expense account that includes entertainment expenses.

There is no minimum educational requirement for salespeople although, generally, they have had experience as service supervisors in either stimulation or cementing. The experience varies from three months to six years; most have had at least two years of field service experience that ranges from running various pieces of equipment to overseeing the total job. The Texas Service Company provides in-house training in the techniques of selling for those who are interested, but attendance is not mandatory. The turnover of field salespersons in the Bryan district is between 6 and 8 percent per year.

Salespeople's performance appraisal

A yearly performance appraisal is completed for each field salesperson. Different weights are given to the performance criteria as follows:

- 50 percent of the evaluation is based on a predetermined dollar amount of sales for which the salesperson is responsible. This figure is agreed on in advance by the district manager and the salesperson based on forecasted drilling activity in the area;

- 15 percent of the evaluation is based on estimated market share of the district;
- 10 percent on overall district profit;
- 5 percent on turnover of field employees;
- 5 percent on call frequency;
- 5 percent on personal development, which is measured by the amount and frequency of sales training and technical training;
- 10 percent on overall contribution to the district, which includes such things as accuracy of reporting of market conditions, competitor activity, and forecasting of trends.

CASE ANALYSIS

CASE 20

The Texas
Service
Company

1. How would you describe the Texas Service Company (TSC) sales-person's job?

_____

_____

_____

_____

_____

_____

_____

_____

_____

_____

_____

_____

_____

2. How accurately do you feel TSC can judge their salespeople's perfor-mance?

_____

_____

3. Does TSC's present method of performance appraisal appear reasonable?

_____

_____

_____

_____

_____

_____

4. Assess the adequacy of TSC's performance appraisal system to motivate salespeople over the long term.

_____

_____

_____

_____

_____

_____

_____

_____

5. Identify the major factor or factors that make compensation, motivation, and performance appraisal difficult for TSC.

    _____

    _____

    _____

    _____

6. Suggest specific changes in the performance criteria or weights assigned to them that might improve TSC's performance evaluation system.

    _____

    _____

    _____

    _____

    _____

    _____

    _____

    _____

    _____

    _____

    _____

    _____

    _____

_____

_____

_____

_____

_____

_____

_____

_____

_____

_____

_____

PART FIVE

PRICING DECISIONS

CASE 21

BARBER FLORIST

Background

Barber Florist is owned and operated by Ron Barber and Galvin Dodd. From the time it began operation, in 1969, annual sales have grown from approximately $30,000 to slightly over $150,000.

Barber Florist is located in Jacksonville, Illinois, a rural town with a population slightly exceeding 20,000 people. Jacksonville is approximately ninety miles northeast of St. Louis, Missouri. Although it is predominantly an agricultural community, industrial employers include Mobil Chemical, Anderson Clayton, Carnation, and Capitol Records.

Jacksonville has two established four-year liberal arts colleges, each with a student body approaching one thousand students. Illinois College, founded in 1829, is the oldest college in Illinois. It has been recognized for its excellent business department. In fact, many of the town's prominent business persons are graduates of Illinois College.

MacMurray College, a prestigious all-female college, became coeducational in the 1960s. MacMurray College is known for its winning soccer teams. The college is also known for its strong special education department, with the largest enrollment as deaf education majors.

There are two institutions in Jacksonville for people with special needs: the Illinois School for the Deaf and the Illinois School for the Visually Impaired. Both of these institutions have been in existence for over one hundred years.

Barber Florist is located on a main street six blocks north of down-

This case was prepared by Professor Martin Meyers, MacMurray College, Jacksonville, Illinois.

Courtesy of Bohdan Hrynewych © 1976/Stock, Boston

town Jacksonville. Since it is located in a residential neighborhood, there are few window shoppers compared to stores in the downtown area. Approximately 40 percent of sales are walk-ins, whereas 60 percent of sales are phone orders.

Barber is the second largest of five local florists, with approximately 30 percent of the town's business. Barber's highest sales volume is for funerals. The second largest segment of the business consists of deliveries made to hospitals. The third largest dollar volume is for anniversaries. Holidays, such as Mother's Day and Valentine's Day, comprise the fourth largest business segment.

Product line

Cut flowers account for approximately 50 percent of Barber's annual sales. Blooming flowers, such as mums and azaleas, account for 30 percent of annual sales. Green plants account for 10 percent of the firm's annual sales. Barber Florist carries a number of gift items, such as stuffed animals, candy, greeting cards, porcelain, and vases. These items account for 10 percent of the firm's annual sales. Barber is seriously considering expanding the gift line.

Recently, Barber and Dodd added balloons to their product line. They have 25 different messages printed on 16-inch round balloons. The balloons are made of a synthetic fabric that permits the helium to last for five days, in contrast to the one- or two-day period for regular helium balloons. Some of the messages printed are "Happy Birthday," "Happy Valentine's Day," "Congratulations," "Kiss Me I'm Irish." The price of the balloon with a printed message is three dollars. It can be combined with eleven regular helium-filled balloons. The bouquet of a dozen balloons sells for $10.

Pricing

Barber Florist has implemented a penetration pricing policy. The company aggressively promotes low prices to attract customers. For example, Barber charges $18 for a dozen roses. Most local florists charge approximately $30 for a comparable box of roses.

Distribution

Barber and Dodd grow many of the plants and flowers that they sell. This includes most of the foliage, such as the philodendron and wandering jews. They grow mums and a variety of other blooming flowers. Several different green plants are also grown by Barber and Dodd.

The plants and flowers not grown by Barber are purchased directly from growers. This differs from the distribution used by most other florists. Presently, most growers sell their products to a jobber. The jobber accumulates flowers from several growers and then sells them to various florists. Since the flowers are generally held by the jobbers for a few days, they are not as fresh as the flowers purchased directly from a grower.

Approximately 15 percent of Barber Florist's income is derived from wholesale business. Many of the plants and flowers grown are sold to other florists, farmer's markets, grocery stores, and discount stores.

Services provided

Barber provides delivery service in a gray unmarked van. If a customer is not satisfied with the flowers, free replacement is provided.

FTD (Florists Transworld Delivery) is not provided by Barber Florist, although its major competitors provide this service. FTD is a service by which a customer can order flowers from a local florist for an out-of-town destination. A participating florist in the area where the flowers are to be sent fills the order and makes the delivery.

Barber does not provide FTD for two reasons. First, the profit margin is 3 percent, compared to a profit margin exceeding 25 percent for regular orders. Second, if an unsatisfactory order was delivered, Barber would be blamed, even though it had not sent the flowers.

Promotion

Barber places two weekly 30-second commercials on the local radio station. Since it has a contractual arrangement with the radio station, each spot costs a discounted $9.40. The central theme of the radio advertising is low prices. Sometimes a weekly special is mentioned; sometimes the balloons are mentioned. During holidays a price reduction is identified in relation to the specific holiday.

Local newspaper advertisements, like the radio commercials, use the theme of reasonable prices. The sizes of the newspaper advertisements range from an eight-line ad to a quarter page.

Barber and Dodd distribute calendars to their customers every year. These are attractive calendars with "Barber Florist" printed on them. Another promotional device is the token. Tokens can be used for a $1 discount on a minimum purchase of $5.

CASE
ANALYSIS

CASE 21

Barber
Florist

1. How can Barber and Dodd market their products profitably at significantly lower prices than local competitors?

_____

_____

_____

_____

_____

_____

_____

2. Should Barber and Dodd increase their prices to the level of other local competitors?

_____

_____

_____

_____

_____

_____

_____

3. What themes besides low prices could be stressed in Barber Florist's promotion? What other promotional devices could be used?

_____

_____

_____

_____

_____

_____

_____

_____

_____

_____

_____

_____

4. Should Barber Florist participate in the FTD program? Why or why not?

_____

_____

_____

_____

_____

_____

_____

_____

_____

_____

_____

_____

_____

_____

5. Describe how Barber and Dodd could expand their balloon product
    line. How would you promote the balloons?

_____

_____

_____

_____

_____

_____

_____

6. Comment on the expansion of gift items. Should a penetration pricing policy be implemented?

_____

_____

_____

_____

_____

_____

_____

_____

_____

CASE 22

HEALTH CRUISES, INC.

Health Cruises, Inc., packages cruises to Caribbean islands such as Martinique and the Bahamas. Like conventional cruises, the packages are designed to be fun. But the cruise is structured to help participants become healthier by breaking old habits, such as smoking or overeating. The Miami-based firm was conceived by Susan Isom, 30, a self-styled innovator and entrepreneur. Prior to this venture, she had spent several years in North Carolina promoting a behavior-modification clinic.

In 1982, Isom determined that many people were very concerned about developing good health habits; yet they seemed unable to break away from their old habits because of the pressures of day-to-day living. She reasoned that they might have a chance for much greater success in a pleasant and socially supportive environment, where good health habits were fostered. Accordingly, she established Health Cruises, Inc., hired 10 consulting psychologists and health specialists to develop a program, and chartered a ship. DeForrest Young, a Miami management consultant, became the chairperson of Health Cruises. Seven of Isom's business associates contributed an initial capital outlay totaling more than $250,000. Of this amount, $65,000 went for the initial advertising budget, $10,000 for other administrative expenses, and $220,000 for the ship rental and crew.

Mary Porter, an overweight Denver school teacher, has signed up

M. I. Mandell/L. J. Rosenberg, *Marketing,* 2nd ed., © 1981, pp. 365–366. Reprinted by permission of Prentice-Hall, Inc., Englewood Cliffs, N.J.

Courtesy of Sunrise Hospital Medical Center

to sail on a 2-week cruise to Nassau, departing December 19. She and her shipmates will be paying an average of $1,500 for the voyage. The most desirable staterooms cost $2,200.

Mary learned of the cruise by reading the travel section of her Sunday newspaper on October 16. On that date, Pittsford and LaRue Advertising Agency placed promotional notices for the cruise in several major metropolitan newspapers. Mary was fascinated by the idea of combining therapy sessions with swimming, movies, and an elegant atmosphere.

Pittsford and LaRue account executive Carolyn Sukhan originally estimated that 300 people would sign up for the cruise after reading the October 16 ads. But as of November 14, only 200 had done so. Isom and Health Cruises, Inc., faced an important decision.

"Here's the situation as I see it," explained a disturbed Ms. Isom at the Health Cruises board meeting. "We've already paid out more than a quarter of a million to get this cruise rolling. It's going to cost us roughly $200 per passenger for the 2 weeks, mostly for food. Pittsford and LaRue predicted that 300 people would respond to the advertising campaign, but we've only got 200.

"I see three basic options: (1) we cancel the cruise and take our losses; (2) we run the cruise with the 200 and a few more that will trickle in over the next month; or (3) we shell out some more money on advertising and hope that we can pull in more people.

"My recommendation to this board is that we try to recruit more passengers. There are simply too many empty rooms on that ship. Each one costs us a bundle."

At this point, Carolyn Sukhan addressed the board: "I've worked out two possible advertising campaigns for the November 20 papers. The first, the limited campaign, will cost $6,000. I estimate that it will bring in some 20 passengers. The more ambitious campaign, which I personally recommend, would cost $15,000. I believe this campaign will bring in a minimum of 40 passengers.

"I realize that our first attempt was somewhat disappointing. But we're dealing here with a new concept, and a follow-up ad might work with many newspaper readers who were curious and interested when they read our first notice.

"One thing is absolutely certain," Sukhan emphasized. "We must act immediately if there's any hope of getting more people on board. The deadline for the Sunday papers is in less than 48 hours. And if our ads don't appear by this weekend, you can forget it. No one signs up in early December for a December 18 sailing date."

Isom interrupted, shaking her head. "I just don't know what to say. I've looked over Carolyn's proposals, and they're excellent. Absolutely first-rate. But our problem, to be blunt, is money. Our funds are tight, and our investors are already nervous. I get more calls each day, asking me where the 300 passengers are. It won't be easy to squeeze another $6,000 out of these people. And to ask them for $15,000—well, I just don't know how we're going to be able to justify it."

CASE ANALYSIS

CASE 22

Health Cruises, Inc.

1. What is the minimum number of passengers that Health Cruises must sign up by November 20 in order to break even with the cruise? Show your calculations.

_____

_____

_____

_____

_____

2. Since Health Cruises had signed up 200 passengers by November 13, should it go ahead with the cruise? Defend your answer.

_____

_____

_____

_____

3. Would it be worthwhile for Health Cruises to spend either $6,000 or $15,000 for advertising on November 20? If so, which figure would you recommend that it spend?

_____

_____

_____

_____

_____

4. How realistic are Carolyn Sukhan's estimates of 20 more passengers for the $6,000 campaign and 40 more passengers for the $15,000 campaign?

_____

_____

_____

_____

5. Should Health Cruises consider cutting its prices for this maiden voyage? Defend your answer.

_____

_____

_____

_____

_____

_____

_____

_____

CASE 23

THE SONY CORPORATION

The television industry is one of the most dynamic industries in the world. Advances in technology and foreign and domestic competition have resulted in a number of significant changes in this industry—particularly in the United States. In 1974 Magnavox was sold to North American Phillips, a Dutch-based electronics and pharmaceutical concern. Rockwell International bought Admiral. In late 1978 it closed its U.S. plants and restricted its television business to Canada and Mexico. Sylvania, owned by General Telephone and Electronics, sells components to other television manufacturers. Much of this change in ownership can be attributed to the saturation of the U.S. color television market and the inability of companies with smaller shares of the market to keep abreast of the new developments through continuous and expensive research. One of the companies that has competed successfully in this market is SONY.

Historical development

The Tokyo Telecommunications Engineering Corporation was founded in May 1946 out of the rubble of World War II. Products were marketed under the trade name SONY. The trade name was adopted for the corporation, and in January 1958 the SONY Corporation was founded. Since its inception, SONY has operated under the concept of being free of preconceived ideas, encouraging creativity, and of marketing new products. This philosophy as well as quality leader-

This case was contributed by Joe Thomas, Northeast Missouri State University, Kirksville, Mo. 63501.

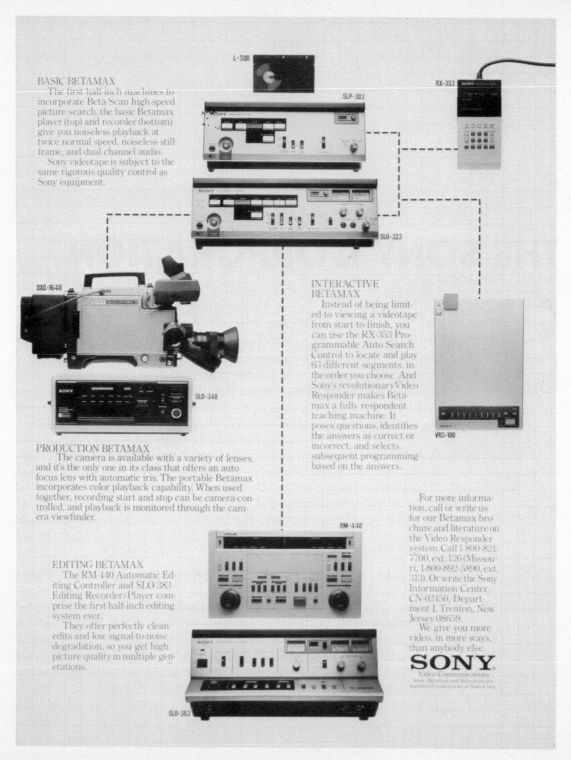

BASIC BETAMAX

The first half-inch machines to incorporate Beta-Scan high-speed picture search, the basic Betamax player (top) and recorder (bottom) give you noiseless playback at twice normal speed, noiseless still frame, and dual channel audio.

Sony videotape is subject to the same rigorous quality control as Sony equipment.

PRODUCTION BETAMAX

The camera is available with a variety of lenses, and it's the only one in its class that offers an auto focus lens with automatic iris. The portable Betamax incorporates color playback capability. When used together, recording start and stop can be camera-controlled, and playback is monitored through the camera viewfinder.

EDITING BETAMAX

The RM-440 Automatic Editing Controller and SLO-383 Editing Recorder/Player comprise the first half-inch editing system ever.

They offer perfectly clean edits and low signal-to-noise degradation, so you get high picture quality in multiple generations.

INTERACTIVE BETAMAX

Instead of being limited to viewing a videotape from start to finish, you can use the RX-353 Programmable Auto Search Control to locate and play 63 different segments, in the order you choose. And Sony's revolutionary Video Responder makes Betamax a fully respondent teaching machine. It poses questions, identifies the answers as correct or incorrect, and selects subsequent programming based on the answers.

For more information, call or write us for our Betamax brochure and literature on the Video Responder system. Call 1-800-821-7700, ext. 126 (Missouri, 1-800-892-5890, ext. 313). Or write the Sony Information Center, CN-02450, Department I, Trenton, New Jersey 08659.

We give you more video, in more ways, than anybody else.

SONY
Video Communications
Sony, Betamax and Beta-Scan are registered trademarks of Sony Corp.

ship have enabled SONY to become a world leader in the electronics field.

The management team at SONY has accumulated many years of experience with the company. Mr. Masaru Ibuka is the Honorary Chairman. He founded the corporation and has been at its helm ever since. Many of SONY's policies of maximizing employee abilities and developing products that no other firm has produced are the result of Mr. Ibuka's leadership. He served as Chairman and Chief Executive Officer of SONY until its reorganization in 1976.

In the reorganization, Mr. Akio Morita was promoted to Chairman and Chief Executive Officer. He has also been with SONY since its beginning. His activities prior to this promotion involved development of SONY's worldwide marketing network. He is now responsible for top management decisions for the entire SONY group.

Mr. Kazuo Iwama is the President and Chief Operating Officer. Previously he was the director of the technical and production sectors of the organization. His achievements include directing the work of transistor development, including the guidance given to Dr. Leo Ezaki (Nobel physicist), which has made the name SONY almost synonymous with transistor. Mr. Iwama is responsible for the overall operation of SONY.

Under the leadership of these three individuals, SONY has made many notable accomplishments. In 1961, it was the first Japanese-based enterprise to offer its shares in the United States. It is now listed on fifteen exchanges in nine countries. Approximately half of SONY's stock is owned by non-Japanese stockholders.

The emphasis on developing new products has enabled SONY to achieve many "firsts." A partial list includes:

*Tape Recorder	1950
*Magnetic Recording Tape	1950
*Transistor	1954
*Transistor Radio	1955
**Pocketable Transistor Radio	1957
**MW/SW 2 Band Transistor Radio	1957
**FM/AM 2 Band Transistor Radio	1958
**Transistor TV	1959
**Transistor Video Tape Recorder	1961
**Micro-TV	1962
**Desktop Calculator	1964
**VTR for home use	1964
**Transistor Condensor Microphone	1965

**Portable VTR	1966
**IC Radio	1966
**TRINITRON System Color TV	1968
**Color Videocassette System	1969
**Color Video Projection System	1972
**114° Wide-Angle-Deflection Trinitron Color TV	1972
**Betamax Videocassette Recorder	1975

One of the key factors in the creation of so many innovative products is SONY's concern for the individual abilities of its employees and its pioneering spirit. This attitude is summarized by the corporate philosophy that:

SONY is a pioneer, always a seeker of the unknown.

SONY never intends to follow others,
and in blazing the path into new fields
where no one has ventured,
SONY hopes to find its own way of progress.
Through progress, SONY wants to serve mankind.
The trail of a pioneer is strewn with difficulties.
But in spite of many hardships,
people of SONY work in harmonious unity,
because they find joy in participating creatively
and pride in contributing their own unique talents
to each pioneering effort.

SONY has the principle
of respecting and encouraging each one's abilities
—the right person in the right post—
and always tries to bring out the best in the person.
SONY believes in each one
and constantly allows the individual
to develop his or her abilities.

This is the vital force of SONY.

Current operations

The cornerstone of SONY's marketing strategy has been its reputation for quality. The company prides itself on being the manufacturer of one of the world's best televisions. One of its most recent successes was the manufacture of the Trinitron. Industry experts generally ag-

*First in Japan.
**First in the world.

Table 23–1
Share of U.S. color television market, 1975–1980

	1975	1976	1977	1978	1979	1980
Zenith	24.0	23.0	22.0	21.3	21.0	20.5
RCA	19.0	20.0	20.0	19.3	20.0	21.0
Sears	8.7	9.0	9.1	9.0	8.0	7.5
SONY	5.8	7.0	7.5	7.7	6.0	6.5
Magnavox	6.6	6.5	6.9	6.8	7.0	7.0
GE	6.2	5.5	6.0	6.1	6.0	7.5
Quasar	5.9	5.0	5.0	5.0	5.0	5.0
Sylvania	4.4	4.5	4.0	4.2	4.0	4.0
Panasonic	3.5	3.0	3.0	3.4	3.0	2.0
Others	17.0	17.0	16.5	18.2	20.0	19.0

ree that SONY products are superior to those of most of its competitors in quality and workmanship.

Two of SONY's most notable accomplishments are its Trinitron picture tube and the first fully transistorized television set in the world. The Smithsonian Institute holds the first Trinitron as a historic product marking an important point in the progress of color television. SONY also received an Emmy award from the National Academy of Television Arts and Sciences for the development of the Trinitron. Awards have also been received in other countries. Trinitron is manufactured in Japan, San Diego, and Wales.

One of the factors contributing to SONY's reputation for quality has been its efforts to avoid price competition and, instead, concentrate on building the best product technically possible. Recently, this policy has created a problem with its U.S. franchised distributors. Since price competition is something that the corporation tries to avoid, large orders are needed to get quantity discounts. To circumvent this problem, some franchisers engaged in transshipping. They ordered large quantities of SONY products, especially color televisions and Betamax recorders, and sell them at a small markup to other retailers. This allowed many small retailers to sell SONY products at reduced prices. SONY recalled all U.S. franchises in order to stop this practice. To get a new franchise, the distributor must agree not to participate in any further transshipping. Some retailers objected and filed suit, charging violation of antitrust laws.

One reason distributors give for their need to sell SONY products at a more competitive price relates to SONY's quality image. Retailers claim that most customers cannot see enough improved quality in SONY products to justify the price differences. While most au-

Table 23–2
Relative net sales by product groups

Product group	Percentage of net sales					
	1980	1979	1978	1977	1976	1975
Video cassette recorders	23	16	17	14	10	7
Television sets	28	29	31	33	37	37
Tape recorders and radios	15	19	17	20	23	25
Audio products	9	11	12	11	13	14
Other (business machines, magnetic audio and video tapes)	25	25	23	21	18	17

thorities agree that SONY products are of above-average quality, other products are of sufficient quality that the average customer cannot appreciate the difference. Due to unappreciated quality, higher-than-average prices, and the decline of the dollar relative to the Japanese yen, SONY's sales in the United States have been rather disappointing.

There have been major shifts in the composition of SONY's sales, as shown in Table 23–2. The sales of television sets comprised about 28% of net sales in 1980. This compares to a high of 37% in 1975 and only 22% in 1965. The biggest increase in sales has been in the VTR units. In 1965, VTRs and audio equipment combined comprised only 3% of sales. By 1971, the VTRs and audio units made up 6%, and 8% of sales, respectively. The VTRs have almost quadrupled to 23% of net sales, with audio equipment sales rising and then dropping to 9%. The biggest loser of market share has been tape recorders and radios. This division fell from 58% of sales in 1965 to 15% in 1980. This compares to 25% of sales in 1975.

The United States is not the only place where SONY's sales are suffering. SONY's share of the Japanese market is also declining. Outlets are one of SONY's key domestic problems. Matsushita, which owns Panasonic and Quasar, is SONY's largest Japanese competitor, with 21,000 exclusive outlets. Toshiba has approximately 10,000 outlets, compared to 1,000 outlets for SONY. These firms have not been averse to cutting prices and have reduced SONY's share of the Japanese color television market from 15% to 12% in three years.

One of the most notable developments in television has been the home video cassette recorder or VCR. In 1975 Sony introduced its recording unit as part of a color television console which sold for

**Table 23–3
Domestic vs. foreign
net sales**
(thousands of U.S.
dollars)

	1980	1979	1978	1975
Domestic sales	1,337,526	1,179,626	1,018,161	925,607
Foreign sales	2,893,578	1,869,924	1,516,991	1,472,611
Total sales	4,231,104	3,049,550	2,535,152	2,398,218

$2,500. Sales were disappointing until SONY introduced the Betamax in February 1976. Matsushita began marketing its video home system (VHS) through its U.S. subsidiary, Panasonic, in 1977. Both the Betamax and VHS can record television programs and play them back to the viewer on a conventional television set. While the two systems are comparable in terms of operation, their components are not interchangeable. The cassette developed by Matsushita holds up to four hours of recording but does not fit the Betamax unit. The Betamax cassette can record five hours of programs. A tape for VHS units that will have a nine-hour playing time is being tested.

The success of the VCR has been rapid in spite of the product's relatively high price. The suggested retail price is about $1,100 for the Betamax and $900 for the VHS. Statistics show that 1.5% of the 75 million households with televisions have VCRs. This penetration has been achieved in less than five years. It took color television five years to acquire 1% of the market.

Much of the market penetration can be attributed to the selling of the units by U.S. television companies. Zenith and Sears sell the Betamax units. RCA, Panasonic, Quasar, and Sylvania market the Matsushita format recorder. Support from such reputable companies and their advertising have speeded the adoption of the recorders. Rapid growth is predicted for the 1980s as prices continue to fall and the unit becomes more affordable for the average consumer.

Within two years of its introduction, market researchers reported sales of the VHS ahead of the Betamax. Much of the credit for this rapid market growth can be attributed to aggressive marketing of the VHS unit and its lower selling price. Some estimates show VHS machines outselling Betas by as much as 2 to 1. SONY is currently developing another new feature which allows the viewer to scan the tape and locate the beginning of a scene or program. Some experts feel that the longer tapes will not succeed without this feature. It is hoped by SONY that this feature will enable the company to regain its position of market leadership.

An outgrowth of the VCR boom has been the demand for recorded material. Prerecorded movies are becoming readily available. Magnetic Video Corporation offers about fifty movies from Twentieth Century Fox. Prices range from $49.95 for *The Grapes of Wrath* to $69.95 for Elizabeth Taylor's version of *Cleopatra.* Pornographic films are available from other distributors. Pirated tapes of popular movies are also available. *Star Wars* tapes were reportedly selling for $1,000 when the film opened. Blank cassettes typically sell for about $17 for a two-hour cassette and $25 for a four-hour unit. Fotomat converts 8mm and Super 8 home movies to cassettes. Although they are more expensive, the cassettes are more convenient than the conventional projector/screen system.

SONY, Matsushita, and others are developing movie cameras which record directly onto the cassettes. Fotomat is in the process of developing a rental system for tapes. Typical rental is expected to be about $12 for five days.

The most obvious challenge to the VCR is the videodisc. These units are less expensive and simpler to operate than the VCRs. Rather than utilizing a tape cassette, programs are bought on discs and played much like a phonograph record. In Atlanta and Seattle Magnavox is test-marketing a laser-equipped machine that sells for $695. RCA says that it will announce a machine using a stylus similar to a phonograph needle. The unit is predicted to sell for about $400. RCA has reportedly invested $50 million in developing this product. Roy Pollack of RCA envisions marketing programs much as phonograph records are marketed. Recording is not as easy with these units as with the video cassette. Two-hour feature movies are available for $12–18 each. Popular movies such as *Jaws* and *Love Story* are available for about $25. Television networks fear that this competition may be a threat to conventional programs, with their many commercials. Some industry authorities predict that people will develop libraries of programs tailored to their viewing preferences and will not watch regular television programs. Some even forecast that movies will be made strictly for the home viewer.

Other new products are being introduced to stimulate television sales. Portable "mini-combos" with three- and five-inch screens, AM-FM radios, audio cassette recorders, and digital alarm clocks are being tested. Selling prices start at $180. The Sharp Corporation of Japan has introduced "dual vision," a set that allows the viewer to watch two channels on the same screen at the same time. The viewer can superimpose a four-inch black-and-white picture on a seventeen-inch color screen. This television set should be especially attractive to sports enthusiasts, who will be able to watch two sports events simultaneously.

Panasonic has developed the Cinema Vision color projection system, which has a sixty-inch diagonal screen and a selling price of about $4,000. Firms that are either unwilling or unable to devote large sums of money to developing such new products are likely to find themselves unable to compete for the consumer's dollar.

The future

SONY is expanding its foreign operations. Approximately two-thirds of the color television sets sold in the United States are manufactured in SONY's San Diego plant. Reasons for this move include restrictions put on Japanese imports by the Orderly Market Agreement, which limited the number of television sets that could be imported. Another factor favoring overseas production is the increase in the value of the yen compared to other currencies. This increase has made wages and materials cheaper in foreign countries. In addition to the San Diego and Wales plants mentioned earlier, a new plant for producing video cassette recorders is being built in Brazil. Other subsidiaries are located in Hong Kong, Panama, Australia, Denmark, Belgium, France, West Germany, and England.

SONY is active in most aspects of electronics. Major fields of electronics include semi-conductors, magnetic tapes, magnetic recording heads and cores, color picture tubes, circuitry, audio components, and precision mechanisms. In keeping with its efforts to produce quality products, SONY manufactures its own key components. This diversity of interests in electronics has enabled SONY to make technological breakthroughs that would not have been attainable by firms with smaller R&D efforts. Technological developments have also been facilitated by the founding of the SONY Research Center.

In addition, SONY is entering new fields on its own or as joint ventures with other firms. SONY currently has sixty-four subsidiaries and joint ventures. It has advertised its willingness to utilize its marketing system to help other firms with quality products enter the Japanese market. These products are often outside the electronics field. One firm that has taken advantage of SONY's marketing system is Whirlpool. And in late 1978 Prudential Insurance Company announced that it was considering a joint insurance venture with SONY. This would be SONY's first venture into the insurance business. Another joint venture has been with Wilson Sporting Goods.

Other SONY diversification moves include the development of a chain of spaghetti shops and a line of French cosmetics called "Sensitive Lady." When questioned about the wisdom of these moves, SONY executives stated that their diversification moves were made to provide opportunities for the development of young executives. Also, the ventures have the potential to be large profit makers in the future.

CASE ANALYSIS

CASE 23

The Sony Corporation

1. What type of pricing strategy is SONY using with its consumer electronics products?

_____

_____

_____

2. Why would SONY pursue such a strategy?

_____

_____

_____

_____

_____

_____

_____

3. Can SONY's pricing strategy be continued in the saturated U.S. color television market?

_____

_____

_____

_____

_____

_____

_____

_____

4.   What would happen to SONY's sales and profits if it made the price of its products more competitive?

_____

_____

_____

_____

_____

_____

_____

_____

5.   Should SONY continue its concentration on marketing television-related products? Why or why not?

_____

_____

_____

_____

_____

_____

_____

_____

_____

_____

_____

6.   Is SONY failing to take advantage of any marketing opportunities for electronics products for which it has the expertise?

_____

_____

_____

_____

_____

_____

_____

_____

_____

7.   Do you think that SONY's recent diversification strategies are in the company's best interest? Explain.

_____

_____

_____

_____

_____

_____

_____

_____

PART SIX

THE MARKETING ENVIRONMENT

CASE 24

THE STATE RETAIL ASSOCIATION: "BLUE LAW" CONFLICT

The State Retail Association (SRA) is a statewide organization whose membership includes both independent merchants and representatives from national companies that retail food, clothing, furniture, and other general merchandise. SRA's primary purpose is to provide legislative, educational, and research programs for the state's retail industry. The association is governed by a 40-member board of directors proportionally divided along trade lines and geographic areas. Charles Odell serves as executive director of the association.

A major agenda item of the board's 1981 fall quarter meeting is to determine the association's position concerning a number of issues which are to be considered by the legislature of this southeastern state when it meets in the spring. One such item relates to a proposal, supported by several state legislators, to abolish the state's Sunday closing law (blue law). (See Exhibit 24–1 for a copy of the law.)

Even though state Sunday closing laws have been upheld as constitutional by the U.S. Supreme Court,[1] many of the state's legislators strongly favor abolishing the state law, arguing that several local areas

Reprinted from J. Barry Mason, Morris L. Mayer, and Hazel F. Ezell, *Cases and Problems in Contemporary Retailing*, copyright © Business Publications, Inc., 1982, by permission of the author and publisher.

[1] The Court, in reviewing four cases relative to Sunday closing laws, concluded that the purpose and effect of these laws were to provide a uniform day of rest for all citizens and that it was merely a matter of convenience and custom that the day chosen was Sunday. Therefore, the Court held that Sunday closing laws as such were not violative of the free exercise of religion provided by the First Amendment to the U.S. Constitution. Further, the Court concluded that even though Sunday closing laws allowed certain businesses of "necessity" and "charity" to remain open on Sunday, these exemptions did not deny the equal protection of the law to all other businesses. Thus, the laws were not violative of the Equal Protection Clause of the 14th Amendment.

Exhibit 24–1
The state Sunday
closing law

> Any person who compels his child, apprentice or servant to perform any labor on Sunday, except the customary domestic duties of daily necessity or comfort, or works of charity, or who engages in shooting, hunting, gaming, card playing or racing on that day, or who, being a merchant or shopkeeper, druggist excepted, keeps open stores on Sunday, shall be fined not less than $10.00 nor more than $100.00, and may also be imprisoned in the county jail, or sentenced to hard labor for the county, for not more than three months. However, the provisions of this section shall not apply to the operation of railroads, airlines, bus lines, communications, public utilities or steamboats, or other vessels navigating the waters of this state, or to any manufacturing establishment which is required to be kept in constant operation, or to the sale of gasoline or other motor fuels or motor oils. Nor shall this section prohibit the sale of newspapers, or the operation of newsstands, or automobile repair shops, florist shops, fruit stands, ice cream shops or parlors, lunch stands or restaurants, delicatessens or plants engaged in the manufacture or sale of ice; provided, that such business establishments are not operated in conjunction with some other kind or type of business which is prohibited by this section. It shall also be lawful to engage in motorcycle and automobile racing on Sunday, whether admission is charged or not; except, that this proviso shall not be construed to prevent any municipality from passing ordinances prohibiting such racing on Sunday.

have passed ordinances to modify the law as it pertains to those areas (counties) and that the law is not being enforced in some areas of the state. On the other hand, many state legislators strongly favor keeping the law, arguing that it is needed to ensure a common day of rest for the citizens of the state.

SRA's board members are also divided on the issue. About one third of them support keeping the closing law; about one third favor abolishing the law, and about one third have no strong feelings one way or the other. Interestingly, the board members' positions are unrelated to trade line, geographic area, or type and size of operation. For example, some food retailers support the law; others favor its abolition. Some independent merchants want the law kept on the books; others want it removed.

Thus, as discussion of the issue continues (at times almost becoming a heated debate), it becomes apparent that the board members cannot reach a consensus concerning the lobbying position that the association should take on the issue.

Finally, Mr. Odell, the executive director, suggests that a consultant be hired to gather information which the board members can use as a basis for determining the association's lobbying position on the blue law issue. The board members unanimously agree, and Mr. Odell is authorized to hire Dr. Katherine Powers, a marketing faculty member at the state university, to serve as the board's consultant.

Mr. Odell promptly sets up an appointment with Dr. Powers. At their meeting he explains the situation to Dr. Powers and solicits her help in providing the board members with the information they need to develop a position statement. Mr. Odell also tells Dr. Powers that only limited funds are available for obtaining the information.

Dr. Powers agrees to serve as the board's consultant and immediately begins planning how to gather the needed information. She realizes that a statewide consumer survey to gather consumers' attitudes and opinions on Sunday closing laws and Sunday shopping would be too costly. Thus, she decides to use the data-collection technique known as the Delphi technique to gather information concerning attitudes toward Sunday closing laws and Sunday openings.

The Delphi technique is useful in determining whether a consensus concerning an issue can be achieved and, if so, the nature of the consensus. The technique elicits opinions from a panel of "experts," or persons highly knowledgeable about an issue. It uses rounds or iterations of questionnaires, with the idea that through these rounds of responses to questionnaires, the individual opinions of the experts will converge toward a consensus. The general procedure of the Delphi technique is as follows:

1. A group of experts are selected to serve as panel members.
2. A questionnaire containing statements related to the issue in question (in this case, Sunday closing laws and Sunday openings of retail stores) is developed.
3. The panel members are asked to evaluate (by indicating their extent of agreement or disagreement) the statements on the questionnaire.
4. Each panel member then receives the list of statements a second time, accompanied by a summary of the responses to each statement. For each of the statements on the questionnaire the following information is provided: the median response of all panel members, the interquartile range (the middle 50 percent of the responses) for all panel members, and the respondent's previous response. A respondent who is in the *minority* (whose response lies outside the interquartile range of the responses to a given statement) is asked to revise his or her opinion or to indicate his or her reasons for wishing to remain in the minority.
5. Each panel member then receives the list of statements a third

time, accompanied by an updated summary and minority opinions, and is given a final chance to revise his or her opinions if still in the minority.

This system of repeated measurement should result in a decrease in the range of responses and in the movement of the group median toward a consensus.

To begin with, Dr. Powers had to select her panel members—those individuals who were defined as "experts" or centers of influence in the area of Sunday legislation and Sunday selling and who were considered capable of expressing informed opinions on the issue of Sunday closing laws. She decided to select panel members from the following groups:

1. *Elected officials (state legislators and municipal officials).* State legislators vote on legislation affecting Sunday openings, and in order to vote intelligently, they should have a thorough understanding of the topic and reflect the attitudes of the majority of citizens. Municipal officials are the ones on whom pressure is often brought to bear in the enforcement of blue laws, and it is often the decisions of these individuals which determine whether the state blue laws will be actively enforced.
2. *Legal experts.* Lawyers and judges are involved when violations of the law occur, and in order to serve in their respective capacities, they must have a thorough understanding of the law and its implications.
3. *Ministerial leaders.* The clergy must be included because, even though blue laws have a secular purpose, religious implications are involved, since Sunday openings may impact directly or indirectly on religious participation.
4. *Retailers.* These individuals must be included because some of their operating strategies will be affected by the nature of Sunday legislation and perhaps by their personal attitudes toward Sunday selling.

Random sampling procedures were not used to select the panel members from within the defined groups. Instead, Dr. Powers took great care to select as panel members only individuals whom she and other knowledgeable persons in the state considered most influential in determining the future course of legislation affecting Sunday retail business activities in the state and most capable of expressing informed opinions on the issue.

The panel consisted of 519 individuals—72 elected officials, 66 lawyers and judges, 63 ministerial leaders, and 318 retailers. All of the panel members agreed to participate in the study and to respond to all three rounds of questionnaires.

Dr. Powers then proceeded to develop the first-round questionnaire. The first part of the questionnaire contained 49 statements concerning attitudes and opinions about Sunday closing laws and Sunday openings. Dr. Powers developed the statements based on secondary research and in-depth interviews with a number of individuals (non-panel members) knowledgeable on the issue of Sunday closing laws and Sunday openings. Of the 49 statements, 23 concerned general social, economic, moral, and political issues related to Sunday closing laws and Sunday openings; 6 dealt with the impact of and problems attendant on Sunday closing laws; 11 concerned the retail strategy implications of Sunday openings; and 9 focused on alternative means of achieving the purpose of the Sunday closing law. Care was taken in the wording of statements to have an equal number of statements reflect favorable and unfavorable attitudes toward Sunday closing laws and Sunday openings and to have the statements randomly arranged on the questionnaire.

A five-point rating scale was used with the questionnaire. In expressing agreement or disagreement with each statement on the questionnaire, the panel members could choose one of the following responses: "highly agree," "agree," "uncertain," "disagree," or "highly disagree." The numbers 5, 4, 3, 2, and 1 were assigned to the five choices, with 1 representing "highly disagree" and 5 representing "highly agree."

The first-round questionnaire contained two other parts. Part 2 requested certain demographic information (e.g., age, occupation, educational level) from all of the panel members. Part 3, which was to be completed only by owners and managers of retail establishments, was included to obtain information on type of ownership, location, the level at which policy decisions were made, hours of operation, and size of establishment. This part of the questionnaire was included because Dr. Powers believed that the board members would be interested in information concerning differences in attitude toward the issue, if any, among retail merchants.

After the first-round questionnaire was complete, it was mailed to the 519 panel members. Within four weeks all of the questionnaires had been returned to Dr. Powers. She then administered the second-round questionnaire. This questionnaire contained the 49 statements which had appeared on the first-round questionnaire. In addition, it provided the following information for each statement: the median response for all panel members, the interquartile range (middle 50 percent of the responses) for all panel members, and the given member's previous response. The panel members were asked to consider the consensus indicators (the median and the interquartile range) for each statement and to change any of their responses if they so desired. If their initial or new response was outside the interquartile range, they were asked to explain why they maintained an opinion deviant from that of the consensus.

Within three weeks the second-round questionnaires had been completed and returned to Dr. Powers. After analyzing the panel members' responses to the second-round questionnaire, Dr. Powers developed the third- and final-round questionnaire. This questionnaire contained the same 49 statements as had appeared on the first two questionnaires. However, in addition to providing updated information relative to the consensus indicators for each statement (the median and the interquartile range), Dr. Powers also provided the panel members with the reasons (presented anonymously on a statement-by-statement basis) that some respondents on the second-round questionnaire had given for maintaining a position deviant from that of the consensus. With this third questionnaire, the panel members were asked to consider the consensus indicators (the median and the interquartile range) and the list of reasons for maintaining a deviant opinion before making a final decision as to their level of agreement or disagreement for each statement. For this final round, reasons were not requested from the panel members for selecting or maintaining a position deviant from that of the consensus.

Within about a month Dr. Powers had received all of the third-round questionnaires. She analyzed the data and prepared her report, which she submitted to Mr. Odell. (See Exhibit 24–2 for Dr. Powers' report.)

Mr. Odell was very pleased with Dr. Powers' work and was eager to share her report with the board members. Copies of the report were mailed to all board members, along with a letter requesting that each member carefully study the contents of the report and come to a meeting scheduled within two weeks to discuss the findings and to develop the association's lobbying position statement on the issue of the state's Sunday closing law.

Exhibit 24–2
Dr. Powers' report

THE STATE UNIVERSITY

Date

Mr. Charles Odell
Executive Director
The State Retail Association
City, State   00000

Dear Mr. Odell:

Enclosed with this letter are tables which present the information collected from my survey concerning attitudes and opinions on Sunday closing laws and Sunday openings. In all of the tables, median responses to individual questionnaire statements are reported.

Tables 1–8 present median responses for the 23 questionnaire statements which relate to general social, economic, moral, and political issues related to Sunday closing laws and Sunday openings. Table 1 presents for the total panel and the four panel subgroups responses to the 14 (of the 23) statements reflecting *unfavorable* attitudes toward Sunday openings; Table 2 presents data for the 9 (of the 23) statements reflecting *favorable* attitudes.

I felt that the board members would be interested in having information concerning differences in attitude, if any, among retail merchants relative to the issue; thus, I have included in my report Tables 3–8, which present this type of information.

Table 3 gives median responses of retailers in three different locational categories (CBD, shopping centers, and isolated locations) to the 14 statements reflecting unfavorable attitudes; Table 4 presents responses for these categories of retailers to the 9 statements reflecting favorable attitudes. Tables 5 and 6 present, respectively, responses to unfavorable and favorable attitude statements of retailers who own and/or manage a single-unit store versus those who own and/or manage multi-unit stores. Tables 7 and 8 present, respectively, for the unfavorable and favorable attitude statements the responses of retailers categorized by type of merchandise sold.

Table 8 gives the total panel's responses to the 6 questionnaire statements concerned with the impact of and problems attendant on Sunday closing laws; Table 9 provides the median responses of only the retail subgroup to the 11 questionnaire statements dealing with the strategic implications of Sunday openings. Please note that I have categorized these statements as economic implication statements, personnel implication statements, and miscellaneous. Lastly, Table 11 presents the responses of the entire panel to the nine questionnaire statements which focus on alternative means of achieving the purpose of the Sunday closing law.

There are a few comments which I would like to make that may be of help to you and the board members in analyzing the information pre-

(cont.)

Exhibit 24–2
(cont.)

sented. First, there was little, if any, attitude change on the part of the panel members over the rounds of questionnaires. Only rarely did a panel member change his or her opinion on a statement after receiving feedback concerning the median response of all panel members and the interquartile range. Thus, it may be that one cannot expect initial convergence or attitude change when individuals are dealing with an issue which involves strong, perhaps emotional, opinions based on individual value systems. *However,* the retail subgroup exhibited more convergence of opinion than any other group—a finding which may indicate that retailers, as a group, are capable of interacting and working toward common goals. Apparently, the retailers are a more homogeneous group than the other groups, with fewer external variables affecting their attitudes. In terms of a power base for influence, this conclusion has value—it seems to indicate that it would be highly advantageous for SRA to develop a position statement on the Sunday closing law issue and make its position very clear to the state legislature.

Secondly, there was no way for me to test the findings of this survey for statistical inference since random sampling procedures were not used in selecting panel members. Thus, it would not be appropriate to extrapolate the findings of this study to any other population.

If you have any questions concerning this report, please call me. Also, if you would like me to attend the board meeting at which you discuss the findings of this survey, please let me know the date of the meeting and I will make every effort to attend. I have enjoyed working with SRA. If I can be of any assistance in the future, please let me know.

Best wishes,

Katherine Powers, Ph.D.

Enclosures

Table 1
Median responses to statements reflecting unfavorable attitudes toward Sunday openings for total panel and for each major panel subgroup

Statement	Total panel	Retailers	Ministers	Elected officials	Legal experts
Allowing retail stores to be open on Sunday would lead to decreased church attendance	3.5	4	3	3.5	2
Sunday shopping hours would disrupt the family living patterns of retail employees	4	4	4	4	2
Selling goods and services on Sunday results in a decrease in family leisure activities	4	4	3.5	4	2
Sunday closing laws are needed to prevent moral decay in our society	2	2	2	3.5	2
Sunday closing laws are needed to provide a common day of rest for all members of society	4	4	4	3.5	2
Laws setting aside Sunday as a day of rest are needed to protect individuals from the physical and mental fatigue which comes from uninterrupted labor	3	4	4	2.5	2
Sunday laws are part of American tradition and should not be abolished	4	4	3	4	2
There is no significant need and, hence, demand for goods and services on Sunday	2	2	4	3	2
People who want to observe Sunday as a day of worship can do so without restricting others	4	4	4	4	4
Employees who wish to observe Sunday as a day of rest and worship would be harassed into working by store managers who wished to remain open on Sunday	4	4	4	4	3

(cont.)

Table 1 (*cont.*)

Statement	Total panel	Retailers	Ministers	Elected officials	Legal experts
Since Sunday is a day of worship for over 90 percent of the population, Sunday should be the day of the week set aside as a common day of rest	4	4	4	4	4
Any law of prohibition will adversely affect some segment of the population, but lack of a Sunday closing law would be even more detrimental to society	4	4	4	3.5	2
Churches should do more to educate people so as to make Sunday openings less profitable	3	3	3.5	3.5	2
People need legislative protection from an economic system which will grind them up for the sake of profit	4	4	4	4	3

Note: Code for median responses: 1 = highly disagree, 2 = disagree, 3 = uncertain, 4 = agree, 5 = highly agree.

Table 2
Median responses to statements reflecting favorable attitudes toward Sunday openings for total panel and for each major panel subgroup

Statement	Total panel	Retailers	Ministers	Elected officials	Legal experts
Sunday closing laws are a violation of the due process clause of the 14th Amendment since they prohibit the right to use one's property as one sees fit so long as the rights of others are not thereby infringed	3	3	2	3	2
Retailers should be allowed to determine for themselves if they wish to remain open on Sunday	2	2	2	2	4
Consumer demand, not legislation, should determine whether retail establishments should be open on Sunday	2	2	2	2.5	4
Sunday closing laws violate an individual's religious freedoms guaranteed by the First Amendment	2	2	2	2	2
Sunday closing laws are an outrage against individual freedom	2	2	2	1.5	2
There should be no restriction whatever on Sunday selling activities	2	2	1.5	1.5	2
All types of retail establishments should be allowed to remain open on Sunday	2	2	2	2	2
Sunday closing laws discriminate against retailers who worship on days other than Sunday	3	3	4	4	4
Since industries can manufacture and transport goods on Sunday, retailers should be allowed to sell on Sunday	2	2	2	2	3

Note: Code for median responses: 1 = highly disagree, 2 = disagree, 3 = uncertain, 4 = agree, 5 = highly agree.

Table 3
Median responses of retailers in certain locational categories for statements reflecting unfavorable attitudes toward Sunday openings

Statement	CBD	Shopping center	Isolated location
Allowing retail stores to be open on Sunday would lead to decreased church attendance	4	4.5	4
Sunday shopping hours would disrupt the family living patterns of retail employees	4	5	4
Selling goods and services on Sunday results in a decrease in family leisure activities	4	4.5	4
Sunday closing laws are needed to prevent moral decay in our society	3	4.5	2
Sunday closing laws are needed to provide a common day of rest for all members of society	4	4.5	4
Laws setting aside Sunday as a day of rest are needed to protect individuals from the physical and mental fatigue which comes from uninterrupted labor	4	4	3
Sunday laws are part of American tradition and should not be abolished	4	4	4
There is no significant need and, hence, demand for goods and services on Sunday	4	4	3
People who want to observe Sunday as a day of worship can do so without restricting others	3	4	2
Employees who wish to observe Sunday as a day of rest and worship would be harassed into working by store managers who wished to remain open on Sunday	4	4	4
Since Sunday is a day of worship for over 90 percent of the population, Sunday should be the day of the week set aside as a common day of rest	4	4	4

Table 3 (*cont.*)

Statement	CBD	Shopping center	Isolated location
Any law of prohibition will adversely affect some segment of the population, but lack of a Sunday closing law would be even more detrimental to society	3	4	4
Churches should do more to educate people so as to make Sunday openings less profitable	3	4	3
People need legislative protection from an economic system which will grind them up for the sake of profit	3	4.4	4

Note: Code for median responses: 1 = highly disagree, 2 = disagree, 3 = uncertain, 4 = agree, 5 = highly agree.

Table 4
Median responses of retailers in certain locational categories for statements reflecting favorable attitudes toward Sunday openings

Statement	CBD	Shopping center	Isolated location
Sunday closing laws are a violation of the due process clause of the 14th Amendment since they prohibit one the right to use one's property as one sees fit so long as the rights of others are not thereby infringed	2	2	3
Retailers should be allowed to determine for themselves if they wish to remain open on Sunday	2	1.5	2
Consumer demand, not legislation, should determine whether retail establishments should be open on Sunday	2	2	3
Sunday closing laws violate an individual's religious freedoms guaranteed by the First Amendment	2	2	2
Sunday closing laws are an outrage against individual freedom	2	2	2
There should be no restriction whatever on Sunday selling activities	2	1.5	2
All types of retail establishments should be allowed to remain open on Sunday	2	1.5	2
Sunday closing laws discriminate against retailers who worship on days other than Sunday	2	3	3
Since industries can manufacture and transport goods on Sunday, retailers should be allowed to sell on Sunday	2	2	2

Note: Code for median responses: 1 = highly disagree, 2 = disagree, 3 = uncertain, 4 = agree, 5 = highly agree.

Table 5
Median responses of retailers in certain ownership categories for statements reflecting unfavorable attitudes toward Sunday openings

Statement	Single-unit	Multi-unit
Allowing retail stores to be open on Sunday would lead to decreased church attendance	4	3.5
Sunday shopping hours would disrupt the family living patterns of retail employees	4	5
Selling goods and services on Sunday results in a decrease in family leisure activities	4	4
Sunday closing laws are needed to prevent moral decay in our society	2	3
Sunday closing laws are needed to provide a common day of rest for all members of society	4	4
Laws setting aside Sunday as a day of rest are needed to protect individuals from the physical and mental fatigue which comes from uninterrupted labor	4	3
People who want to observe Sunday as a day of worship can do so without restricting others	4	4
Sunday laws are part of American tradition and should not be abolished	4	4
There is no significant need and, hence, demand for goods and services on Sunday	2	2.5
Employees who wish to observe Sunday as a day of rest and worship would be harassed into working by store managers who wished to remain open on Sunday	4	4
Since Sunday is a day of worship for over 90 percent of the population, Sunday should be the day of the week set aside as a common day of rest	4	4
Any law of prohibition will adversely affect some segment of the population, but lack of a Sunday closing law would be even more detrimental to society	3	4
Churches should do more to educate people so as to make Sunday openings less profitable	3	4
People need legislative protection from an economic system which will grind them up for the sake of profit	4	4

Note: Code for median responses: 1 = highly disagree, 2 = disagree, 3 = uncertain, 4 = agree, 5 = highly agree.

**Table 6
Median responses of
retailers in certain
ownership categories
for statements
reflecting favorable
attitudes toward
Sunday openings**

Statement	Single-unit	Multi-unit
Sunday closing laws are a violation of the due process clause of the 14th Amendment since they prohibit the right to use one's property as one sees fit so long as the rights of others are not thereby infringed	3	3
Retailers should be allowed to determine for themselves if they wish to remain open on Sunday	2	2
Consumer demand, not legislation, should determine whether retail establishments should be open on Sunday	2	2
Sunday closing laws violate an individual's religious freedoms guaranteed by the First Amendment	2	3
Sunday closing laws are an outrage against individual freedom	2	2
There should be no restriction whatever on Sunday selling activities	2	2
All types of retail establishments should be allowed to remain open on Sunday	2	1.5
Sunday closing laws discriminate against retailers who worship on days other than Sunday	2	3
Since industries can manufacture and transport goods on Sunday, retailers should be allowed to sell on Sunday	2	2

Note: Code for median responses: 1 = highly disagree, 2 = disagree, 3 = uncertain, 4 = agree, 5 = highly agree.

Table 7
Median responses of retailers in certain merchandise-sold categories for statements reflecting unfavorable attitudes toward Sunday openings

Statement	Food and drug	Furniture/ appliance	General merchandise
Allowing retail stores to be open on Sunday would lead to decreased church attendance	3	4	4
Sunday shopping hours would disrupt the family living patterns of retail employees	4	4	4
Selling goods and services on Sunday results in a decrease in family leisure activities	4	4	4
Sunday closing laws are needed to prevent moral decay in our society	2	3	2
Sunday closing laws are needed to provide a common day of rest for all members of society	3	4	4
Laws setting aside Sunday as a day of rest are needed to protect individuals from the physical and mental fatigue which comes from uninterrupted labor	4	3	3
People who want to observe Sunday as a day of worship can do so without restricting others	4	4	4
Sunday laws are part of American tradition and should not be abolished	4	4	3.5
There is no significant need and, hence, demand for goods and services on Sunday	2	4	2.5
Employees who wish to observe Sunday as a day of rest and worship would be harassed into working by store managers who wished to remain open on Sunday	4	4	4
Since Sunday is a day of worship for over 90 percent of the population, Sunday should be the day of the week set aside as a common day of rest	4	4	4
Any law of prohibition will adversely affect some segment of the population, but lack of a Sunday closing law would be even more detrimental to society	4	3	4
Churches should do more to educate people so as to make Sunday openings less profitable	3	4	3
People need legislative protection from an economic system which will grind them up for the sake of profit	3	2	4

Note: Code for median responses: 1 = highly disagree, 2 = disagree, 3 = uncertain, 4 = agree, 5 = highly agree.

Table 8
Median responses of retailers in certain merchandise-sold categories for statements reflecting favorable attitudes toward Sunday openings

Statement	Food and drug	Furniture/ appliance	General merchandise
Sunday closing laws are a violation of the due process clause of the 14th Amendment since they prohibit the right to use one's property as one sees fit so long as the rights of others are not thereby infringed	3	3	3
Retailers should be allowed to determine for themselves if they wish to remain open on Sunday	2	4	2
Consumer demand, not legislation, should determine whether retail establishments should be open on Sunday	2	3	2
Sunday closing laws violate an individual's religious freedoms guaranteed by the First Amendment	2	3	2
Sunday closing laws are an outrage against individual freedom	2	2	2
There should be no restriction whatever on Sunday selling activities	2	2	2
All types of retail establishments should be allowed to remain open on Sunday	2	2	2
Sunday closing laws discriminate against retailers who worship on days other than Sunday	2	3	2.5
Since industries can manufacture and transport goods on Sunday, retailers should be allowed to sell on Sunday	2	2	2

Note: Code for median responses: 1 = highly disagree, 2 = disagree, 3 = uncertain, 4 = agree, 5 = highly agree.

**Table 9
Median responses of
the total panel for
statements concerned
with the impact of and
problems attendant on
Sunday closing laws**

Statement	Median
Permitting the sale on Sunday of items in one store but not in another discriminates against those not allowed to remain open to sell the items	4
Retailers who must remain closed on Sunday are at a competitive disadvantage compared with merchants who are allowed to remain open on Sunday	4
Sunday laws are invalid because they are subject to unequal and sporadic enforcement	4
Blue laws are ill equipped to be used as a vehicle for establishing a common day of rest for members of society because many employees who labor the hardest on Sunday are often excluded from coverage in the statutes	4
The purpose of Sunday closing laws (providing a common day of rest) has been prostituted into a weapon of economic warfare due to the growing fight between the discount operator and the downtown merchant	4
Statutes restricting business operations on Sunday are outdated in our socially and economically affluent society	4

Note: Code for median responses: 1 = highly disagree, 2 = disagree, 3 = uncertain, 4 = agree, 5 = highly agree.

	Statement	Median
Table 10 **Median responses of retailers for statements indicating strategy implications**	Economic implications	
	Selling goods and services on Sunday results in net decreases in retailers' business profits	3
	Sunday openings would only lead to increased costs for retailers with no material increases in total revenue	4
	Sunday openings merely redistribute retailers' weekly sales without materially adding to them	4
	Small, independently owned retail stores would be at an economic disadvantage compared to large chain stores if Sunday openings were permitted	4
	Stores located in downtown areas would be at a competitive disadvantage compared to stores located in shopping centers if Sunday openings were permitted	4
	Personnel implications	
	Retailers would have a problem obtaining qualified personnel to work on Sunday	4
	With fewer store personnel working in retail stores on Sunday, problems such as shoplifting, pilferage, and robberies will increase	4
	Many employees might choose to work on Sunday in order to have a weekday off to take care of business that can only be conducted Monday through Friday	3
	Miscellaneous	
	Sunday openings would disrupt certain retail store activities such as stocking shelves, taking inventory, and store maintenance	3
	Most retailers who remain open on Sunday do so not because of a change in philosophy relative to Sunday openings but in order to meet competition	4
	Sunday shopping will be a form of leisure activity for many families	4

Note: Code for median responses: 1 = highly disagree, 2 = disagree, 3 = uncertain, 4 = agree, 5 = highly agree.

**Table 11
Median responses
of total panel for
statements suggesting
alternative means of
achieving purpose of
Sunday closing law**

Statement	Median
To allow for differences in local needs and desires, local governments should have the authority to establish their own Sunday opening requirements rather than being controlled by a statewide measure	3.5
Sunday closing laws should provide for a forced day of rest with the particular day being optional (each retailer would choose a day to be closed)	2
Since public opinion on the issue of Sunday closing laws is so diverse that it is impossible to obtain a satisfactory legal solution to the problem, the only feasible solution is to permit Sunday openings	2
The law should allow limited Sunday afternoon openings in all retail stores with fewer than eight employees	2
Only retail establishments selling necessities absolutely essential to the health and well-being of the community should be open on Sunday	4
With the exception of certain stores selling necessity items, retail stores should be closed on Sundays; for those classes of necessity stores, arrangements would have to be worked out for only one store of a particular type to be open on a specified Sunday	3
Sunday closing laws should be strictly enforced against all businesses except those exempted under the law	4
The problem in passing Sunday legislation is primarily in determining which types of retail outlets will be permitted to stay open	4
Sunday closing laws should not be abolished but should be studied, updated, and made more equitable	4

Note: Code for median responses: 1 = highly disagree, 2 = disagree, 3 = uncertain, 4 = agree, 5 = highly agree.

CASE ANALYSIS

CASE 24

The State Retail Association: "Blue Law" Conflict

1. What is the major question facing the board of directors of the State Retail Association (SRA)?

   _____

   _____

   _____

   _____

2. What are the major alternatives available to the board?

   _____

   _____

   _____

   _____

   _____

   _____

   _____

   _____

   _____

   _____

3. What seems to be the consensus of the panel regarding Sunday clos-
    ing laws? Are there differences in attitude among panel subgroups
    (i.e., retailers, ministers, elected officials, legal experts) and, if so,
    what are they?

    _____

    _____

    _____

    _____

    _____

    _____

    _____

    _____

    _____

    _____

    _____

    _____

    _____

    _____

_____

_____

_____

_____

_____

4. Are there differences in the attitudes of the retail merchants and, if so, what are they?

_____

_____

_____

_____

_____

_____

_____

_____

_____

_____

_____

_____

_____

_____

_____

_____

_____

_____

_____

_____

_____

_____

5. What problems or limitations were identified regarding the present law?

_____

_____

_____

_____

_____

_____

_____

_____

6.   Based on retailers' perceptions concerning strategy implications of Sunday openings, for what reasons may retailers not be in favor of expanding Sunday openings?

_____

_____

_____

_____

_____

_____

_____

_____

_____

7.   What is the consensus of the panel concerning alternative means of achieving the purpose served by Sunday closing laws?

_____

_____

_____

_____

_____

_____

8. On the basis of your analysis of the data, assess the alternatives available to the board and propose a course of action.

_____

_____

_____

_____

_____

_____

_____

_____

_____

_____

_____

_____

_____

_____

_____

_____

_____

_____

_____

_____

_____

_____

_____

9.   Propose a plan of action.

_____

_____

_____

_____

_____

_____

_____

_____

_____

_____

_____

_____

_____

_____

_____

_____

_____

_____

_____

_____

_____

_____

CASE 25

CENTRAL HOSPITAL

Public Relations Problems
Plague New Construction Project

Central Hospital in Bloomington, Illinois, is a 400-bed, multi-speciality community hospital providing ambulatory care, acute care and psychiatric care services to residents living within a 30-mile radius of Bloomington–Normal, twin cities. The non-profit hospital is located within close proximity to a large state university. Central Hospital is also located close to what is recognized as the poorest neighborhood in the twin cities, an area of rundown homes with a population that is 90 percent black, 5 percent white, and 5 percent "other."

Three years ago, the Board of Directors of Central Hospital approved a plan to seek approval to build a new ambulatory care facility to replace its inadequate facilities located within the existing hospital structure. Last year, the hospital was awarded a Certificate of Need by the Illinois Health Facilities Planning Board to construct a new 40,000-square-foot ambulatory care building.

The hospital's chief executive officer, health planner and vice president of operations worked exclusively with the architect to plan the new facility, taking the plan to the hospital's Board of Directors for ultimate approval.

Case prepared by Charles H. Patti, Associate Professor of Marketing, and Debra Low, Faculty Associate, Department of Marketing, Arizona State University.

Courtesy of Owen Franken/Stock, Boston

The plan they took to the board proposed a two-story ambulatory care facility with an attached parking garage, extending from the west end of the existing hospital structure, which housed the current out-patient area. The only drawback of the plan was that the new facility would extend across a section of Moon Street. It was determined by the architect that the facility could not be built over the street, and that a portion of Moon Street would therefore have to be purchased from the City of Bloomington to accommodate the new facility.

Twelve of the thirteen board members heartily endorsed the plan, providing that the street could be purchased for less than $50,000 from the city. The 13th board member, Bill Smith, the board's only black, noted that the proposed street was the only major arterial street to the poor neighborhood located just south of the hospital. He noted that the local residents would have to drive three blocks around the proposed facility to get to and from the closest boulevard under the proposed plan. Moon Street was currently the most convenient access street.

Paul Jones, the hospital's chief executive officer, noted that the proposed plan was the most efficient and cost effective plan possible. He further noted that he was certain that the neighborhood would support any project that Central Hospital sponsored. "What's more important," he argued, "a health care facility or a three-block detour?"

The Board of Directors voted. Ten approved the project, two voted against the project and one abstained. The project was passed.

The day before the public hearing, Florence Cummings, an outspoken black who was highly respected in the area, charged that Central Hospital had "ignored the needs of the area residents by proposing to close down our street." She further stated, "Central Hospital is insensitive to our needs. We were never informed of their plans until after the fact. Nobody ever asked us how we felt—or what services we'd like to get from Central Hospital."

Paul Jones' response to the press was: "Central Hospital is providing area residents with the highest quality health care. Our health care professionals have developed this excellent facility for the people we serve. We care."

Florence Cummings and a cadre of 60 local residents picketed the hospital on the day of the public hearing. They also testified against the plan at the public hearing. Despite the protest, the Health Systems Agency voted in favor of the project, and the state ultimately awarded the Certificate of Need.

On the day of the groundbreaking, Hospital Administrator Paul Jones was quoted by the press as saying, "It is obvious that Central Hospital is sensitive to the needs of our health care consumer." Florence Cummings and a number of persons picketed the groundbreaking ceremonies.

CASE ANALYSIS

CASE 25

Central Hospital

1. Should Central Hospital's proximity to a poor neighborhood affect the hospital's basic mission, objectives, and goals? Why or why not?

_____

_____

_____

_____

_____

_____

2. Should the two negative votes at the board level, one of which was given by Bill Smith, the board's only black member, have been considered in more depth in the decision to approve the project? Why or why not?

_____

_____

_____

_____

_____

_____

_____

3. What concept is Central Hospital employing: a product-oriented concept or a consumer-oriented concept? Explain.

_____

_____

_____

_____

_____

4. Were Florence Cummings' criticisms appropriate? Was Paul Jones' response to the press appropriate? Explain both.

_____

_____

_____

_____

_____

_____

_____

_____

_____

5. In order of priority, what steps should have been taken from the outset to facilitate a better relationship between Central Hospital and its constituents?

_____

_____

_____

_____

_____

_____

_____

6. Now that the groundbreaking is over, what steps can Paul Jones take to create a more amicable relationship between the hospital and the community?

_____

_____

_____

_____

_____

_____

7. Is the Florence Cummings contingent an important constituent group for Central Hospital?

_____

_____

_____

_____

_____

_____

8. Is the Health Systems Agency product-oriented or consumer-oriented? Explain.

_____

_____

_____

_____

_____

_____

9. How should Central Hospital deal with the picketers? Explain.

_____

_____

_____

_____

_____

CASE 26

HEUBLEIN, INC.

A Socially Questionable Product

Stuart D. Watson, chairman of the board at Heublein, Inc., sat in his office to review a speech he was to give that evening. The occasion was the annual meeting of the Wine Institute, a trade association of wine producers and distributors. Watson had selected as his topic, "The Corporate Responsibilities Function at Heublein." He would focus in the speech on the importance of monitoring the social and political environment for contingency planning purposes.

In particular, Watson intended to discuss the role at Heublein, Inc., of public affairs and the Corporate Responsibility Committee. Watson was proud of the research sponsored by Heublein on the causes and treatment of alcoholism. He was also pleased that the Corporate Responsibility Committee had provided strong guidance to senior executives on advertising, product, and distribution policies. As an example of the Committee's efforts, he intended to show some recent advertisements that were sensitive to the social consequences of alcohol consumption. The ads depicted people with and without cocktails, all having fun. The intention was not to glamorize drinking as the socially desirable thing to do. The text of the ads stressed moderation. Figure 26–1 shows an example of the ads Watson intended to show the group.

Adler/Robinson/Carlson, *Marketing and Society: Cases and Commentaries,* © 1981, pp. 30, 32, 34–39. Reprinted by permission of Prentice-Hall, Inc., Englewood Cliffs, N.J. This case is not intended to provide a precise account of the thinking of the parties involved.

Figure 26–1
Advertisement for Malcolm Hereford's Cows

Courtesy of Malcolm Hereford's Cows

Just as Watson completed his review, he received a call from John J. Moran, vice president of public affairs. Moran began by saying, "Stuart, did you see the Today Show this morning? Well, I did. I could not believe my eyes. Betty Furness got some fifth graders drunk on Cows and then told America, 'this proves that Heublein is trying to appeal to kids.' Stuart, we cannot let this one lie like we did in November with the MacNeil–Lehrer Report." Watson agreed and asked Moran to prepare his recommendations for an appropriate response. He further requested Moran to add the issue to the agenda of the Corporate Responsibility Committee meeting scheduled for the following day.

Company background

Heublein, Inc., was, in 1977, the largest producer and distributor of distilled spirits and wines in the United States. Corporate-wide revenue was over $799 million for the first half of fiscal 1977. Table 26–1 shows a steady growth pattern in both revenues and profits for the period 1972–1976. Prior to 1976, the company was organized in three major profit centers: beverage, food, and international. In January 1976, the company reorganized into five groups: spirits, wines, food service and franchising, grocery products, and international. Of these, spirits was the largest, in both sales and profits, with 1976 sales over $300 million and profits of approximately $35 million.

The Heublein product line featured over 200 well-known consumer product brand names, including Smirnoff Vodka, Black and White Scotch, A-1 Steak Sauce, Ortega Chiles and Sauces, Italian Swiss Colony, Lancers, Inglenook, Annie Green Springs, T. J. Swann, Jose Cuervo Tequilla, Black Velvet Canadian Whiskey, Irish Mist, Harvey's Bristol Cream, and Snap-E-Tom Cocktails. In addition, the company had acquired, in 1971, Kentucky Fried Chicken.

Heublein had been plagued by several serious problems in recent years which had the net effect of plummeting Heublein stock from 40½ down to the 20s, even though sales and profits continued to be strong. The Christmas quarter of 1976, normally the strongest sales period, was disappointing, with sales down by 13 percent from the previous year. Preliminary estimates showed that company profits for the first half of the fiscal year 1977 would be up only 1 percent over the previous year.

Several reasons were cited by management for the declining performance of company products. First, in 1975, the Federal Trade Commission challenged Heublein's acquisition of United Vintners, a

Table 26–1
Heublein, Inc., consolidated summary of operations
(Dollars in thousands)

	1976	1975	1974	1973	1972
REVENUES					
Beverage	$ 858,706	$ 772,576	$ 697,018	$ 586,423	$ 507,125
Food	489,302	446,792	387,272	315,096	273,154
International	235,125	195,047	155,852	64,620	33,721
	1,583,133	1,414,415	1,240,142	966,139	814,000
Cost of sales	1,099,416	988,474	855,134	660,173	546,674
Selling, advertising, administrative, and general expenses	338,454	290,151	265,660	211,523	181,185
Operating income	$ 145,263	$ 135,790	$ 119,348	$ 94,443	$ 86,141
OPERATING INCOME					
Beverage	$ 72,732	$ 63,226	$ 52,044	$ 42,005	$ 39,080
Food	52,211	55,985	51,458	45,170	43,456
International	20,320	16,579	15,846	7,268	3,605
	145,263	135,790	119,348	94,443	86,141

328

Interest expense	18,494	16,910	9,830	6,357	7,381
Interest income	2,810	2,147	1,384	1,683	646
Miscellaneous income (expense)—net	763	632	122	(225)	367
Income taxes	64,433	61,661	58,683	46,877	41,474
Income from continuing operations	65,909	59,998	52,341	42,667	38,299
Income (loss) from discontinued operations, less tax effect	7,184	1,498	2,069	1,544	(607)
Income before extraordinary items	73,093	61,496	54,410	44,211	37,692
Extraordinary items, less tax effect	—	—	—	(13,800)	(15,250)
NET INCOME	73,093	61,496	54,410	30,411	22,442
Preferred dividends	—	—	—	—	293
Earnings applicable to common stock	73,093	61,496	54,410	30,411	22,149
Common and common equivalent shares	$21,536,526	$21,216,540	$21,166,002	$20,932,055	$19,607,538
Earnings per common and common equivalent share					
Continuing operations	$3.06	$2.83	$2.47	$2.04	$1.94
Discontinued operations	0.33	0.07	0.10	0.07	(0.03)
Before extraordinary items	3.39	2.90	2.57	2.11	1.91
Extraordinary items	—	—	—	(0.66)	(0.78)
NET EARNINGS	$3.39	$2.90	$2.57	$1.45	$1.13

Source: Heublein Annual Report (May, 1978), pp. 17–18.

prestigious and profitable wine group, second only to the E & J Gallo Winery in market share. In negotiations with the FTC, Heublein offered to divest itself of the Petri, Italian Swiss Colony, and Lejon product lines while retaining the Inglenook, T. J. Swann, and Annie Green Springs brands. The FTC rejected this proposal and the case was expected to go to court in late 1977.

Another problem area had been the declining performance of Kentucky Fried Chicken (KFC). As of June 1976, the KFC chain included 4,340 company-owned or franchised outlets, which spent over $30 million on advertising. KFC ranked second in fast-food-industry sales, behind McDonald's, and the company had planned to retain this position by relying on its superior marketing capabilities in spite of a trend of continuous and substantial price increases. Problems occurred when, as one industry analyst put it, "the oil shortage and the nation's economic problem resulted, the economics of a burger meal for the family began to look a lot more attractive than a $9 bucket of chicken . . . they priced themselves into a bind."[1] KFC planned to reduce prices and return to emphasizing a smaller sales package to recapture its declining market share.

The spirits groups also suffered problems during this period. The Black Velvet Whiskey campaign was given the "Keep Her in Her Place" Advertising Award in 1974 by the National Organization for Women for a campaign described as a demeaning "sex-sell." This was followed by an attack from the Oregon State Liquor Commission for "sexually suggestive" advertising.[2] Black and White Scotch, the leading brand of scotch in the 1950s, acquired by Heublein in 1974, experienced a decreasing market share. The company found itself unable to stop the decline. The trend, averaging a decrease of 110,000 cases per year since 1974, represented a drain on corporate profitability.

On the positive side, Heublein had Smirnoff Vodka, which was acquired in 1939 for a mere $14,000 and a small royalty by John G. Martin, grandson of Heublein's founder. Smirnoff was the largest-selling vodka in the country, with sales of 5.5 million cases in 1976. Smirnoff accounted for nearly $15 million in profits in 1976. Smirnoff was the most heavily advertised distilled spirits product in the industry, as suggested by Table 26-2.

Beyond its more traditional liquor lines, Heublein was the industry leader in the prepared cocktail market, with a market share of over 75 percent. Although experts tended to see the company's expertise primarily in marketing, Heublein's research and development divi-

[1] "Top 100 Advertisers," *Advertising Age*, August 18, 1976, pp. 145–146. (Reprinted with permission. Copyright 1976 by Crain Communications, Inc.)
[2] Ibid.

**Table 26–2
Advertising expenditures for distilled spirits, 1976 leading 10 brands, magazines***

1. Smirnoff	$4,067,353
2. Johnnie Walker	3,678,147
3. Canadian Club	3,614,095
4. J & B	3,423,641
5. Chivas Regal	2,817,170
6. Seagram's V.O.	2,390,809
7. Dewar's	2,298,070
8. Hereford's Cows	2,195,269
9. Beefeater	2,146,536
10. Heublein Cocktails	2,102,771

*_1977 Liquor Handbook_ (New York: Gavin-Jobson Associates, 1977): 320.

sion was the largest and most active in the liquor industry. Researchers worked on developing and testing new products ranging from bottled martinis, manhattans, and canned whiskey sours through plum and peach wines to the "softer" coffee and chocolate liqueurs.

Over 1,000 ideas were generated by the marketing department and other sources throughout the year, and of that number, perhaps 100 were considered practical from a marketing or production viewpoint. The time span from conception to full distribution often took several years. A new product had to be salable and also retain quality and flavor over the months it might sit on a store shelf. Thirteen new drinks were introduced in 1974, the success of which contributed to the spirits division market increase from 9.9 percent to over 13 percent of the total market for distilled spirits.

Heublein noted a sharp trend toward lighter and sweeter drinks, with lower alcohol content. As shown in Table 26–3, the prepared cocktail market was growing at over 20 percent per year. The forecast for 1976–1980 showed a continued trend for this category of distilled spirits. As a result, Heublein had its R&D division working on new prepared cocktail drinks. One result was the introduction in 1975 of Malcolm Hereford's Cows—a sweet 30-proof, milk-type drink—first conceived 6 years earlier.

Hereford's Cows was test marketed in Chicago in the spring of 1975.[3] The product was available in five flavors—banana, strawberry, coconut, chocolate mint, and mocha. The successful results of the Chicago test market led to a decision to distribute nationally in March

[3] The details that follow were drawn from John J. O'Connor, "Heublein's Hereford's Cows Success Tips Marketers to Hot New Liquor Area," _Advertising Age_, December 1, 1976, pp. 1, 75. (Reprinted with permission. Copyright 1976 by Crain Communications, Inc.)

Table 26–3
Distilled spirits products, percentage sales increases, 1961–1980*

	1961–66	1966–71	1971–76	1976–80	1961–76
Wine	25.4	29.9	11.5	—	+ 81.68
Vodka	58.6	51.6	55.4	55.4	+ 273.6
Gin	37.7	18.9	4.4	4.4	+ 70.9
Canadian whiskey	66.9	70.6	31.4	31.4	+ 274.0
Scotch	55.1	54.5	8.2	8.2	+ 159.1
Brandy/cognac	46.5	41.3	15.2	15.2	+ 138.5
Prepared cocktails	109.7	30.3	113.5	113.5	+ 483.7
Rum	57.8	77.1	43.1	43.1	+ 300.1

*1977 Liquor Handbook (New York: Gavin-Jobson Associates, 1977): 280–319.

1976. The product had originally been targeted for women in the age group 18 to 35. It was subsequently found to have strong appeal for other groups as well, including blacks, young males, and women over 35. Hereford Cows was budgeted for over $3 million in advertising for 1976.

The product achieved market acceptance far in excess of forecasted levels. In fact, with first-year sales at over a million cases, it was the most successful distilled spirits new product introduction in the history of the industry. William V. Elliott, vice president—marketing, stated:

> There's a huge market here because Cows even appeal to non-drinkers. . . . We could spend triple our promotional budget and it still won't be enough. . . . The repeat business on this product has been phenomenal.[4]

Having seen the success of Cows' appearance on the market, Heublein introduced Kickers, a product almost identical to Cows except for packaging. Kickers was designed to increase demand for milk-type "fun" drinks by appealing to those individuals who considered themselves energetic, activity-minded, and "young at heart."

The controversy

Robert MacNeil, in the introduction to a November 5, 1976, airing of the MacNeil–Lehrer Report on the subject of teenage alcoholism, said:

[4]Ibid.

The appearance of Cows and similar drinks from other manufacturers has alarmed doctors and others concerned with alcoholism. In particular, they are worried that these pop drinks will exacerbate an already serious social problem, teenage drinking.[5]

The show, which focused on Heublein's 30-proof Hereford's Cows, represented a summation of the social objections which surfaced shortly after the product was successfully test marketed and introduced nationally.

Susan Papas, a spokesperson for Odyssey House, a New York center for the rehabilitation of teenage alcoholics, said the sweet-tasting Cows "can cause the start or beginning of teenage problems." She explained:

Kids that don't like Scotch or Vodka or other types of hard liquors might be more inclined to drink something that is like a milkshake. And milk is a very acceptable form of something to drink. And with a bottle like this, that's equal to two and a half cans of beer, I think they probably get a little surprised very quickly.[6]

Although Papas admitted that she had no statistics on Cows specifically, she said her experiences at Odyssey House taught her that teenage alcoholics begin by drinking sweet-tasting products. "It's the pop, the lightness; it's the way it's presented."[7]

In addition to objecting to the ready accessibility of these drinks to potential young alcoholics, Papas and others cited advertising that promoted alcohol as the answer to numerous adult situations, "which happen to be the very ones that teenagers find particularly frightening and painful."[8]

Referring to one of Heublein's ads for Kickers, a companion product to the Cows, Nicholas Pace, assistant professor of medicine at New York University–Bellevue Medical Center, president of the New York City Affiliate of the National Council on Alcoholism, and chairman of the New York State Advisory Commission on Alcoholism, told Robert MacNeil:

It seems as if an awful lot of Madison Avenue . . . is sort of geared towards showing the use of the drug alcohol in a romantic way that would allow

---

[5] "Teenage Alcoholism," *The MacNeil–Lehrer Report*, Library No. 290, Show No. 245, November 4, 1976.

[6] Ibid.

[7] Ibid.

[8] Ibid.

people an escape or a method to dull their senses or to increase their sexual activity and so on.[9]

Other individuals active in fighting alcoholism objected to Heublein's attitude. Morris Chafetz, a medical psychiatrist who was a former head of the National Institute on Alcohol Abuse and Alcoholism, stated:

I must say that I am concerned about the Cow drinks. Not because I think they are designed to hook people to alcoholic problems, but because it reflects a lack of sensitivity on the part of the liquor industry.[10]

He further stated:

The liquor industry could be moving ahead faster. . . . It's taking them a little longer to learn that there is no advantage to their product in people suffering from alcohol abuse and alcoholism.[11]

Pace, Chafetz, and Papas all agreed that they didn't believe government regulation of business practices and advertising was the answer to the types of problems they saw represented in Heublein's Cow. Chafetz, in summary, stated that he believed that the people in the liquor industry "are socially responsible and I would like them to downplay their product or remove it."[12]

Heublein did not respond publicly to the allegations and comments made on the MacNeil–Lehrer Report.

Heublein, the manufacturer of Hereford's Cows, declined to send a representative to join us tonight. A company spokesman objected that this program "was making a direct reference to certain products and had already made a decision that we (that's Heublein) were part and parcel of the problem." The Heublein man added, "It's like we're being placed on trial. Besides we had late notice." In fact, our reporter first contacted Heublein a week ago. We should note that Heublein also refused to send a representative to a Senate hearing on this subject last March. The industry's main lobbying organization in Washington, the Distilled Spirits Council of the United States, also declined to join us. So did the advertising agency that handles the Cows account, and the American Association of Advertising Agencies. The U.S. Brewers Association and the Association of National Advertisers did not respond to our phone calls.[13]

[9] Ibid.
[10] Ibid.
[11] Ibid.
[12] Ibid.
[13] Ibid.

In response to objections raised that advertisements for Kickers seemed to be primarily directed at teenagers, Heublein dropped its advertising campaign even though it disputed the complaint. A spokesman for the Institute of Alcohol Abuse later stated that "Heublein acted very responsibly in acknowledging our concern about the problem of teen drinking, which appears on the rise."[14]

The current crisis occurred against this background. Betty Furness, former Special Assistant for Consumer Affairs to President Johnson and currently consumer affairs reporter for NBC-TV, handed out Dixie cups filled with a beverage which later was found to be Strawberry Hereford's Cows to a classroom of 12- to 14-year-olds.[15] The students were unaware that the cups contained an alcoholic beverage. This action was taped for a segment on NBC's Today show to back up earlier statements made by Furness in criticism of Heublein products.

In an effort to prove that kids were attracted by advertising for sweet milk-type drinks, and without disclosing her intentions to either school officials or the students' parents, Furness gave the teenagers a cup of the beverage. She then recorded their enthusiastic responses to her question of whether they preferred the sweet-cream Cows "rather than a shot of scotch." Furness closed the Today show segment with the statement: "This is proof that Heublein is trying to appeal to young people." Furness did not question the students about whether they had seen any of the advertisements being challenged or if they had heard of the product.

The alternatives

Moran hung up the phone after his brief conversation with Watson. He began to consider the options available to Heublein in response to the latest incident involving the Hereford Cows.

Before laying out the alternatives, Moran reviewed the data provided by research and development and by marketing on the Hereford Cows. First, it was clear that most people could not drink more than two or three Cows at one sitting. The product was quite sweet and had a milk base. In fact, research in the R&D Laboratory showed a high probability that a drinker would get physically sick before he or she would become drunk. Also, marketing research

---

[14] The account of the incident was drawn from Mitchell C. Lynch, "The Day All the Kids Got Booze in Class from Betty Furness," *The Wall Street Journal,* February 12, 1978, pp. 1, 30.

[15] Ibid.

showed that the primary adopters of the product were 25- to 30-year-old women.[16] Further, an awareness study showed that only 8 percent of teenagers polled were aware of the product. Perhaps of most importance, the retail price of Cows, $4.50 to $6.00 per fifth, was well above the cost of the alcohol products typically consumed by teenage alcoholics. These data suggested to Moran that the charges were without factual basis.

He looked at his watch. It was nearly noon. The Corporate Responsibility Committee meeting was scheduled for 8:00 A.M. the following day. That left little time to prepare his recommendations for response to the latest incident which threatened the continued success of the Malcolm Hereford's Cows line of packaged cocktails.

[16]"The Furness Fiasco," *Advertising Age,* February 6, 1978, p. 16. (Reprinted with permission. Copyright 1978 by Crain Communications, Inc.)

CASE
ANALYSIS

CASE 26

Heublein, Inc.

1. What environmental factors led Heublein to develop the Hereford Cow product? Why was the product so successful?

_____

_____

_____

_____

_____

_____

_____

_____

_____

_____

2. What were the MacNeil–Lehrer Report's objections to Heublein's new star product? Do you feel that these objections are justifiable?

_____

_____

_____

_____

_____

_____

_____

_____

_____

_____

3.   The case states that Heublein did not respond publicly to the Mac-
      Neil–Lehrer Report and refused to send a representative to a Senate
      hearing on the subject of teenage alcoholism. How do you explain
      this?

_____

_____

_____

_____

_____

_____

_____

4.   What recommendations can Mr. Moran make to the Corporate Re-
      sponsibility Committee concerning the Betty Furness episode in par-
      ticular and the Hereford Cow situation overall?

_____

_____

PART SEVEN

MARKETING MANAGEMENT

CASE 27

SOCIÉTÉ BIC

Marcel Bich founded in France what has become one of the most successful consumer marketing companies in the world. He named it "Société Bic," dropping the final letter from his name in the belief that a three-letter word was more marketable. He continues to direct the company (at the time of this writing) worldwide from his headquarters in Clichy, an industrial suburb of Paris. BIC Corporation, headquartered in Milford, Connecticut, is responsible for the manufacture and marketing of BIC products in the United States.

The Bic philosophy

M. Bich directs his business with one central philosophy: Manufacture and sell only products that can be made cheaply, used relatively briefly, and then thrown away. Bich began applying this philosophy in 1953 with the disposable pen. Since then he has added disposable lighters and disposable razors.

Bich developed his philosophy from experience, prior to the founding of his company, as a salesman of office supplies and then as a manufacturer of inkwells. Now he directs a firm whose products are sold in 90 countries and manufactured in four—France, Greece, Italy, and the United States.

Bich's products have not been his inventions. Instead of innovating, he has relied on improving products and marketing them worldwide.

This case was prepared by Professor O. C. Ferrell, Texas A&M University. Most of the material in the first half of the case was reprinted from the February 28, 1977, issue of *Business Week* by special permission, © 1977 by McGraw-Hill, Inc., New York, NY 10020. All rights reserved. Other facts have been abstracted from BIC Corporation 1982 Annual Report, published April 15, 1983, and from other information supplied by BIC Corporation in August 1984.

Courtesy of BIC Corporation

For instance, he developed a world market for the disposable razor, a product that had, in fact, been around for years, although its market had been confined mainly to hospitals.

It is conceded by competitors that Bich's strategy makes him a formidable competitor. For example, *Business Week* published the following statements:

> *"Marcel Bich came up with the fantastic idea of disposable, cheap consumer goods," says Jean Plé, president of Gillette France. "With each new product he simply pursues that basic philosophy a bit further. So far he hasn't made a mistake."*
>
> *Bich does agree that he does seem to have uncanny marketing insight, but he also maintains that even disposable products cannot sell unless their quality is high. "My personal marketing strategy has been never to promote a product until it is equivalent to the No. 1 product on the market. I continue to finance development of the product until I know that we can outdo the competition."*

Principal products

BIC competes in the wetshave market with a disposable razor for men called the BIC Shaver and one for women called the BIC Lady Shaver. As Figure 27–1 shows, BIC Shaver sales have increased significantly and represent 15 percent of the total blade market. BIC disposable razors have increased their market share to 35 percent.

BIC is the leading manufacturer of disposable butane lighters in the United States. As Figure 27–2 illustrates, BIC's market share has held at over 50 percent. BIC disposable lighters have had a phenomenal growth over the past 10 years. They compete in a market that has matured and is beset with increased price competition. By holding down expenses, BIC has been able to translate modest increases in sales into substantial increases in profits.

BIC is the largest manufacturer and distributor of ball pen writing instruments in North America. These pens, which are marketed under trademarks owned by the corporation, are available in both nonretractable, nonrefillable models as well as a retractable refillable model. Each model is available in various ink and barrel colors and point sizes. In addition to ball pens, BIC manufactures the BIC Roller, which is a pen that has the combined writing characteristics of a fountain pen and a ball pen. In 1982, BIC introduced Biro, a competitively priced, round-barreled ball point which was well received by the trade and consumers. The company's best-selling pen remains the BIC Stic, its original see-through hexagonal-barreled ballpoint pen, which was introduced in 1958. In order to maintain a leadership posi-

Figure 27–1
The domestic razor
blade market

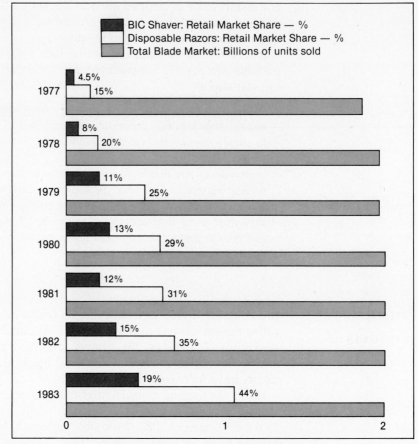

BIC Shaver: Retail Market Share — %
Disposable Razors: Retail Market Share — %
Total Blade Market: Billions of units sold

1977   4.5%   15%

1978   8%   20%

1979   11%   25%

1980   13%   29%

1981   12%   31%

1982   15%   35%

1983   19%   44%

Industry and Market Share are BIC estimates as of year end.

tion in the writing instruments industry, BIC introduced two new products in March 1983, the BIC Erasable Ink Pen and the BIC Ultra Fine Marker. These two new products add depth to BIC's product line and enable them to compete in two growing segments of the writing instruments market.

BIC Leisure Products is a subsidiary responsible for importing and marketing BIC sailboards in the United States. It ended its first fiscal year of operation in 1982 with sales that made it the second largest selling sailboard in the United States.

In October 1982, BIC acquired the assets of the SportRack business of Pinso Sports Ltd., Quebec, Canada. The SportRack is a multipurpose car-top carrier that employs conversion kits to enable it to carry a variety of sporting goods. The SportRack System is expected to com-.

**Figure 27–2
Disposable lighter
market**

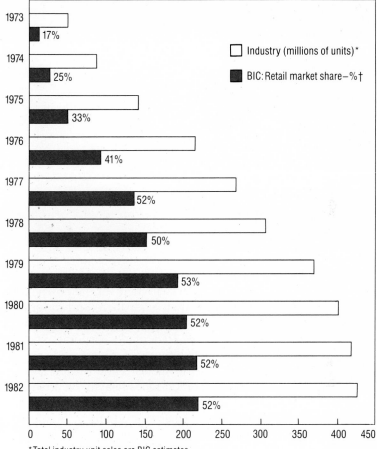

Industry (millions of units)*

BIC: Retail market share—%†

*Total industry unit sales are BIC estimates.
†BIC's market share as reported by independent survey organization.

pliment BIC's sailboard operations and has been made part of the BIC
Leisure Products subsidiary.

Table 27–1 summarizes BIC sales and income by product line for
1980 through 1982.

**Sales/
marketing**

The corporation's products are sold through its sales force to approximately 10,000 accounts, which include variety, drug, and food retail
chains, as well as tobacco, drug, and stationery wholesalers, who in
turn distribute the products widely to retail outlets. Sales to industrial

Table 27–1
Sales and income
by product line
In millions of dollars

	1982	1981	1980
Net sales			
Lighters	$105.2	$103.3	$ 85.6
Writing instruments	73.9	85.4	78.1
Shavers	35.4	29.0	28.1
Other	4.1		.2
	$218.6	$217.7	$192.0
Income (loss) before income taxes			
Lighters	$ 15.4	$ 12.8	$ 15.0
Writing instruments	(2.1)	3.9	16.0
Shavers	2.3	(2.2)	(6.3)
Other	(.8)	(.1)	
	$ 14.8	$ 14.4	$ 24.7

and commercial customers for their own use are generated both by the corporation's own sales force and by office supply distributors and retailers. Writing instruments, lighters, and shavers carrying the purchaser's name, trademark, corporate symbol, or other such imprint are sold to customers for advertising specialty or premium purposes through outside agencies and by specialized salespersons.

The corporation relies heavily on advertising on national television networks, in national publications with broad circulation and in publications for specialized audiences. In addition, the corporation maintains a cooperative advertising program pursuant to which it shares the cost of certain advertising by retailers. The corporation also provides a wide variety of product displays, seasonal sales promotion materials, and other advertising and merchandising aids to retail outlets.

BIC supported Shaver with a new campaign featuring John McEnroe which they consider to be very successful and effective both on national television and in selected print. Although at a reduced level from 1981, BIC continued to support the BIC Roller in 1982. For the lighter, BIC produced ads appearing at the beginning of movies featuring animated BIC Lighters which tell theater patrons where they can or cannot smoke. A unique combination of commercial and public service messages, these ads are offered free to theaters and are seen daily in over half the theaters and drive-ins in the United States. The "Flick Your BIC" Lighter commercials also received extensive play on spot radio.

Competition

Although the corporation is the leading domestic manufacturer of disposable lighters and ball pens, it is subject to intense competition with respect to price and product performance in all areas of its business. Competitors include both smaller specialized firms and larger diversified companies, some of which have broader product lines and substantially greater financial resources than the corporation. The corporation's major competitor in writing instruments, lighters, and shavers is the Gillette Company.

CASE ANALYSIS

CASE 27

Société Bic

1. Write an exact statement of Marcel Bich's strategy. Would you say that this is a marketing strategy or a corporate strategy?

_____

_____

_____

_____

_____

_____

_____

_____

_____

2. How important has that strategy apparently been in the success of Société Bic? Would you recommend that all enterprises, private or public, likewise adhere closely to a basic strategy?

_____

_____

_____

_____

_____

_____

_____

_____

_____

_____

_____

_____

3.   Is Bich's chosen strategy the best one for all consumer goods manu-
     facturers? What alternative strategies might have been logical for
     Bich? Would Bich's strategy be logical for Zenith television, for Her-
     shey candy, for Vic Tanny health clubs?

_____

_____

_____

_____

_____

_____

_____

_____

_____

_____

_____

_____

_____

_____

_____

_____

_____

_____

_____

_____

CASE 28

A. H. ROBINS—ROBITUSSIN

The company

A. H. Robins, Inc. has evolved from a small community pharmacy opened in 1866 in Richmond, Virginia, by Albert Hartley Robins to a diversified multinational corporation operating in more than 100 countries. It was incorporated under the laws of Virginia in 1948, and in 1963 went public with the sale of 350,000 shares to the general public and 75,000 shares to employees. It was listed on the New York Stock Exchange on May 6, 1965. There were four more secondary offerings of the stock and three stock splits with more than 26 million shares outstanding in 1976.

The present operating organization was established in 1969 and Exhibit 28–1 shows the structure of the company as of January 1, 1977. Mr. E. C. Robins, Sr., served as the Chairman of the Board and E. C. Robins, Jr., served as executive vice president.

The corporate headquarters, which housed both corporate and pharmaceutical division offices, are located in Richmond, Virginia. Corporate distribution centers are located in the Richmond area, with branch offices in Los Angeles, California, Des Plaines, Illinois, and Dallas, Texas. The research center was opened in 1963 with more than 325 scientists and technicians engaged in research in many product areas.

By 1976 Robins had grown to assets of more than $260 million, sales of $284 million, and earnings of $31 million. The company attained

This case was prepared by Professors Thomas D. Giese and Thomas J. Cossé of the University of Richmond and Mr. Ian Stewart of A. H. Robins Company, Inc., as a basis for class discussion rather than to illustrate either effective or ineffective handling of an administrative situation.

Exhibit 28–1
A. H. Robins Company, organization chart (January 1977)

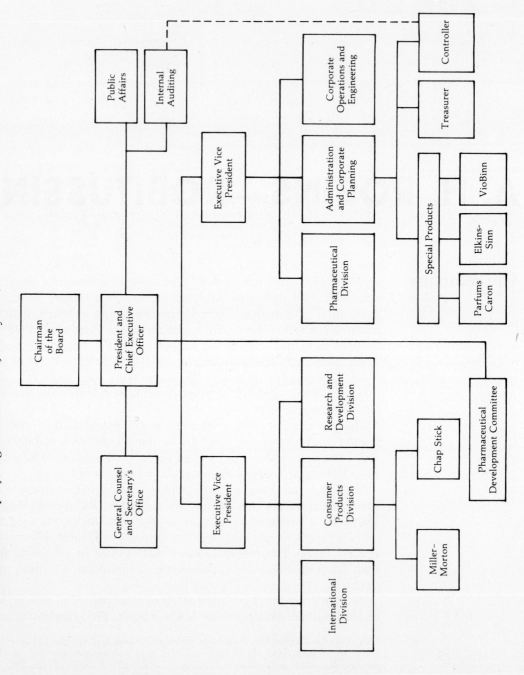

356

Courtesy of Mike Mazzaschi/Stock, Boston

•Robitussin weather is back•

It's that time again. Time to remember the Robitussin formulas that are right for the different actions you want for your patients.

ROBITUSSIN®
For the expectorant action of guaifenesin.

ROBITUSSIN-DM®
Guaifenesin with the nonnarcotic cough suppressant dextromethorphan.

ROBITUSSIN-PE®
Guaifenesin with the nasal decongestant pseudoephedrine.

ROBITUSSIN-CF®
Guaifenesin with the nonnarcotic cough suppressant dextromethorphan and the decongestant phenylpropanolamine.

©A.H. Robins Company 1982

A·H·ROBINS
Consumer Products Division
Richmond, Virginia 23230

outstanding growth in the ten-year period with sales increasing from $74 million in 1966 to over $280 million in 1976. Recent trends in the 1970's revealed that the Consumer Division and the International Division were growing faster than the domestic Pharmaceutical Division, although pharmaceutical sales were keeping pace with the rest of the industry.

The A. H. Robins Company is engaged principally in the manufacture of finished dosage forms of pharmaceutical products. Finished products are manufactured and packaged from raw materials purchased from suppliers of pharmaceutical grade chemicals. The company's principal products are ethical OTC drug products which are promoted nationally by 1,350 field representatives to physicians, dentists, and pharmacists. Some of Robins' best known brand names are Robitussin, a cough and cold syrup; Donnatal, an antispasmodic drug; and Robaxin, a skeletal muscle relaxant.

Robins' products are distributed to drug wholesalers which sell to retail drug stores and to hospitals. This distribution system has proven successful in the past. But, in the current drug market the chains do more than 50% of the industry volume. If the large chains do buy direct from a manufacturer (at a lower price), they give those brands in-store marketing support; such as end aisle displays, extra shelf facings and co-op advertising.

While maintaining its major position as manufacturer and researcher of pharmaceuticals, A. H. Robins has diversified into consumer products. In 1963, Robins acquired Morton Manufacturing located in Lynchburg, Virginia, the producer of Chap Stick lip balm. In 1967, Robins acquired Polk Miller Products of Richmond, Virginia, producer of the Sergeant's line of pet care products. These two companies were later consolidated into Miller-Morton Company in an effort to consolidate consumer product activities. Robins enjoyed further success in the consumer goods area with the introduction of Lip Quencher, a lipstick utilizing the moisturizing qualities of Chap Stick. In 1967, it continued its entry into the consumer field with the acquisition of Parfums Caron, a leading producer of French fragrance products. Consumer products are advertised nationally and marketed through department stores, specialty shops and drug outlets.

A. H. Robins entered the international markets in the 1960's by establishing manufacturing and distribution centers in England, Mexico, Australia and Colombia. Foreign expansion was precipitated by both a demand for Robins products abroad and increasing foreign government regulation which restricted imports into these countries. Subsidiaries in Australia, Brazil, Canada, Colombia, France, Mexico, the Philippines, South Africa, the United Kingdom, Venezuela and West Germany provided a base for the company's growing international operations. International operations in 1976 accounted for 33% net sales and 34% earnings before tax, interest and amortization expenses applicable to international operations.

The drug industry

The pharmaceutical industry is highly competitive, with the largest U.S. drug company holding only a 7.5% share of the U.S. market in 1972. By 1976, the top 150 pharmaceutical companies each had in excess of $1 million in sales of both ethical and proprietary drugs, representing 95% of the reported hospital and drug store purchases of pharmaceuticals. At that time, A. H. Robins ranked number 21 out of the 150 largest firms.

Robins competes principally in the therapeutic segment of the ethical pharmaceutical market. This segment has sales of more than $2 billion annually, and Robins had in excess of 5% of this segment in 1974. Competition is stimulated by direct promotion by field representatives and product performance. Of the 55 pharmaceutical products produced by Robins in 1976, 19 were among the 200 most widely prescribed drugs in the United States. It was ranked fifth among U.S. pharmaceutical manufacturers on the basis of new prescriptions written in the United States in 1976.

Worldwide drug demand has averaged a 10% rate of growth for the past decade. Sales in 1965 were $15 billion and in 1976 had risen to $43 billion with estimates for 1985 as high as $100 billion in constant dollars. Over the same period, sales of U.S.-based pharmaceutical companies grew from $5 billion in 1965 to approximately $14 billion in 1976 with estimates for 1985 at $35 billion.

The industry experienced severe inflation problems for the first time in 1974–75. Currency translations for the multinationals masked improving trends in operating profits in 1976. Fewer new products were introduced to the market due to increased Food and Drug Administration (FDA) regulations which caused money designated for research on single-entity drugs to be diverted to preserving present drugs' market penetration. Research and development became more expensive and less productive with the time for introduction of a new drug being 7–12 years and an investment of $15–20 million. Thus, new researched products declined while there was a proliferation of duplicate drugs. According to drug industry analysts, the industry image suffered as a result of these trends.

Increased institutionalization of health care has created other problems for the drug industry. The Medicare, Medicaid and third-party payment programs changed a larger portion of medical care to group practice settings, clinics and hospital out-patient facilities. Physicians prescribed more drugs in these institutional settings, and their prescribing habits were influenced more by government regulations. Antisubstitution laws in some states had been repealed, thereby permitting a pharmacist to substitute a generic version of the same drug prescribed by the physician. Therefore, the hospital and clinical pharmacies grew in importance as prescribers of drugs.

The product

Robitussin, a cough and cold syrup, is marketed in five forms, one of which is an ethical prescribed form; the other four are ethical over-the-counter forms. The product to date has been marketed only through wholesalers and directly to non-proprietary hospitals. Demand is stimulated by detailmen calling on the medical profession and detailing the drug, i.e., describing its advantages and features so that they would either prescribe or recommend the use of the product.

The promotion of the product is complemented by sampling, trade deals, and trade and medical profession journal advertising. However, the demand for the product is now static as it reached the mature stage in its present market segment.

The cough syrup market totaled $183 million annually by 1975 having grown at a 5% rate from the previous year. Within the overall market, the largest growth was in food stores. Table 28–1 shows the growth for the years 1972 through 1975.

Sales in food stores, which accounted for 24% of total sales, are increasing at a faster rate than drug stores. The sales in drug stores are polarizing towards the chains and large independents who wanted to purchase directly from the manufacturer rather than through the wholesaler, which resulted in lower margins for retail outlets.

While the ethical segment of the cough syrup market was still trending up slightly in dollars, in 1975, the proprietary brands in food and drug outlets exhibited a healthy 10% increase in dollar terms as compared with a 2% increase for the ethical segment.

In unit terms, the cough syrup market was not growing, but within the segments, food store sales were moving up in importance while drug store units were declining. One study showed that the average housewife visited the supermarket about three times a week and the drug store twice a month. Exhibit 28–2 shows the unit sales of 1972 through 1975. In the drug stores it was the ethical brands that were holding their share while proprietary brands were declining as seen in Exhibit 28–3.

By way of comparison with other cold remedy products, the cough syrup market is 12% larger than the cold tablet market and more than three times larger than the nasal spray market.

The heavy users of cough syrup preparations differ from most cold products categories since the heaviest users usually do not purchase their own product because 50% of actual users are under eighteen years of age. The prime prospect households can be described as follows:

- Female head of household 25–49 years old
- Households with children 2–17 years old and with 5 or more persons
- Household annual income of $15,000 or lower
- Less educated
- Heavy usage among non-whites*

The breakdown of unit sales, by brand, within the total market can be seen in Exhibit 28–4. Robitussin has 21.6% share of unit sales in drug stores compared to Vicks' 16% and in food/drug stores combined, an estimated 14% share versus Vicks' 27%. Based on a survey conducted in 1973, the leading brands of cough syrup used are Formula 44, doctor's prescription and Nyquil (see Exhibit 28–5).

In 1975 a sample of branded proprietary lines were spending over $7 million in media advertising as shown in Table 28–2.

The four Robitussin ethical over-the-counter lines are fully described in Exhibit 28–6. The share trend on a consumer dollar basis and share by store type are shown in Exhibits 28–7 and 28–8.

Towards the end of the 1976 financial year, as the planning stage for 1977 was being finalized, George Mancini, the product manager for the Robitussin line of cough syrups, had noted that over the past several years the line had only been growing in the 1 to 2% range in comparison with the 6 to 8% growth in the overall cough syrup market. Robitussin was becoming a mature product in its present segment of ethical over-the-counter drugs.[1]

*Source: T.G.I.

[1] Drug industry practice was to classify products as either "ethical" or "proprietary" depending on the marketing method employed. Ethical products were marketed by promotion directly to the medical profession. The ethical classification was further subdivided into those drugs which required prescription and those which could be purchased without a prescription called "over-the-counter" (OTC) drugs. Proprietary products were promoted directly to the consumer.

Table 28–1
Cough syrup annual
dollar sales
In millions

	1972	1973	1974	1975
Drug stores	125.1	135.6	135.2	139.1
Food stores	34.6	36.1	38.6	44.2
Food and drug stores	159.7	171.7	173.8	183.3

Source: A. C. Nielson.

Table 28–2
Competitive media
spending
In 1,000 dollars

	1973	1974	1975
Formula 44	3,850	2,470	2,590
Formula 44D	670	1,020	1,050
Silence Is Golden	1,370	500	70
Breacol	1,190	1,750	1,370
Halls	—	1,900	2,115
Total	$7,080	$7,640	$7,195

Exhibit 28–2
Cough syrup annual
unit sales
In millions

	1972	1973	1974	1975
Drug stores	65	66	64	63
Food stores	34	43	42	43
Total	99	109	106	106

Source: A. C. Nielson and SSC & B.

Exhibit 28–3
Cough syrup unit
sales in drug stores
In millions

	1972	1973	1974	1975
Proprietary	28.1	28.3	26.7	25.3
Ethical	36.5	37.7	37.6	38.0

Source: A. C. Nielson.

**Exhibit 28–4
Share of market for
leading brands, food
and drug**

	Unit share
Proprietary	
Formula 44	18.0
Formula 44D	5.9
Vicks	2.7
Breacol	2.0
Silence Is Golden	1.2
Halls	1.8
All other proprietary	23.4
Ethical	
Robitussin	14
All other ethicals	31

**Exhibit 28–5
Brand of cough syrup
used most often**

	% of all cough syrup users
Formula 44	29
Doctor's prescription	26
Nyquil	16
Robitussin	8
Pertussin	4
Romilar	3
Cheracol	3
Silence Is Golden	3
Triaminic	2.5
All others	10

Exhibit 28–6
The product

The Robitussin Ethical line consists of four cough medicines and one cough lozenge. The following outlines the active ingredients in each formula.

Robitussin	*Guaifenesin,* NF (in a palatable, aromatic syrup) enhances the output of lower respiratory tract fluid to make unproductive coughs more productive and less frequent.
Robitussin DM and cough calmers	*Guaifenesin,* NF and Dextromethorphan Hydrobromide, NF enhance the output of lower respiratory tract fluid to make unproductive coughs more productive and less frequent. Plus, antitussive effectiveness which depresses the nervous system's cough response mechanism.
Robitussin CF	*Guaifenesin, Phenylpropanolamine Hydrochloride, Dextromethorphan Hydrobromide, NF*—expectorant action, antitussive action and a mild vasoconstrictor action resulting in a nasal decongestant effect.
Robitussin PE	*Guaifenesin,* NF, Pseudoephedrine HCl, NF—expectorant action and a sympathomimetic amine, helps reduce mucosal congestion and edema in the nasal passages.

*Formerly Glyceryl Guaiacolate

Exhibit 28–7
Robitussin share trend—total U.S. drug stores, consumer dollar basis

	1971	1972	1973	1974	1975
Robitussin Plain	5.5	5.6	5.6	5.7	5.9
Robitussin DM	6.2	6.6	7.1	7.9	8.2
Robitussin PE	0.5	0.7	1.0	1.2	1.2
Robitussin CF	N/A	N/A	N/A	0.5	1.2

Source: A. C. Nielson.

Exhibit 28–8
Robitussin share by store type, consumer dollar basis

	Total cough syrup market, percentage	Robitussin sales share of market, percentage	
		1974	1975
Chain	31.7	17.3	18.4
Large independent	47.1	17.4	18.8
Medium independent	16.9	17.3	19.2
Small independent	4.2	17.5	20.2
Total	100.0	17.4	20.2

Source: A. C. Nielson.

CASE ANALYSIS

CASE 28

A. H. Robins— Robitussin

1. What area of strategic analysis has not been utilized by A. H. Robins in respect to the cough syrup industry?

_____

_____

_____

_____

_____

_____

_____

_____

_____

2. What problems are confronting Mr. Mancini at the end of the 1976 financial year?

_____

_____

_____

_____

_____

_____

_____

_____

_____

_____

_____

_____

_____

_____

_____

_____

_____

_____

3. Explain the significance of Robitussin's position in the "mature" stage of the product life cycle and show how this position affects the promotion of the product.

_____

_____

_____

_____

_____

_____

_____

_____

_____

_____

4.   What can be done to alleviate the problems?

_____

_____

_____

_____

_____

_____

_____

_____

_____

_____

_____

_____

_____

_____

_____

_____

_____

_____

_____

_____

_____

5. Would any marketing organization changes have to be made if Robitussin were to be marketed more intensively to chain stores, large independents, or food stores?

_____

_____

_____

_____

_____

_____

_____

_____

_____

_____

_____

_____

_____

_____

_____

_____

_____

_____

_____

_____

_____

6. What long-range strategic planning would you advise for Robitussin (A. H. Robins Corporation)? Why?

_____

_____

_____

CASE 29

GOLDPAR'S

Mike Goldpar sat back in his chair in deep concentration. In the fifteen years he has worked at Goldpar's, he has never encountered such a perplexing situation. If only it weren't late October, with the Christmas season coming soon, he would have more time to sort out the facts. Regardless, he knew he had to start making decisions about the proposed computer system. Mike began to think back over the events of the last several months and about what he should do.

Background

Goldpar's is a small, family-owned department store located in Newdale, Georgia. Herman Goldpar, Mike's grandfather, started the business in 1921 by opening a general merchandise store, the first of its kind in Newdale. Goldpar's downtown store has been located in the same building since 1921. Mike believes that expansion and new, modern fixtures have made Goldpar's one of the best stores in town today. The merchandise mix includes ladies', men's, and young adult fashion clothing as well as cosmetics and small gifts. The profile of the typical Goldpar's customer is middle-aged, with a relatively high income and education, and probably best labeled as "conservative."

At present the 30,900 Newdale residents are served by a regional mall, the central business district, and numerous smaller shopping centers. Two years ago, Goldpar's opened its first and only branch

Written by Stephen B. Castleberry, the University of Georgia. Reprinted from J. Barry Mason, Morris L. Mayer, and Hazel F. Ezell, *Cases and Problems in Contemporary Retailing*, copyright © Business Publications, Inc., 1982, by permission of the author and publisher.

Courtesy of Mike Mazzaschi/Stock, Boston

store in the new regional mall. The mall store is much smaller than the downtown store and only carries fashion clothing. Approximately five miles separate the two stores. All merchandise for the mall store is delivered by a truck, owned and operated by Goldpar's, from the downtown store.

Decision to search

Mike first became interested in a computer system for Goldpar's while at a trade show in Atlanta. He was amazed at what the computer could do and began to wonder if it could be used to save (or possibly "make") money for Goldpar's. Mike was no stranger to the world of computers himself since he had worked on a computer in some of his undergraduate classes at a nearby private college. However, in earning his B.B.A. degree, Mike only used the computer in a first-level COBOL class. He was not aware of its retail uses.

When Mike returned to Newdale, he couldn't get computers off his mind. Goldpar's accountant gave him the name of several reputable computer companies to contact. Mike contacted the sales office of one of these companies, Vendor T, and was told that a salesman would call on him in the next several days.

The search

Vendor T's representative, Scott Barasca, arrived the next day and discussed the procedure he would use to come up with a proposal. An intensive investigation of the current system was first on the list. Mike wasted no time in introducing Scott to his bookkeepers and, in fact, accompanied Scott as he gathered his information.

Edna Parker, a bookkeeping clerk, provided Scott with information concerning Goldpar's accounts payable (A/P) and accounts receivable (A/R). Goldpar's has 300 A/P accounts, most of which are paid on a monthly basis. Goldpar's has approximately 10,000 credit accounts, of which 5,000 are considered active (used at least once in the past six months). All billing is currently being processed by a local service bureau for a fee of $200 per month plus 15¢ per bill sent. Mrs. Parker spends about fifteen hours per week on A/R preparing the sales information for the service bureau. Because of the way the service bureau set up Goldpar's computer A/R, no service charges are being added to customers' bills. Mike remembered telling Scott that any computer purchased should have the capability of adding service charges. The system should also be able to access credit customers for special uses (e.g., letters to Goldpar's credit card holders who had not used their credit in the past six months, specials aimed exclusively at target groups, etc.).

As Mike and Scott discussed these topics, Mrs. Parker seemed a little upset about something and spoke softly to herself (but Mike heard it): "I wonder who they're going to get to run that stupid computer. I certainly don't have time, and wouldn't want to anyway!" Mike didn't comment, and instead decided to act as though he had not heard it.

Scott left after talking with Mrs. Parker but promised to be back the next day to complete his investigation. Mike could not remember anything else that happened that day, except a bad case of indigestion. He hasn't eaten at Brandy's Pizza and Grill since!

Mike remembered arriving at work the next day only to be greeted

**Table 29–1
Breakdown of
employees at
Goldpar's**

Downtown store	Mall store
15 salespersons	5 part-time salespersons
5 office workers	1 manager
3 managers	6
1 janitor/delivery boy	
24	

coldly by his office crew. Mrs. Parker had obviously been on the phone the night before telling other office workers about the computer. Scott arrived around 8:30 to finish his investigation. His first interview was with Mrs. Peters, the payroll clerk. From Mrs. Peters, Scott learned that Goldpar's has thirty employees (see Table 29–1) and that all payroll was done by hand. Mrs. Peters had commented to Scott, "Where do you think you're going to put that computer? We hardly have enough room to move around in here as it is!" Scott had said, "Computers are much smaller than most people realize," but Mike remembered his looking around the cramped office quarters rather carefully.

After talking with Mrs. Peters, Scott finished his investigation by asking Mike several questions. Scott was told that Goldpar's had six departments, but Mike had no idea how many SKUs (stock keeping units). Mike hoped the new computer would provide a better inventory control system that, among other things, would provide selling reports by department and by salesperson. In addition, Mike wanted the computer to have the ability to evaluate the success of promotion tools used (e.g., how many pairs of X-brand slacks are sold after a newspaper ad is run). Also, a cashier should be able to check the customer's credit at the cash register before issuing additional credit. Mike also wondered about the possibility of using a scanning device.

Scott promised to have a proposal together by the end of the week and left. As he was leaving, James Goldpar, the general manager of Goldpar's (and Mike's father) walked in. James told Mike that several of the office staff had talked to him about the computer. Apparently, they were quite upset, fearing that their workloads would increase or become more difficult, or possibly that their jobs would be terminated. Mike looked at his father as he continued talking and realized that he would also have to convince his father that a computer was the best step to take. James was not one to rush in a new direction without a great deal of thought. However, it was James who had made the decision to move into the new mall two years ago, because he realized that everything in Newdale was moving away from the CBD. When James finished talking, Mike assured him that he was only "looking" and that he would talk to the office crew and calm them down.

Proposal for a new system

The following week, while Mike was sitting in his office thinking about the computer system, he suddenly straightened up in his chair and reached for the bottle of Maalox. Maybe it wasn't only the pizza that had caused his indigestion before. He opened his top drawer and pulled out the proposal of Vendor T. As he thumbed through its pages, he thought back to the end of last week, when Scott had confidently presented the proposal to Mike.

The "total retail system" proposed by Vendor T was a real-time online system. In this system, each of the eight electronic cash registers (ECRs), equipped with scanners, is tied directly to the main computer. The operation is simple: As the cashier enters the transaction information (with the scanner or manually), this information automatically and immediately goes to the inventory control system, updating the inventory count for those items purchased. At the end of the day, totals for department and/or salesperson can be generated. Additionally, purchase orders can be printed automatically to revive inventory to its service level. This same information also goes automatically to the accounts receivable file, if it is a credit purchase, and updates that customer's file. Statements can be printed automatically with service charges added or deleted.

In addition, the "total retail system" has many other features: a complete perpetual inventory system with a wide array of management-oriented reports; complete payroll, accounts receivable, accounts payable, and general ledger systems; a ReportWrite computer program that will allow Goldpar's to have the computer print any type of report or letter (e.g., letter to credit card users who have not used their credit in the past six months) using any or all information stored in the computer; and the ability to check a customer's credit at the time of purchase.

Mike had been impressed up to this point but wondered what such a great system would cost. He did not have to wonder long, because he saw the tab in the proposal (at the back, of course) labeled "investment considerations." On turning to that section, he found that this "total retail system" of Vendor T's was going to cost him plenty! The entire system could be placed on a standard three-year lease agreement for a mere $2,200 per month (the price includes maintenance). Or, according to option two, the system could be purchased in installments with $8,000 down and 48 monthly payments of $2,360 (plus a

$398 per month maintenance fee). At the end of the 48 months, Gold-par's would own the computer. Option three was an outright pur-chase option of $75,000 (plus a $398 per month maintenance fee).

After Scott had left the office the week before, Mike had decided to check with other vendors. Vendor R proposed a less elaborate system that did not have the capability to update inventory or accounts re-ceivable files automatically, as Vendor T's system could. Vendor R's proposed system is considered a batch system. Each of Goldpar's present eight cash registers has the capability to accept a cassette unit which can capture all transaction information as it is entered at the cash register terminal. Although Goldpar's is not currently using this feature, Vendor R's proposal intends to use it. At the end of the day, these cassettes are carried to the central computer and all the files (accounts receivable, inventory) are updated. This would require some of Mike's time, since he would have to deliver the cassettes from the mall store to the downtown store each night. Also, it is not possi-ble to check a customer's credit at the cash register or write letters to customers at will. However, a great deal of money can be saved be-cause Goldpar's can use their existing cash registers. The three-year lease rate of this system is $1,830.30. The system can be purchased in 36 installments of $2,182.50 after a $5,000 down payment, or it can be purchased outright now for $50,080. Monthly maintenance costs for purchase options are $305.

Finally, Mike had talked to the service bureau that was processing Goldpar's A/R at that time. The service bureau was happy to propose a system for Goldpar's that included payroll, accounts payable, gen-eral ledger, and accounts receivable. However, the service bureau's computer did not have the capability to accept either online input (like Vendor T's proposed system) or cassette input (like Vendor R's pro-posed system) from Goldpar's. It would be necessary for bookkeepers in Goldpar's office to prepare for the service bureau the input sheets that summarized the daily accounting information. It would also be impractical to put inventory control on the service bureau's computer. However, the price for these services was much lower than the other quotes. The service bureau would handle the mentioned tasks for $800 per month plus 7¢ per check written, bill written, report written, or inquiry processed. As a bonus, the service bureau would make it possible to add service charges on customer billing.

The decision

This little think session had not done Mike much good. He still did not know what decision he should make. Any computer located at Goldpar's would take up room, possibly even a little of the present selling space. The office personnel were much less than enthusiastic about having a computer around the office. He felt sure that they would eventually accept it but was not sure of the immediate impact. He wondered how Goldpar's customers would react to such a change.

Supposing that Goldpar's changes its present system, which proposal would be in Goldpar's best interest? The online "supersystem" of Vendor T, the batch system of Vendor R, or giving additional business to the service bureau? Mike was somewhat concerned that no company making a proposal had a retail installation of its system close enough to show Goldpar's.

Even after Mike makes his decisions on these issues, he realizes that his toughest job is yet to come. How can Mike convince his father that he has made the best decision?

CASE ANALYSIS

CASE 29

Goldpar's

1. Assess the pros and cons of keeping the current system.

_____

_____

_____

_____

_____

_____

_____

_____

_____

_____

_____

_____

_____

_____

_____

_____

_____

_____

_____

_____

_____

_____

_____

2.   Assess the pros and cons of the service bureau's proposal.

_____

_____

_____

_____

_____

_____

_____

_____

_____

_____

_____

_____

_____

_____

_____

_____

_____

_____

_____

_____

_____

_____

3. Assess the pros and cons of Vendor T's proposal.

_____

_____

_____

_____

_____

_____

_____

_____

_____

_____

_____

_____

_____

_____

_____

_____

_____

_____

_____

_____

_____

_____

_____

_____

4. Assess the pros and cons of Vendor R's proposal.

_____

_____

_____

_____

_____

_____

_____

_____

_____

_____

_____

_____

_____

_____

_____

_____

_____

_____

_____

_____

_____

_____

5. Propose and defend a course of action for Mike.

    _____

    _____

    _____

    _____

    _____

    _____

    _____

    _____

    _____

    _____

    _____

    _____

    _____

    _____

    _____

    _____

    _____

    _____

_____

_____

_____

_____

_____

_____

CASE 30

CANFARM COOPERATIVE

After almost ten years as an agency of the Canadian federal government, the Canfarm Service Agency fell victim to government budget cuts in early 1979. This left the organization with no source of revenue to support its computerized farm record-keeping development, processing, and delivery activities. Thanks to the efforts of several concerned farm organizations, and a $4 million loan guarantee from the federal government, the company was able to continue operating until it could reorganize. Mr. Dick Mitchell, the new marketing manager, faced the task of converting the agency, which had been heavily dependent on government support, into a profitable, private business venture. He knew that this would require a totally new strategy for the organization and that marketing would become the key ingredient in any future success.

Background   The Canfarm computerized farm record-keeping service was first offered to Canadian farmers in 1969 through the federal government's Canfarm Service Agency. Located in Guelph, Ontario, at its high point, the Canfarm Service Agency employed approximately 250 staff members, many of whom were highly trained agricultural economists and computer experts with high-level civil service appointments. The products they developed were designed to capitalize on computer technology to keep farm records and provide information to assist

This case was prepared by Jane G. Funk, Thomas F. Funk, Allan Gowan, and Jack Britney of the University of Guelph, Ontario, Canada. It is intended as a basis for classroom discussion and is not designed to present either correct or incorrect handling of administrative problems. Copyright 1983 by the University of Guelph.

farmers in making better production and financial management decisions. At its peak of popularity in the mid-1970s, approximately 14,000 farmers were using the Canfarm system.

Prior to 1978, the Canfarm system consisted of three parts: the Canfarm Service Agency, the Canfarm Contact Agency, and the Canfarm Advisory Board. The Canfarm Service Agency, which was an agency of the Federal Department of Agriculture, had responsibility for developing software packages for the farm record-keeping and management programs and providing data-processing facilities and services to process customer information. The Canfarm Contact Agency was a joint venture of all Provincial Departments of Agriculture and had the responsibility for obtaining customers and providing follow-up service to farmer clients. The last group, the Canfarm Advisory Board, consisted of representatives from the Contact Agencies and acted as an Advisory Committee to the Executive Director of the Service Agency.

The Canfarm product consisted of a software system designed to perform record-keeping functions for Canadian farmers. Although early versions were quite primitive, in 1979 the system was based on accepted accounting principles and current tax legislation. The system was designed to be used by any type or size of farm. Individual farmers could choose from a wide variety of reports ranging from simple income and expense summaries to detailed enterprise accounting and tax management reports. The prices farmers paid for the reports varied from nothing in some provinces to a maximum of $30 a year in others. In all cases, the fees charged were substantially below the cost of generating the reports.

Distribution was the primary function of the contact agency. This was accomplished through the cooperation of the government agricultural extension services in each province. Local agricultural extension people (Ag. Reps. and their assistants) in each county or district were given the responsibility of soliciting farmer clients and helping them register on the Canfarm System. Even though the Ag. Reps. were not trained in accounting or financial management, and had many other responsibilities, this was considered a very desirable system at the outset because of their close contact with farmers and the low cost associated with using an established system. Some training of Ag. Reps. and their staffs was undertaken by Canfarm Service Agency personnel over the years.

Federal pullout

When Agriculture Canada, the Federal Department of Agriculture, withdrew its support in 1979, the Service Agency would have disappeared had not a group of concerned farm organizations and a financial cooperative negotiated with Agriculture Canada to take it over. As part of the agreement, the organizations invested $200,000 in the new company, and the financial cooperative provided a loan of $4 million, which was guaranteed by the federal government. The only condition the new owners insisted on was that they be given the right to deal directly with the farmer instead of necessarily working through the various provincial contact agencies. In most cases, the provinces were glad to get out of the sales and service end of the business. Their only concern was to make sure their current clients would continue to receive some record-keeping service.

The newly formed company was called Canfarm Cooperative and replaced the agencies which had been in the Canfarm System before. Mr. Mitchell recognized that he had to "retool" the former government agency to run in the competitive business world. As a government agency, Canfarm was never encouraged to show a profit; as a private company profit was essential for survival. Although Mr. Mitchell had a year in which to get a new plan in place, he decided to attempt to generate more revenue by initiating a substantial price increase to all customers. He felt this would be necessary sooner or later, so he decided he might as well get customers used to paying a price closer to the real cost of the service right away. Following this, he formed a new sales department and hired Mr. Roger Knox to the position of sales manager. Together they began gathering information and identifying and evaluating the organization's marketing alternatives.

Attitudes toward Canfarm

As a first step in their assessment of the situation, Mr. Mitchell and Mr. Knox attempted to determine current farmer attitudes toward Canfarm. A recent market research study showed that 65% of farmers surveyed were aware of Canfarm. Unfortunately, indications were that although the Canfarm name was recognized, farmers were not at all clear about exactly what Canfarm really did. Management speculated that awareness among the "commercial" farmers (those with gross sales above $50,000) was certainly considerably higher than 65%.

Management was also aware that they had to deal with some rather negative attitudes which had developed toward Canfarm. In some cases these attitudes were the result of past experiences with Canfarm; in other cases, they were the result of hearing negative comments from friends and neighbors. Management realized that many Canfarm representatives themselves had not thoroughly understood either the system or basic accounting fundamentals. This, coupled with farmers' lack of interest in or knowledge of bookkeeping, led to many mistakes in data inputting. This, in turn, led to rejected transactions and much frustration. Farmers were frequently overwhelmed by the perceived complexity of the system and the masses of paper printed out by the computer. Slow computer turnaround added to their frustration and that of their accountants. Other farmers were suspicious about Canfarm's past association with government. Despite assurances of complete confidentiality, they were afraid that the government could have access to their records whenever it so desired. Management found that some farmers were also suspicious of any association with computers. In extreme cases, Canfarm representatives were greeted with definite hostility on their farm visits.

Current record-keeping practices

Farmers vary considerably in their interest in and methods of accounting. Canfarm executives estimated that in 1979 approximately 50 percent of all farmers used the so-called shoebox method of accounting in which they kept bills in one box and receipts in another. At the end of the year they used these records to estimate their profit or loss and to prepare their taxes. The other 50 percent of farmers used bookkeeping firms, accountants, or programs such as Canfarm to keep records on their farming operations.

Although some farmers kept records to provide information for making management decisions, the vast majority kept records only for tax purposes. Mr. Mitchell estimated that about 50 percent of all farmers had their tax forms completed by specialized tax filing organizations, about 10 percent used chartered accountants, and the remaining 40 percent either completed the tax forms themselves or did not file a tax form at all. The tax filing organizations used by many farmers were similar in concept and operation to the H&R Block type of business common in the consumer market. Only the very large farms were thought to use chartered accountants because of the substantial cost involved. In addition, although most rural communities had chartered accountants available, many rural accountants had little experience with the specialized tax legislation that affected farming operations.

Target market

As a government program, Canfarm had been developed for the use of all Canadian farmers, and the transfer agreement stipulated that the program must continue to be offered nationwide. Mr. Mitchell and his staff wondered whether in reality their sophisticated com-

Exhibit 30–1
Number of farms by value of sales, Canadian provinces, 1976

Province	Under $2,499	$2,500 to $24,999	$25,000 to $49,999	$50,000 to $99,999	$100,000 and over
Newfoundland	575	166	29	36	42
P.E.I.	1,146	1,784	367	224	149
Nova Scotia	2,900	1,594	368	313	244
New Brunswick	2,045	1,668	403	271	147
Quebec	14,242	24,144	9,173	3,000	953
Ontario	21,107	39,949	13,309	9,838	4,517
Manitoba	4,787	17,704	5,877	2,711	973
Saskatchewan	4,416	38,194	18,299	8,070	1,695
Alberta	9,062	33,242	10,231	5,732	2,692
British Columbia	9,384	6,707	1,252	1,114	937
Canada	69,683	165,157	59,309	31,309	12,349

Source: Selected Agricultural Statistics for Canada, Agriculture Canada.

puter-based offering might be more likely to appeal to the commercial farmers whose gross sales were above $50,000 per year. In the past, the livestock operations had been most receptive to the Canfarm offerings. No one was quite sure why this was the case. Exhibit 30–1 shows the distribution of farms by province and gross sales for 1976.

Product

The current product line carried by Canfarm Cooperative consisted of one of the most advanced farm record-keeping systems in the world. Indeed, delegations from many foreign countries visited the Canfarm head office to learn more about the system. The system which was being utilized in 1979 had been developed so it could be used by any type of farmer in any part of Canada. The exact product any farmer received was determined by the contact agent and by the farmer when he first decided to register on the system and completed a Request for Reports Form (see Exhibit 30–2). By checking the appropriate boxes on this form, a farmer could receive anything from a simple annual farm operating statement to all the reports provided on a monthly basis. Because all users paid the same price regardless of the number or frequency of reports, there was some tendency for many farmers to order all the reports. The flexibility inherent in this system, and the fact that one basic program could be used to serve the needs of all

Exhibit 30-2

REQUEST FOR REPORTS

NAME

R90

FISCAL YEAR STARTING — MONTH — 1 9 | FARM ID

To request a report put a checkmark in the appropriate box, eg. ☑ To indicate a report is no longer wanted put a circle around the Reference No., eg. ⑫③

To change the frequency of a report, record new checkmarks for the entire year for that particular report only.

REPORT TITLE	REF. NO.	EACH TIME DATA IS SENT	OR	JAN	FEB	MAR	APR	MAY	JUN	JUL	AUG	SEP	OCT	NOV	DEC
STATEMENT OF ASSETS, LIABILITIES & OWNERS EQUITY	310*	☐													
FARM INCOME STATEMENT	312*	☐													
FARM OPERATING STATEMENT	313	☐													
FARM OPERATING STATEMENT WITH PHYSICAL QUANTITIES	314	☐		☐ 1	☐ 2	☐ 3	☐ 4	☐ 5	☐ 6	☐ 7	☐ 8	☐ 9	☐ 10	☐ 11	☐ 12
INVENTORY BALANCE REPORT	321	☐													
STATEMENT OF CHANGE IN FINANCIAL POSITION	331*	☐		☐ 1	☐ 2	☐ 3	☐ 4	☐ 5	☐ 6	☐ 7	☐ 8	☐ 9	☐ 10	☐ 11	☐ 12
CASH FLOW STATEMENT	341	☐													
BANK ACCOUNT REPORT	342	☐													
CURRENCY REPORT	343	☐													
CREDIT ACCOUNT REPORT	344	☐		☐ 1	☐ 2	☐ 3	☐ 4	☐ 5	☐ 6	☐ 7	☐ 8	☐ 9	☐ 10	☐ 11	☐ 12
SUMMARY CREDIT ACCOUNT REPORT	345														
STATEMENT OF OWNER'S CONTRIBUTIONS AND WITHDRAWALS	351	☐													
TAX STATEMENTS (CASH METHOD)	510														
TAX STATEMENTS (ACCRUAL METHOD)	520														
SCHEDULE OF FIXED ASSETS & C.C.A.	610														
SCHEDULE OF FIXED ASSETS & DEPRECIATION	620														
ENTERPRISE ANALYSIS REPORTS (If you want only some of these reports or if you want them in differing frequencies use R91)	400	☐													

SPECIFIC MONTHS

* These reports can be received only if inventories have been submitted

394

potential customers, was felt by Mr. Mitchell to be a major advantage of the Canfarm System. Mr. Knox appreciated these points, but was somewhat concerned about a farmer's ability to choose the right set of reports for his operation. Even when assisted by the Canfarm contact representative, Mr. Knox felt there could be some problems in making the proper choice.

In addition to its basic package, Canfarm offered a number of other products. These included CanChek, a single-entry cash accounting system. This system was not marketed through Canfarm but rather through national banks such as the Bank of Montreal, Toronto-Dominion Bank, and the Bank of Nova Scotia. Some confusion had developed among farmers when the service subsequently was not recommended by Canfarm because it did not utilize the more widely accepted double-entry accounting system. Many technical, service, and design problems had been associated with CanChek and had undoubtedly contributed to the negative attitudes farmers had about Canfarm. Mr. Mitchell and Mr. Knox considered dropping the program but realized there were some very loyal CanChek users. Both the banks and Canfarm were reluctant to jeopardize their loyalty by discontinuing the program.

Other products offered by Canfarm included a Swine Breeding Management Service, a Beef Finishing Service, and a Dairy Ration Feed Formulation Service.

Pricing

As a government agency, Canfarm's objective was to meet targeted numbers within approved budget plans, not to earn a profit or even break even. As a result, prices to users reflected only a fraction of the costs of developing and operating the system. Actual prices varied from province to province depending on the provincial government's philosophy. In Ontario, for example, the total price to any user was set at $30 per year for any combination of reports; in Nova Scotia the same combination of reports was provided free of charge. Even the higher Ontario prices did not cover the estimated direct costs of $50 associated with providing the service to one farmer for a year. One of Mr. Mitchell's first decisions in trying to convert Canfarm into a profitable business was to establish separate prices for individual reports and to increase substantially the overall cost to users. After his price increases, a fairly basic set of reports sold for approximately $200 per year. A farmer buying all the reports would be charged about $500 per year.

Despite the price increase, Mr. Mitchell felt Canfarm was in a good position in relation to competition. Several banks offered computerized record systems (CanChek and others) but these were only suitable for very basic cash accounting purposes. They cost less than the new Canfarm rate, but Mr. Mitchell felt they were not comparable in value terms. Other competition came from some larger accounting firms that had their own computer programs for general business financial purposes. All could be adapted to farm businesses but were not developed especially for the farm situation as was Canfarm. These programs also cost several times more than Canfarm and management believed few farmers utilized them.

Distribution policies

As a government agency, Canfarm services had been offered nationwide, mainly through provincial government extension branches and the Federal Farm Credit Corporation. A few accounting, bookkeeping, and farm management firms also carried the service. Many of the distributing organizations had proven unwilling or unable to enthusiastically promote Canfarm products to potential customers, or to provide adequate service to existing clients. The original Canfarm Service Agency had identified inadequate training and backup support of local field personnel as a major problem. As a result, neither the agent nor the farmer received a clear idea of the technical aspects of the Canfarm Computer System or of general farm management principles. Both agent and farmer felt considerable frustration and dissatisfaction with the product. It was not unusual for an annoyed farm user to simply toss the entire "report" into the wastebasket (see Exhibit 30–3 for a sample Canfarm report).

Mr. Mitchell and Mr. Knox realized the absolute necessity of developing a distribution system suitable for handling the highly sophisticated Canfarm product. Mr. Knox encouraged the development of a system based on personal selling. Under this system, marketing representatives could sell and service Canfarm products while providing an effective mechanism for Canfarm to learn about and respond to the needs of the market. A decentralized marketing structure of 5 regions and 67 territories across Canada was envisioned. Staffing this new organization would require 72 representatives and supervisors at an approximate cost of $40,000 each. Under this plan, Canfarm would change from a research and operations organization into a marketing organization.

Ontario itself would be broken into 14 territories, each centering around a "primary trading center." The plan was to establish a Canfarm "store" in each of these centers. The marketing representative

Exhibit 30–3

MARTIN FARMS
FARM OPERATING STATEMENT
JAN 1, 1977 TO DEC 31, 1977

DESCRIPTION	1ST QUARTER	2ND QUARTER	3RD QUARTER	OCTOBER	NOVEMBER	DECEMBER	YEAR-TO-DATE	ITEM NO
INCOME								
WHEAT	6,499	6,940	17,980		4,500		35,919	111
BARLEY	1,663	284	2,414				4,361	112
TOTAL CROPS							40,280	
BEEF BULL	500	415	750			534	1,665	311
BEEF COWS	232						766	312
BEEF BREEDING HEIFER	608	750		2,790	1,518	2,380	8,046	314
FEEDER CATTLE			4,021	4,050		1,250	9,321	316
TOTAL LIVESTOCK							19,797	
PATRONAGE PAYMENTS		505					505	817
CWB PYMT	7,131						7,131	841
TOTAL SUPPLIES & SERVICES							7,636	
TOTAL INCOME	$16,633	$8,894	$25,164	$6,840	$6,018	$4,164	$67,713	
EXPENSES								
HAY		150					150	141
TOTAL CROPS							150	
BEEF BULL		875					875	311
BEEF COWS				840			840	312
FEEDER CATTLE	2,625						2,625	316
TOTAL LIVESTOCK							4,340	
COMMERCIAL FEEDS						760	760	51
RAPESEED MEAL		31		82		19	131	5133
SALT			3	7		3	13	5141
COMMERL MINERAL SUPP	115			19		31	166	5146
VITAMINS						17	17	5148
VETERINARY SERVICES	81	23	73	35		98	309	521
GENERAL LVSTK S/S						200	200	53
STABLE SUPPLIES	50						50	534
LVSTK REGISTRATION				75			75	5363
FEED TESTING	33						33	5364
INSECTICIDES					19		19	541
HERBICIDES	674						674	542
CHEMICAL FERTILIZER		1,300			879		2,179	551
GENERAL CROP S&S					20		20	56
SEED CLEANING	190						190	5621
BALER TWINE		254	529				783	5645
CROP TOOLS & EQUIP.		72					72	565
GASOLINE		135	668	122			925	611

(cont.)

Exhibit 30-3 (*cont.*)

MARTIN FARMS
FARM OPERATING STATEMENT (CONT'D)
JAN 1, 1977 TO DEC 31, 1977

731943 PAGE 6
PRODUCED ON 04/10/76

1ST QUARTER	2ND QUARTER	3RD QUARTER	DESCRIPTION	OCTOBER	NOVEMBER	DECEMBER	YEAR-TO-DATE	ITEM NO
			EXPENSES (CONT'D)					
64	23	138	CAR GAS	48			273	6114
		205	DIESEL FUEL				205	612
74			HEATING FUELS	89			162	614
129		15	MOTOR OIL				144	6161
39	308	295	EQUIPMENT R&M	42	84	15	783	62
251	24	35	TRACTOR R&M		24		309	621
18	17	16	TRUCK R&M		27		57	622
			AUTOMOBILE R&M		45		45	623
		187	HARVEST EQUIP R&M	70			258	625
67		57	BUILDING R&M				125	631
242			HOUSE R&M				288	6311
	180		FENCE R&M			190	370	633
		21	R&M HARDWARE		12	9	42	642
		131	TOOLS				131	643
81	671	60	HIRED LABOUR	142		38	992	651
		250	HIRED LABOUR				250	651 G
	10		CUSTOM HAULING			145	155	671
			CUSTOM HARVESTING		240		240	675
7		37	ADVERTISING				43	711
150	137	1,194	INTEREST		5,855	800	8,137	721
7	6	6	SERVICE CHARGE	1	2		22	723
438			BLDG/FIRE INSURANCE				438	731
25			EQUIP & MACH INSUR				25	732
		160	CAR INSURANCE				160	7321
		489	CROP INSURANCE				489	733
		200	HAIL INSURANCE				200	7331
18	7	30	TELEPHONE		11		66	741
77	124	95	HYDRO/ELECTRICITY				296	742
		897	PROPERTY TAX				897	751
	45		TRUCK LICENCE				45	762
	14		DRIVERS LICENCE				14	764
3			FEES & SUBSCRIPTIONS	14			17	781
	147		OFFICE SUPPLIES		12		158	785
			TOTAL SUPPLIES & SERVICES				22,450	
$5,457	$4,552	$5,790	TOTAL EXPENSES	$1,587	$7,230	$2,325	$26,940	
$11,176	$4,341	$19,374	EXCESS OF INCOME OVER EXPENSES / EXCESS OF EXPENSES OVER INCOME	$5,253	$1,212	$1,840	$40,773	

398

would operate out of this store, selling and servicing the complete range of Canfarm products. Mr. Knox realized that these representatives would need to have a wide variety of expertise and skills ranging from technical understanding of Canfarm systems to knowledge of financial management. It was felt that the presence of these representatives would upgrade the Canfarm image. Mr. Knox explained "We aren't selling record-keeping here—our product is financial management." He felt the local service center would encourage area farmers to drop by and discuss Canfarm and their management needs with local representatives. He foresaw the center expanding in the near future to include an in-store computer terminal with direct access to the head office in Guelph.

Along with the direct selling proposal, Canfarm was considering wholesaling its services through various agencies. This program, which had the support of Mr. Mitchell, concentrated on wholesaling Canfarm products through selected agencies such as accountants and banks. Marketing representatives would concentrate not on farmers, but rather on selling Canfarm benefits to the retail agencies. Farmers would be directed to go to various accounting firms or banks which were Canfarm Agencies. Direct selling to farmers would be almost nonexistent. Mr. Mitchell felt this program had several advantages. One major advantage was that it would provide Canfarm with qualified accounting and management agents at a fraction of the cost of hiring such people directly. Under the proposed system Mr. Mitchell felt that only two marketing representatives per region would be needed to service the retail agencies. He questioned, however, whether or not accountants would be willing to actively support and promote the product. He knew that many accountants were not familiar with Canfarm and that some viewed it negatively from the past. He also wondered whether or not current Canfarm users, whose accountants were not agents, would be willing to switch to an accountant using the Canfarm system.

Mr. Mitchell thought many accountants would view Canfarm as a tool to increase their billing time. They would receive the Canfarm packages at a discount of approximately 10 percent from retail price. He figured that a farmer purchasing a complete package (Canfarm reports plus accountant's time) would spend approximately $2,000 per year. He felt that both accountants and farmers would benefit from using Canfarm's program.

Accountants who would become Canfarm agents were not required to invest any capital; rather they would agree to enroll a minimum of 20 clients in the program in the first year and to continue with a "clear, aggressive plan for continued growth" in future years. Canfarm promised a backup staff of qualified chartered accountants and farm management specialists to support product quality and service functions. Agents would receive intensive training in the Canfarm system at the Guelph office.

Mr. Mitchell's decision

By mid-1979, Mr. Mitchell realized that a new plan would have to be finalized soon if it were to be in place by the beginning of 1980. Although his major concern centered on selecting a method of distribution, he was also wondering what, if any, changes should be made in Canfarm's product line and pricing policies. He also realized that he would need to formulate a promotional program to support the distribution system he selected. Although he thought the direct selling and wholesaling proposals were the most relevant, he did not rule out the possibility of continuing to use the present system, which utilized provincial government extension people. He wondered, too, whether there were other distribution alternatives which should be considered. As he prepared to make his decision, he was alarmed to learn that the number of Canfarm users had declined from nearly 14,000 in 1978 to 5,000 in 1979.

CASE ANALYSIS

CASE 30
Canfarm Cooperative

1. What distribution alternatives are available to Canfarm Cooperative?

_____

_____

_____

_____

_____

_____

_____

_____

2. What factors should be considered in assessing the distribution alternatives?

_____

_____

_____

_____

_____

_____

3. Assess the major distribution alternatives.

_____

_____

_____

_____

_____

_____

_____

_____

4. Summarize what is known about the needs, attitudes, and behavior of farmers in Canfarm's trading area.

_____

_____

_____

_____

_____

_____

_____

_____

_____

5. Summarize what is known about the needs, attitudes, and behavior of accountants.

6. Summarize what is known about the needs, attitudes, and behavior of bankers.

7. Outline an appropriate promotion program consistent with your preferred distribution strategy.

_____

_____

_____

_____

_____

_____

8.   What changes, if any, would you recommend in Canfarm's product
     policies?

_____

_____

_____

_____

_____

_____

9.   What changes, if any, would you recommend in Canfarm's pricing
     policies?

_____

_____

_____

_____

PART EIGHT

SELECTED APPLICATIONS

CASE 31

LECTRON CORPORATION

The Lectron Corporation was founded in the early 1970s by William Patton with the objective of developing new electrical products for industrial and commercial markets. Prior to founding Lectron, Mr. Patton had been the executive vice president of a leading electrical products manufacturing company and had had twenty years' successful experience in the electrical products industry.

After two years of extensive research and development at a cost of approximately $300,000, the Lectron control was developed. Although the product was being marketed primarily as a motor control, the general design of the unit made it suitable for many electrical switching applications, including temperature controls and lighting controls.

Since its development, annual sales have been in the $250,000 range, with a manufacturing margin of about 50%. Mr. Patton, however, was not satisfied with the market response to the Lectron control, since the potential market was believed to be, at a minimum, $100 million. The product, by all estimates, fit a market need, was technically sound, was priced competitively, and had many superior performance characteristics, yet it was still far from reaching its full market potential. As a result, a great deal of discussion and planning was being done to identify the type of marketing program that would lead to increased sales growth and the "take off" stage in the product life cycle.

This case was prepared by David McConaughy, Graduate School of Business, University of Southern California. Revised 1980.

Product

The Lectron motor control was a completely solid-state device; that is, it was totally electronic and had no mechanical moving parts. It used only top-quality electrical components, such as those manufactured by RCA and Westinghouse. Its design used the latest digital technology and had been well tested. It met appropriate National Electrical Manufacturers Association standards and was the first such device approved for switching applications by Underwriter's Laboratory, a safety and circuit certification company. Underwriter's approvals are accepted and often required by state and industry safety departments and insurance companies.

The primary function of the Lectron control was to provide a "soft start," i.e., to reduce the heavy current inrush and starting torque of an electric motor. Avoiding the high initial current flow and torque results in the following benefits:

1. Starting power requirements are reduced.
2. Line voltage drop during motor starts is reduced.
3. Possible damage to the motor and the equipment that it drives is reduced.
4. Thermal and electrical stress on motor and electrical circuits is reduced.

The Lectron control was more trouble-free, provided smoother operation, was quieter, operated in a wider range of environments, and was less expensive than other types of "soft-start" equipment. Because of its solid-state design, the Lectron control did not cause the electromagnetic interference common with mechanical types of switching and thus reduced "electromagnetic pollution," a topic of growing concern to the FCC.

One highly successful application on a Coast Guard cutter electrical system created a great deal of interest in the marine industry and received widespread publicity in new product and new application sections of trade publications.

Competition

At the moment, there was only fragmented competition, but this could change in the future because many solid-state control circuits were being developed. Various solid-state circuit designs were being published in the application literature of component manufacturers as well as in the journal of the Institute of Electrical Engineers. However, Mr. Patton had several comprehensive patents on the Lectron circuit.

Electromechanical starters that provided a similar function were, of course, competition in that they were an accepted method of "soft-start" control. Of these, the principal control being used was the auto-transformer. While this device did limit initial power surge, it made a jerky shift to each power level as the current was increased. This jerky movement resulted in a higher burn-out risk and greater mechanical stress compared to the Lectron control, which was smooth throughout the entire starting cycle. Other "soft-start" controls included the part winding starter, which usually required a specially designed (and costly) motor, and the primary resistor starter, which mechanically switched an electrical resistor bank in series with the motor as it was started. Exhibit 31–1 provides a brief comparison of the costs and features of various starting devices. Exhibit 31–7 shows typical wiring diagrams of these different devices.

Market potential

The exact market potential for the Lectron control was unknown because the control could be used in a large amount of industrial equipment as well as in electrical control applications. The total market for motor and related controls of all types was in excess of $1 billion a year, with the relevant control market perhaps as large as $500 million a year. Exhibit 31–2 lists these data.

To aid in market planning, Mr. Patton collected available market data and developed a list of potential industrial applications in which he felt the Lectron control offered distinct advantages. Exhibit 31–3 lists the value of shipment of selected industries in which the Lectron control could be used, and Exhibit 31–4 lists possible applications.

Shipments of industrial equipment closely followed capital investment plans of industry, but even in those years when such spending declined, the demand for labor-saving devices and motors rarely declined by much. Thus Mr. Patton thought that general economic conditions would not affect the demand for the Lectron control. However, marketing to an industry that was experiencing rapid growth might produce built-in growth once the Lectron control was adopted. Examples of such industries were the pump and compressor industry, which was growing as a result of energy-related capital expansion, and food processing, mining, and pulp and paper mills.

The current Lectron customers seemed unrelated by product or industry, but usually purchased the Lectron control for very limited and unusual applications in which no other starter would work. This could change, since two major crane manufacturing companies were in the process of testing the Lectron control, and Mr. Patton hoped to sell 2,000 to 3,000 units in this market. Several brewing and bottling companies had successfully tested the Lectron device to control pumping operations and had expressed great enthusiasm for the product; however, no formal commitments from these markets had been received.

Mr. Patton employed six sales representatives in the major industrial areas of the country. Most orders, however, were placed directly with the company as a result of press releases and limited advertising describing the Lectron control, or as a result of Mr. Patton's work with selected customers. Typical orders were for only one or a few controls, and the controls were shipped by United Parcel Service after being built to order by the small production department.

Marketing strategy

After five years of focusing his attention on problems of product development and manufacturing, Mr. Patton became increasingly aware of the need for a comprehensive marketing plan if Lectron was to reach its full business potential. He was not sure that his sales representatives were effective in developing new markets, although with this approach his sales cost was only 10% of sales. Company-employed salesmen would be more committed to selling the product; yet they were expensive, and Mr. Patton was not sure toward which companies and market areas they should be directed. Exhibit 31–5 lists average sales cost data he had collected. He recognized that selling costs were higher in major metropolitan areas such as New York, Chicago, and San Francisco, where costs were 40–60% higher than average. In the smaller cities of the Southeast, such as Greenville, near the textile industry, costs were 15–20% below average.

Mr. Patton also developed a list of possible trade publications in which he might place Lectron advertising (Exhibit 31–6), and observed that in many the cost of advertising seemed quite high. Before he did any extensive advertising, however, he wondered whether he should concentrate on establishing wholesale distribution so that customers could get local service and delivery of the product. He was not strongly in favor of distribution through wholesalers because his earlier experience with electrical wholesalers had led him to the conclusion that: (1) wholesalers don't make an effort to push the product; (2) wholesalers carry too many other products; and (3) wholesalers really lack the technical knowledge to understand potential applications. It seemed to him that some form of personal selling was required. If this was done properly, he might not have to advertise until he could better afford it.

Finally Mr. Patton cleared a work space on his desk and on a fresh sheet of paper outlined some of his thoughts:

Whom to sell to?

Specifiers such as electrical designers and original equipment manufacturers.

End users such as equipment buyers and industries that use conveyors, pumps, cranes, etc.

Manufacturing and maintenance buyers who are looking for products to solve a particular problem.

Other manufacturers of controls even though there seems to be little interest in competing equipment.

Government agencies such as the Coast Guard or TVA.

Sales representatives and smaller wholesalers who are looking for unique products to distribute.

What to sell?

Control only.

Control system including wiring, enclosure and connecting equipment.

Complete control and motor package.

At this point, Mr. Patton stopped writing and wondered whether other pioneers in the electrical industry, such as Thomas Edison, had gone through this process and, if so, what they would have done to hasten the success of the Lectron control.

Exhibit 31–1
Comparison of features and prices for selected 10-horsepower motor starters

Type of control	Type of start	Size (in.)	Weight (lb.)	List price	Comments
Magnetic starter	On-off only	12 × 7 × 6	15	$ 162	Switches full power only
Primary resistor	Stepped-smooth	29 × 18 × 10	120	$ 839	Low efficiency
Autotransformer	Stepped-smooth	34 × 24 × 12	450	$1139	Most widely used reduced voltage starter
Part winding	Stepped-smooth	21 × 14 × 7	100	$ 448	Requires special motor with winding taps
Star-Delta	One-step start	35 × 35 × 12	210	$ 695	Three-phase motors only
Lectron	Continuous-smooth	12 × 10 × 5¾	15	$ 875	Solid-state—no moving parts

Source: Company records.

Exhibit 31–2
Value of shipments of selected switchgear and control apparatus, 1974

SIC code	Product	Number of producing companies	Value of shipments (in millions of dollars)	Growth, 1973–74 (%)
3613 701	Magnetic Control Circuit Relays	56	256.5	9.3
3613 704	Starter Accessories Inc. Overload Relays	25	17.2	3.6
3622 012	A.C. Full Voltage Starters 600 Volts or Less	42	182.9	27.4
3622 013	A.C. Connectors, 600 Volts or Less	30	37.5	–6.0
3622 011	A.C. Reduced Voltage Controls	19	25.2	NA
3622 015	Synchronous Motor Starters	6	NA	NA
3622 016	Motor Control Centers	55	145.1	54.0
3622 018	Starters and Contractors for Motors over 600 Volts	21	37.3	33.2
3622 081	Rheostats and Resistors	17	20.1	39.6
3622 097	All Other General Industry Devices	48	268.1	28.5
3622 045	Marine and Navy Auxiliary Controls and Accessories	18	27.0	0.4
3622 048	Metal Mill, Crane and Hoist Controls, Constant and Adjustable Voltage	30	66.3	11.6
3633 049	Definite Purpose Contractors and Starters for Refrigeration and Air Conditioning	9	23.5	NA

Source: U.S. Department of Commerce.

Exhibit 31–3
Selected industry data

Industry category	1975 shipments SIC code	Value (in millions of dollars)	Average annual growth rate, 1967–75		Exports (%)	Major producing areas
			Establishments	Shipments (%)		
Pumps and compressors	3561 3563	4,700	643	10.8	15.6	North Central, Northeast
Material handling equipment	3534	3,720	1,250	5.7	17.9	Middle Atlantic
	3535 3536 3537					North Central, Western
Mining machinery	3532	1,550	240	14.5	16.4	Pennsylvania, West Virginia, Ohio
Oil machinery	3533	3,250	314	20.6	28.6	Texas, Oklahoma, California, Louisiana
Food products machinery	3551	1,745	675	10.8	16.1	North Central, California, New York
Textile machinery	3552	845	578	1.8	12.7	Northeast, Southeast
Switchgear	3613	2,760	898	5.9	NA	NA
Motors and generators	3621	3,125	775	4.0	NA	NA
Industrial controls	3622	2,093	1,173	6.0	NA	NA
Shipbuilding	3731	4,710	455	8.6	NA	Great Lakes, East, West, and Gulf Coasts

Source: U.S. Department of Commerce.

**Exhibit 31–4
Potential applications**

Blowers
  Centrifugal
  Constant pressure

Brick plants
  Augers
  Conveyors
  Dry pans
  Pug mills

By-product coke plants
  Door machines
  Leveler rams
  Pusher bars
  Valve reversing machines

Cement mills
  Conveyors
  Dryers—rotary
  Elevators
  Grinders, pulverizers
  Kilns

Coal mines
  Car hauls
  Conveyors
  Cutters
  Fans
  Hoists—slope
  Hoists—vertical
  Jigs
  Picking tables
  Rotary car dumpers
  Shaker screens

Compressors
  Constant speed
  Varying speed
    Centrifugal
    Plunger-type

Cranes—general purpose
  Hoist
  Bridge or trolley—sleeve bearing
  Bridge or trolley—roller bearing

Concrete mixers

Flour mills
  Line shafting

Food plants
  Butter churns
  Dough mixers

Hoists
  Mine hoists—slope
  Mine hoists—vertical
  Contractor's hoist
  Winch

Larry car

Lift bridges

Machine tools
  Bending rolls
  Boring mills
  Bulldozers
  Gear cutters
  Grinders
  Hobbing machines
  Lathes
  Milling machines
  Presses
  Punches
  Saws
  Shapers

Material handling
  Coal & ore bridges
    Holding
    Closing
    Trolley
    Bridge

Metal mining
  Ball, rod or tube mills
  Car dumpers—rotary
  Converters—copper
  Conveyors
  Crushers
  Tilting furnace

Paper mills
  Beaters
  Calendars

Pipe working
  Cutting and threading
  Expanding and flanging

(cont.)

Exhibit 31–4 (cont.)

Power plants
  Clinker grinders
  Coal crushers
  Conveyors—belt
  Conveyors—screw
  Pulverized fuel feeders
  Pulverizers—ball-type
  Pulverizers—centrifugal-type
  Stokers

Pumps
  Centrifugal
  Plunger

Rubber mills
  Calendars
  Crackers
  Mixing mills
  Washers

Steel mills
  Accumulators
  Casting machines—pig
  Charging machines
    Bridge
    Peel revolving
    Trolley
  Coiling machines
  Conveyors
  Converters—metal
  Cranes
    Hoist
    Bridge & trolleys, sleeve
      bearing
    Bridge trolleys, roller bearing
  Crushers
  Furnace doors
  Gas valves
  Gas washers
  Hot metal mixers
  Ingot buggy
  Kick off
  Levelers

  Manipulator fingers
  Pickling machine
  Pliers—slab
  Racks
  Reelers
  Saws—hot or cold
  Screw downs
  Shears
  Shuffle bars
  Side guards
  Sizing rolls
  Slab buggy
  Soaking pit covers
  Straighteners
  Tables
    Approach
    Roll
    Shear approach
    Lift
    Main roll
    Transfer
  Tilting furnaces
  Wiring stranding machines

Textiles
  Weaving
  Knitting
  Throwing
  Winding
  Tufting

Wood-working plants
  Boring machines
  Lathe
  Mortiser
  Moulder
  Planers
  Power trimmer and mitre
  Sanders
  Saws
  Shapers
  Shingle machines

Exhibit 31–5
Productivity and costs for selected types of salesmen

Type of salesman	Average direct cost	Metropolitan area		Suburban area	
		Calls/year	Cost/call	Calls/year	Cost/call
Account representative—calls on already established customers; selling is low key with minimal pressure to develop new business.	$37,800	1,195	$32	598	$63
Detail salesman—performs promotional activities and introduces new products; actual sale is ultimately made through a wholesaler.	$33,200	$1,912	$17	1,195	$28
Sales engineer—sells products where technical know-how and technical aspects are important to sale; experience in identifying and solving customers' problems is required.	$39,100	1,045	$37	665	$59
Industrial products salesman—sells a tangible product to industrial or commercial purchasers; a high degree of technical knowledge is not required.	$35,800	1,673	$21	956	$37
Intangibles/service salesman—must be able to effectively sell intangible benefits such as design services or application concepts.	$37,250	2,151	$17	1,195	$31

Source: S&MM *Sales and Marketing Management,* 1980.

Exhibit 31–6
Cost and circulation data on selected trade publications

Publication	Circulation	Cost of full page ad, black and white	Comments
Production Engineering (formerly *Automation*)	92,238	$ 3,180	Production engineering emphasis; has trade show issues.
Control Engineering	74,308	$ 2,690	Instrumentation and automatic control emphasis
Design News	139,090	$ 3,275	Design engineer's idea magazine
Electrical Apparatus	14,920	$ 995	Magazine of electromechanical operation and maintenance; rebuilding apparatus and selling replacement equipment
Electrical Construction and Maintenance	71,615	$ 3,145	Electrical contractors, electrical consultants and in-plant maintenance supervisors
Electrical Contractor	47,121	$ 1,850	Electrical construction and maintenance; contractors
Electrical Equipment	93,521	$ 2,625	Edited for electrical and electromechanical engineers who research, design and install electrical or electromechanical products
Electrical Wholesaling	15,675	$ 1,785	Controlled circulation to electrical distributors; sourcebook of electrical wholesaling, marketing and selling
Food Processing	56,517	$ 1,690	New product reports, case histories; covers processing equipment material handling, etc.

Industrial Equipment News	185,451	$11,085	What's new in equipment, parts and materials; covers literature and catalogues that are available
Industrial Maintenance	105,529	$ 4,585	News tabloid magazine for those responsible for maintenance and operation of industrial plants
Machine Design	157,297	$ 3,450	Technical and "how to" information for machine designers and engineers
Marine Engineering/Log	23,272	$ 1,100	Covers new developments in marine engineering and naval construction
Materials Handling Engineering	97,009	$ 2,700	Technical magazine for material handling, packaging and shipping specialists
Modern Materials Handling	97,950	$ 2,865	For materials-handling professionals who have responsibility for recommending, selecting, or buying materials-handling equipment
New Equipment Digest	182,872	$ 6,450	Condensed descriptions of new equipment, materials, processes and design literature and catalogues (tabloid size)
Pit and Quarry	22,077	$ 1,480	Directed to management professionals who specify and buy equipment, supplies and services for mining, quarrying and processing nonmetallic minerals
Purchasing	89,954	$ 3,375	News magazine for industrial buyers

Source: Standard Rate and Data Service.

Exhibit 31–7

Auto-transformer control

Auto-transformer-type starters are the most widely used reduced voltage starters because of their efficiency and flexibility. All power taken from the line, except transformer losses, is transmitted to the motor to accelerate the load. Taps on the transformer allow adjustment of the starting torque and inrush to meet the requirements of most applications. The following characteristics are produced by the three voltage taps:

Tap	Starting torque % locked torque	Line inrush % locked ampere
50%	25%	28%
65%	42%	45%
80%	64%	67%

Part-winding controls

Part-winding starting provides convenient economical one-step acceleration at reduced current where the power company specifies a maximum or limits the increments of current drawn from the line. These starters can be used with standard dual-voltage motors on the lower voltage and with special part-winding motors designed for any voltage. When used with standard dual-voltage motors, it should be established that the torque produced by the first half-winding will accelerate the load sufficiently so as not to produce a second undesirable inrush when the second half-winding is connected to the line. Most motors will produce a starting torque equal to between ½ to ⅔ of NEMA standard values with half of the winding energized and draw about ⅔ of normal line current inrush.

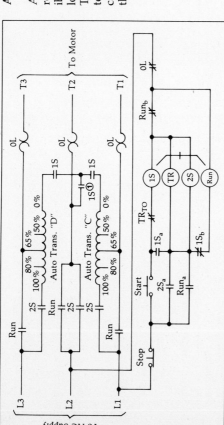

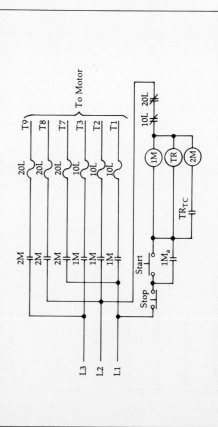

Primary resistor

Primary resistor-type starters, sometimes known as "cushion-type" starters, will reduce the motor torque and starting inrush current to produce a smooth, cushioned acceleration with closed transition. Although not as efficient as other methods of reduced voltage starting, primary resistor-type starters are ideally suited to applications such as conveyors, textile machines, or other delicate machinery where reduction of starting torque is of prime consideration. Starters through size 5 will limit inrush to approximately 80% of locked rotor current and starting torque to approximately 64% of locked torque. Larger sizes will be custom designed to the application.

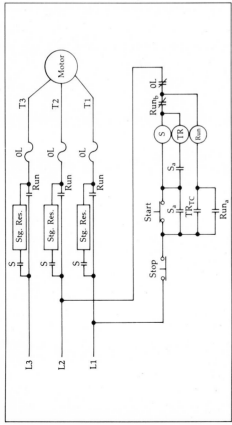

Star-Delta control

Star-Delta-type starters have been applied extensively to industrial air conditioning installations because they are particularly applicable to starting motors driving high inertia loads with resulting long acceleration times. They are not, however, limited to this application. When six or twelve lead delta-connected motors are started star-connected, approximately 58% of full line voltage is applied to each winding and the motor develops 33% of normal locked rotor current from the line. When the motor has accelerated, it is reconnected for normal delta operation.

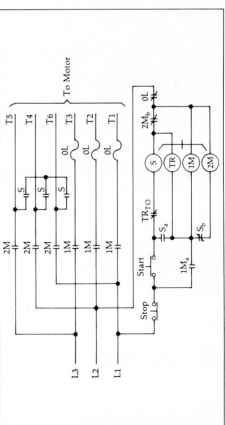

CASE
ANALYSIS

CASE 31

Lectron Corporation

1. How would you assess the product benefits and liabilities in the marketplace?

   a. Product benefits

   _____

   _____

   _____

   _____

   _____

   _____

   _____

   b. Product liabilities

   _____

   _____

   _____

   _____

   _____

   _____

   _____

2.   What barriers do you see to the product reaching the growth stage of the product life cycle?

_____

_____

_____

_____

_____

_____

_____

_____

_____

_____

_____

_____

_____

_____

_____

_____

_____

_____

_____

3. Are there possibly better strategies that Mr. Patton should consider?

_____

_____

_____

_____

_____

_____

_____

4. What common elements in a marketing strategy and plan might apply to all of the alternatives?

_____

_____

_____

_____

_____

_____

CASE 32

ST. PETER'S HOSPITAL
Development of a Hospice Program

Background

St. Peter's Hospital, a 200-bed acute care hospital in central Illinois, is owned and operated by an order of religious sisters. In 1978, the hospital's Board of Directors conducted a search to replace its retiring chief executive officer. Within six months, a successor was named: John Rowe, 40, who previously served in a similar institution as an assistant administrator. Mr. Rowe was selected for a variety of reasons, but primarily because of his reputation as an aggressive and innovative marketer of new health services. He was also considered an extremely diplomatic administrator with a proven track record in obtaining every C.O.N. he pursued. This was attributable to his skills in working with the regulatory agencies.

Current developments
A plan of action

Within six months following Rowe's appointment to St. Peter's, he developed a priority plan for the hospital. Among the areas he hoped to develop were:

1. a home care dialysis center
2. an ambulatory care program (outpatient clinic)
3. expanded radiologic and laboratory facilities
4. the addition of 20 medical/surgical beds

This case was prepared by Charles H. Patti, Associate Professor of Marketing, and Debra Low, Faculty Associate, Department of Marketing, Arizona State University.

5. recognition as an approved Trauma Center
6. remodeling of 90% of the existing facility
7. designation as a university teaching hospital

In a presentation which Rowe made to the hospital's Board of Directors he outlined his seven-point program. The Board was receptive to his assessment of needs; however, one member, an oncologist, stated the need to assign an eighth priority area, a hospice program. Dr. Bell, the oncologist, explained that,

> Hospice is essentially an innovative program of palliative and supportive services to provide physical, psychological, social and spiritual care to the terminally ill and their families. St. Peter's is an ideal sponsor of a hospice program because of its already established acute care program.

Another board member, Sr. Marie Davis, noted that hospice care would be consistent with the healing mission of a Catholic health care apostolate. After minimal discussion, the Board overwhelmingly approved establishing hospice as the top priority area.

Determining
hospice feasibility

The first action of the Board was to appoint a team to study the feasibility of implementing a hospice program. The in-house team proceeded to visit a variety of hospices around the U.S. and discovered several existing models. Included in these models were:

- free-standing facilities
- home care programs
- combination home care/in-patient palliative care beds
- multi-institutional arrangements

The team discovered that the pricing of hospice programs was difficult to assess given the variety of existing hospice models, the newness of the hospice concept, and the lack of accurate cost data. They also discovered that the Midland Illinois Health Systems Agency which served the 12-county area encompassing St. Peter's service area would recommend only one hospice per health systems area to the State's regulatory agency. It was learned that three other hospitals within the health systems area were also studying the feasibility of launching a hospice program.

In speaking to hospice program directors, the team learned that most persons in the U.S. (including many physicians) have never heard of hospice care. Although hospice care had been featured in a number of television news programs and was the subject of numerous newspaper and magazine articles, the fact remained that the hospice movement was suffering from a lack of sustained media exposure.

Three months after its appointment, the team reported its findings to the Board. Several conflicting points of view emerged at the meeting. For example:

- Four of the Board members proposed to abandon the hospice program until additional information could be obtained on pricing and reimbursement.

- John Rowe stressed that he would like to postpone commitment to the hospice program until the hospital achieved the other seven priority areas.

- Six nuns stressed that the Board already made a commitment and should therefore pursue the hospice program as the top priority.

- Four persons believed the proposed St. Peter's Hospice should be a free-standing facility; four believed it should be a home care program coordinated by the hospital's home health department; and three others believed it should be a combined home care/in-patient program.

Ultimately, all of this confusion led the Board to decide to hire a marketing consultant to make recommendations. The consultant's mandate was to develop a complete marketing plan for the proposed St. Peter's Hospice. The plan was to focus on:

1. Service Development
   Major issues:
   a. determination of the most feasible hospice model to implement.
   b. what needs exist among consumers?
   c. what services should be offered?
2. Pricing of Hospice Care
   Background facts:
   a. The room rate for an acute care bed in the oncology unit was priced at $140/patient day (semi private) and a nursing home room was priced at $80 for a similar arrangement.
   b. Blue Cross/Blue Shield would not yet reimburse the costs of hospice care in the State of Illinois (see Exhibit 32–4).
   c. The availability of federal funds was limited due to a demonstration grant program awarded to 26 hospice programs over a two-year period by D.H.H.S. (previously D.H.E.W.).

Exhibit 32–1
Summary of promotion studies*

Question 1: "Have you heard of hospice care?"

Results (1% of population responding "yes"):

Doctors:	88%
Nurses:	74%
General public:	18%

Question 2: "Indicate your level of knowledge about hospice care."

Results:

General public	Very low	42%	28%	20%	8%	2%	Very high
Doctors	Very low	0%	5%	8%	34%	53%	Very high
Nurses	Very low	4%	12%	43%	23%	18%	Very high

Note: Questions 1 and 2 were asked to a nationwide sample of doctors, nurses, and the general public.

Question 3: "How appealing is hospice care to you?"

Results:

Very unappealing	21%	10%	32%	22%	15%	Very appealing

Question 4: "How likely is it that you would prefer hospice care to conventional care?"

Results:

Very unlikely	15%	20%	46%	11%	8%	Very likely

Note: Questions 3 and 4 were asked only of the general public. Also, respondents were told to assume that they were in a position to consider hospice care.

Question 5: "If there was a hospice in your area, how likely is it that you would contribute your time as a member of a volunteer staff?"

Results:

Very unlikely	8%	12%	62%	15%	3%	Very likely

Note: Question 5 was asked to the general public only and they were told to assume that they had an appropriate amount of time available for volunteer work.

Question 6: "How likely is it that you would refer patients to a hospice?"

Results:

Very unlikely	20%	30%	23%	12%	15%	Very likely

Question 7: "Rank order the following sources of information in terms of their importance in keeping you up-to-date on current trends in health care facilities. One (1) means the most important source of information and six (6) means the least important source of information."

Results:

Information source	Rank
talking with health care professionals	1
direct mail	2
tv, special topic tv programs	3
health care journals	4
health care columns in daily newspapers	5
medical journals	5

(cont.)

Exhibit 32–1 *(cont.)*

Question 8: "Rank order the following sources of information in terms of their importance to you as a source of general news."

Results:

Information source	Rank
newspapers	1
television	2
magazines	3
radio	3
direct mail	5

Note: Questions 6, 7, and 8 were asked of doctors only.

---

*During the past few years, several studies have been conducted among the various publics which are influential in the potential success/failure of the hospice movement. The above data have been extracted from some of the studies.

3. Distribution of Hospice Services
    Major questions to address:
    a. 24 hours a day or less?
    b. pain control medication as needed or on demand?
    c. who will refer to hospice?
    d. who should staff the hospice? who should direct it?
    e. should volunteers be used?
4. Promotion of Hospice Services
    Major questions to answer:
    a. who are the target market(s)?
    b. how to best create awareness among the target market(s)?
    c. how to stimulate ongoing patient referrals?
    d. what media are most effective in achieving communications goals?

Although the Board wanted to encourage maximum objectivity and creativity in the consultant's solutions, it decided to supply him with the information contained in Exhibits 32–1 through 32–4. The Board also told the consultant that:

1. The proposed hospice would service approximately 200 dying patients per year, based on the projections of anticipated cancer deaths in the hospital's service area.
2. The health care environment was extremely competitive.
3. The Board was reliant upon his recommendations due to their differing assessments of the situation.
4. He would have no more than three months to complete his analysis. He would also have up to $5,000 to spend on a suitable research project.

**Exhibit 32–2
Summary of
distribution-related
facts**

- Population of the area which St. Peter's serves is 150,000.
- Population growth has averaged 5% during each of the past five years.
- There are no unusual demographic or economic characteristics of the geographic area in which St. Peter's is located. The city is one of the ten largest in Illinois and is supported by agriculture, light manufacturing, service, and retailing.
- There is a rapid development of housing and shopping in areas away from the "downtown" district. Furthermore, there are no immediate plans for renewal of the "downtown" area.

**Exhibit 32–3
Summary of service-
related information**

Note: In early 1978, a government health agency conducted a nationwide survey on attitudes about hospice care. The following table has been taken from the final report.

Hospice care preferences: type of facility			
Type of care	General public	Doctors	Hospital administrators
Home care	53%	5%	23%
In-patient	15%	82%	62%
Home care/in-patient combination	5%	10%	14%
No opinion	27%	3%	1%
	100%	100%	100%

**Exhibit 32–4
Summary of price-
related information**

1. The room rate for an acute care bed in the oncology unit was priced at $140/patient day (semi private) and a nursing home room was priced at $80 for a similar arrangement.
2. Blue Cross/Blue Shield would not yet reimburse the costs of "hospice care" in the State of Illinois. However, many hospice-type programs are reimbursed through other designations such as "acute care," "home health care," and "extended nursing care."
3. The availability of federal funds is limited due to a demonstration grant awarded to 26 hospice programs over a two-year period by D.H.H.S. (previously D.H.E.W.).
4. The general public does not consider pricing a highly relevant variable in the selection of the type of health care they can have because most health care is covered by third party reimbursement. This is particularly true when the health problem involves terminal illness. The cost of health care for terminally ill patients is relevant in the decision process only at the extremes of a cost continuum—that is, both "free" care and care costing $7,000–$10,000 per month are relevant decision variables.
5. Cost is more relevant to relatives of terminally ill patients than it is to the patient.
6. Hospice care *can* be a profitable unit for a hospital, but the nature of the service creates a comparatively low profit potential for doctors.

CASE ANALYSIS

CASE 32

St. Peter's Hospital

1. Given John Rowe's seven priority areas, is it appropriate for the Board of Directors to designate the development of a hospice as its number one priority? Explain.

_____

_____

_____

_____

_____

_____

2. Discuss the rationale used by the Board in concluding that a hospice should be developed. Support or refute the rationale.

_____

_____

_____

_____

_____

_____

_____

3. Do the four topic areas to be covered in the marketing consultant's study include all of the basics of a good marketing study? Should other areas be included? If so, what?

_____

_____

_____

_____

_____

_____

_____

_____

4. How should Exhibits 32–1 through 32–4 be utilized by the consultant? Would other information be useful in making marketing decisions? If so, what?

_____

_____

_____

_____

_____

_____

_____

5. Are the marketing questions raised by the Board valid? Should other topics be covered? If so, what?

    _____

    _____

    _____

    _____

    _____

    _____

6. Demonstrate how the "four P's" of marketing can be integrated in this situation.

    _____

    _____

    _____

    _____

    _____

    _____

    _____

    _____

    _____

    _____

    _____

_____

_____

_____

_____

_____

_____

_____

_____

_____

_____

_____

_____

_____

CASE 33

SIOP: A POISON PREVENTION PROGRAM

Introduction

It is a sad fact that each year in the United States over 1,500,000 children are the victims of accidental poisoning. While the number of poisonings has not varied appreciably, the kinds of poisonings have certainly changed. In 1968 22% of the recorded poisonings were due to salicylates (a crystalline compound used, for example, in aspirin for relieving pain). In 1981 only 3% of poisonings were caused by these agents. The decrease is due to child safety containers and the effectiveness of poison prevention efforts. The most tragic aspect of accidental poisoning is that 95% of the children poisoned are under adult supervision at the time. Most incidents could be averted if parents took ordinary safety precautions.

These statistics have prompted the development of poison control centers based in hospitals throughout the country. Brokaw Hospital's Poison Control Center in Bloomington–Normal, Illinois, is typical of many of these facilities; it is coordinated by the hospital's pharmacy department. Brokaw Hospital's pharmacy staff decided they had an obligation to do more than efficiently treat poisonings. They felt that attempts had to be made to lower the number of accidental poisonings within the community. This resolution initiated a movement to investigate the basic problem and implement an effective marketing strategy to prevent poisonings.

Through marketing research, it became apparent to the staff members that children will eat or drink just about anything. They found

Most of the material in this case was developed by Terry Trudeau, Howard University, Department of Pharmacy, Washington, D.C.

that most poisoning agents are located in and around the house. The most commonly ingested substances are plants, household cleaning products, aspirin, vitamins and cold medicines—in that order.

Plants rank number one among poisoning substances (12% of reported poisonings). They are rarely toxic (depending on the species encountered), but they provide a challenge for the development of poison prevention and identification efforts.

Four basic factors have been identified as leading to childhood poisonings: (1) accessibility of toxic agents; (2) the inquisitive nature of children; (3) the limited space of a small house or apartment which causes children to play near poisonous substances (as in the kitchen or basement); and (4) the problems of communicating with children who are too young to understand the dangers of toxic products. The communications aspect was seen as the most crucial factor in establishing an effective poison prevention program.

Development of the SIOP Program in Bloomington–Normal, Illinois

Presented with these facts, Terry W. Trudeau, director of the Poison Control Center, set about the task of developing an educational program that would teach children to avoid poisons and instruct teachers and parents in the basics of poison prevention. This year-round program drew on existing ideas concerning poison prevention, as well as new ideas provided by staff members and professionals within the community.

A key aspect of poison prevention is the use of an easily recognized symbol. The traditional symbol for poison has been the skull and crossbones, but research shows that children are often attracted to this symbol because it suggests "playing pirate for fun" rather than danger or death. Symbols developed by other poison control centers in the United States were also ruled out, since none had sufficient impact to inspire a year-round poison prevention effort. It was decided to develop a new, easily recognizable poison symbol that would be repellent to all age groups.

Designed with the help of the Illinois State University art staff, the symbol shown in Figure 33–1 has proved effective in tests with preschool and kindergarten children. Named "SIOP," the symbol is a stylized green snake against a bright orange, circular background. The symbol is effective both because of its colors (green has proved to be repellent, and orange is among the hues that are first recognized) and because of its shape (the circle is the first shape children recog-

Figure 33–1
SIOP Symbol

A PARENT
AND TEACHER'S
INTRODUCTION
TO THE

SIOP
POISON
PREVENTION
PROGRAM

Courtesy of Terry Trudeau, R.Ph., M.B.A., Howard University, Washington, D.C., and Frank Braden, M.H.A., Vice President, Operations, Brokaw Poison Control Center, Normal, Illinois

nize and remember). The SIOP symbol comes with an adhesive band long enough to fit around most household products. The band is also orange, a color not frequently used in commercial packaging, and increases the visibility of the symbol from all angles.

SIOP was designed to be as frightening to children as possible. This improves the chances that children will stay away from the symbol, even though they might not know what it stands for. However, the key to making the SIOP symbol an effective deterrent was the creation of an educational program that conditions children to stay away from SIOP. Whenever and wherever children see the fanged green snake, they are taught to say, "No! SIOP!" ("poison" spelled backward). In addition, "Happy," the Poison Prevention Dog, was developed to serve as a foil to SIOP and teach children to avoid poisons. Happy barks whenever SIOP is near. This theme of good versus bad is carried throughout the program.

Some local programs have recruited a clown to attract children when program materials are displayed at malls, fairs and parties. Her name is Eppy Kak (Ipecac) and she is billed as the Poison Prevention Clown. Ipecac, by the way, is the drug used to promote vomiting of ingested poison. Eppy Kak entertains by juggling, making balloon animals, telling jokes (bad ones) and playing kid games. A babysitter's guide to poison prevention has proven to be the most popular promotional piece to date.

The launching of the SIOP Program coincided with the beginning of National Poison Prevention Week. Much publicity was used in the area, including newspaper, television, and radio coverage of the new poison symbol. The telephone company's mailing list was used to send SIOP stickers and a guide to poison prevention to each family in the country. Educational materials were delivered to all kindergartens, nursery schools, and day-care centers. Teachers received a packet of materials containing instructions for using the program year round. Each child received an activity book, a story pamphlet, a poison prevention guide, and a button. Additional materials were supplied on request.

Today, when new residents arrive in the community, they receive SIOP stickers and pamphlets through the mail. The materials are also distributed through the school system. Natural childbirth classes, the public health department, and Brokaw's pediatrics ward help perpetuate the program by distributing SIOP materials. Grants from such organizations as the Jaycees and the Brokaw Hospital Service have permitted free distribution of the materials. Many pharmacists serve on a speaker's bureau to present educational programs to schools and PTA groups.

Development of the program was a joint effort of the Bloomington–Normal Jaycees, area universities and the hospital. Project Chairman and Brokaw Hospital Poison Control Director Terry Trudeau described the SIOP Program:

> *The educational materials teach children to stay away and say "No! SIOP!" (poison spelled backward) whenever they see the symbol. What makes SIOP different from other poison sticker programs is that SIOP is also a comprehensive educational program geared at doing two things: teaching children to stay away from poisonous products and teaching poison prevention rules to children and adults. The SIOP Program does not rely on a simple symbol scaring children away from poison, but rather educates through a coordinated total program.*

Expansion of SIOP beyond Bloomington–Normal, Illinois

Through strategic publicity, the program has become worldwide. The SIOP Program at Brokaw Hospital continues to receive inquiries each day from various locations. Each program participant is encouraged to use and expand the materials in order to make them effective for their geographic area. Materials have been translated into Spanish and German, and a poison prevention plant brochure has been expanded to include plants found in the specific region where the program will be implemented.

Terry Trudeau and others involved in developing the SIOP Program have been highly commended since the program's inception eight years ago. Among the many awards received is a federal grant from the Consumer Product Safety Commission for continued service in poison prevention. Several research studies (for example, *American Journal of Public Health*) indicate that the SIOP Program creates intellectual awareness of poisons and an ability to distinguish poisonous from nonpoisonous products. SIOP warning labels have been shown to have a greater effect on visual discrimination than any other symbol available for testing. Most important has been the decrease in the number of calls made to the Poison Control Center. And the severity of reported poisonings has diminished to an appreciable extent. But as the program has gained national and international acceptance, there has been some criticism.

Analysis of effectiveness

Dr. Morris K. Jackson, Department of Anatomy, Louisiana State University Medical Center, Shreveport, offered the following opinion concerning the use of a stylized snake as the central focus of the SIOP Program:

Most ophiologists become quite ired at the use of a snake, symbol or not, which is designed to create an adverse and negative reaction about snakes. The reinforcement of negative thoughts and false conceptualizations about snakes, we fear, might create animosity towards an already overhated creature. We argue that SIOP might establish a new generation of hardened snake-phobes in the future and likewise stir the "dragons of Eden" within adults today. Most of us would like for the American public to think of the snake as the two entwined serpents on the staff of the eaduceus—the symbol of healing and the physician, instead of SIOP, the poison bearer. Can we afford to overlook another onslaught (however subtle) against the snake, even though SIOP was never intended to be a snake? Conversely, SIOP is very effective in his role and many parents are grateful. Can we afford not to have a SIOP?

In 1981 an attitudinal study was conducted in Springfield, Illinois, to test whether the SIOP Program negatively influenced children's conception of snakes. The sample for this study included 90 three- and four-year-old children from four different nursery school classrooms. Two of the classrooms were used as an experimental group and two as the control, with 45 children in each group. The results were published in *Hepatological Review.*

The results from the analysis of data suggested that there was no significant difference between the groups tested. The data collected in the study indicated that the SIOP Program has no significant effect on a child's attitude toward snakes. Nor does the program have a significant effect on a child's conception of good and bad snakes.

Those involved in the SIOP Poison Prevention Research and Education Program believe that the program is based on thorough research and creates no negative attitudes toward snakes. The program has been proven effective by the dramatic reduction of accidental poisonings in those communities where the program has been implemented. Therefore, according to the SIOP supporters, the answer to Dr. Jackson's final question is evident. Where the health and welfare of our children are involved, we can ill afford not to have a SIOP.

A study of the effectiveness of the SIOP Poison Prevention Program in improving verbal and visual discrimination of poisonous and nonpoisonous products among preschool children has been published in the *American Journal of Public Health.* The study examined both the educational program and the use of warning labels. The study sample consisted of 156 day-care and nursery school children randomly assigned to one of four treatment groups: (1) educational program with SIOP warning labels; (2) educational program; (3) SIOP warning labels; and (4) control.

A combination of the educational program with the use of SIOP warning labels proved to be the most effective approach in producing both verbal and visual discrimination. The educational program proved more effective for verbal discrimination and the SIOP warning labels proved more effective in improving visual discrimination. The results suggest two goals of an effective poison prevention program: an intellectual awareness of poisons and an ability to visually distinguish poisonous from nonpoisonous products.

Future directions

New ways are constantly being sought to improve and spread the SIOP Program and materials. The program is now becoming a national effort; Texas and Louisiana have adopted it, and other areas are in the process of doing so. Worldwide recognition is extending the program, with inquiries coming from nations as far as Australia and France. New ideas about distribution and target markets (such as industrial chemicals) are being explored in an effort to develop a single, comprehensive poison prevention program for the country. While accidental poisonings will always be a problem, the SIOP Program is taking positive steps to prevent them.

Overall, the SIOP Program remains one of the most scientifically based and validated prevention programs of any type in existence. Terry Trudeau provides the following summary of the current challenge:

Our main problem is that of coordination. The program has become so large that it is no longer a part-time effort. Orders roll in for materials that must be handled by our printer as he has time. I feel that if an educational publisher could be recruited to handle the program its continued success would be assured. However, to date we have had no serious inquiries. Personally, I'm happy that SIOP has done so well, yet because we are involved in a number of other things, the developers of SIOP are hesitant to make the program our life's work. The questions we are asking are whether we should be content with the success we have had (and the research we have added to the field) or should we reach for new levels and markets? Time and geographic considerations will have the major impact on our decisions.

Summing up my thoughts, we have certainly achieved our local goals of decreasing the number and severity of childhood poisonings in our area. The Brokaw Poison Center has become a visible entity within the community. Due to lack of full time personnel connected with the SIOP Program, the program will spread mainly by diffusion of materials and information. If an educational publisher is recruited to spear-head the program, it will be actively promoted. This would represent a new phase in program development.

CASE ANALYSIS

CASE 33

SIOP: A Poison Prevention Program

1. What marketing tasks have been performed by the people involved in the SIOP Program?

_____

_____

_____

_____

_____

_____

_____

_____

2. Compare the objectives of the SIOP Program with previous poison prevention sticker programs.

_____

_____

_____

_____

_____

_____

_____

_____

_____

_____

3.   How is the SIOP product unique? What are its advantages?

_____

_____

_____

_____

_____

_____

_____

_____

4.   What price do consumers pay for this product?

_____

_____

_____

_____

_____

_____

_____

_____

_____

5. Describe the promotion and distribution activities employed in the SIOP Program.

_____

_____

_____

_____

_____

_____

_____

_____

_____

_____

_____

_____

_____

_____

_____

_____

_____

_____

_____

_____

_____

6. Has the SIOP Program achieved its goal? What are future possibilities for the program?

_____

_____

_____

_____

_____

_____

_____

_____

_____

_____

_____

_____

_____

_____

_____

_____

_____

_____

_____

_____

_____

7. What problem has resulted from the success and subsequent growth of the SIOP Program? Suggest a marketing strategy for the future.

_____

_____

_____

CASE 34

SCIENTIFIC INSTRUMENTS COMPANY, INC.

Company background

The Scientific Instruments Company is a small manufacturer of scientific laboratory instruments used in biochemical research. Its manufacturing plant and the executive offices are located in the state of Iowa. The company, which employs a full-time staff of 135 persons, was formed in 1961 by James Colburn, a scientist with extensive research experience. Until 1960 Colburn was employed as a researcher by a major corporation. In this capacity he became interested in designing a product used in biochemical research. He decided, therefore, to leave his employer and to form, in collaboration with several other persons, the Scientific Instruments Company. Scientific Instruments is, as might be expected, a research-oriented firm.

The company produces and markets ten different products for biochemical research, the best known being ultraviolet analyzers, fraction collectors, and environmental chambers. These products are extremely sophisticated instruments used primarily by biochemists in laboratory work and, therefore, are purchased principally by universities, research foundations, corporations engaged in biochemical research and by scientists for personal research use. The products fall into two categories, standardized and custom-made. The company has a published price list for standardized products, but the prices of custom-made products vary depending on the specifications of the buyer. Prices of the products range from $125 to $250,000 per item. The company uses a few specialized distributors located in key cities to market its products in the United States, and direct sales also are made to certain large research laboratories and universities.

This case was prepared by A. H. Kizilbash of Northern Illinois University. Used by permission.

Courtesy of Richard Wood © 1980 The Picture Cube

Special characteristics that affect the sale of these products are (1) high unit value, (2) long life, (3) limited market, (4) demonstration requirements, and (5) required negotiation period before sale.

Export operations

Scientific Instruments Company made its first export sale in early 1964, when an order for ultraviolet analyzer equipment was received unsolicited from a Canadian research group. The company shipped the product ordered and the transaction was easily completed. Later that year, when a few requests for literature about the various products were received from several Canadian and European research organizations, the company responded by sending detailed information about the products and their uses. Contacts established in this manner with several Canadian and European research groups resulted in sales of several thousand dollars.

When the sales figures for 1971 were tabulated, the export sales volume astonished the management, which then conducted an informal investigation of the export potential of the company's products. Results showed that each of several products had unique characteristics and that only one other manufacturer (a Swedish firm) produced similar types of products. In mid-1972 a decision was reached to try to solicit distributors in all foreign markets (except Canada) that have sizable sales potential. It was agreed that Canadian sales would be handled directly from the home office and that no Canadian distributor need be appointed.

As a result of the decision to enter the export business, the company sent inquiries through the mail to several hundred distributors throughout the world (except Canada, of course). From those who responded, a selected few were visited personally by the company staff and a final selection was made. The distributors were selected on the basis of two considerations: (1) due to the technical nature of the products, after-sale service was considered very important, and therefore, only those distributors were selected who had qualified staff to perform this service; (2) it was felt that those distributors who carry complementary lines of products would be most desirable since the sale of several products of the Scientific Instruments Company is closely tied to the sale of other research equipment which is not produced by the firm. Ultraviolet analyzers, fraction collectors, and environmental chambers, for example, generally are used by scientists in conjunction with other research equipment, whose availability can be helpful in the sale of the Scientific Instruments Company's products.

In 1972, the first full year of export business, the company attained an impressive export volume of $53,600, representing 10 percent of corporate sales. Export sales increased to $191,240 in 1974, representing by then 28 percent of corporate sales. In 1976 export sale again increased, this time to $751,740, representing 33 percent of corporate sales. According to the vice president of sales, the increase in export sales has been "beyond the most optimistic expectations of the corporate staff."

The company divides its foreign sales into three major market areas. Europe, Canada, and the rest of the world. Exhibit 34–1 shows export sales by major market areas.

Exhibit 34–1
Sales by major market areas for 1972, 1974, and 1976

	1972		1974		1976	
	Amount	Percent	Amount	Percent	Amount	Percent
Total corporate	$536,000	100	$683,000	100	$2,278,000	100
Total export	53,600	10	191,240	28	751,000	33
Europe	21,440	4	109,240	16	364,480	16
Canada	26,800	5	54,640	8	250,580	11
Rest of world[a]	5,360	1	27,320	4	136,680	6

[a]Excluding United States, Canada, and Europe.

From the figures in Exhibit 34–1, it may be seen that export sales as a percent of total corporate sales have steadily increased from 1972 to 1976. Furthermore, the data show that with respect to export sales Canada lost in relative importance to the European market from 1972 to 1974 but began to gain in relative importance from 1974 to 1976.

The Canadian market

From 1971 to 1973 distribution in Canada was achieved directly from the home office. Promotional literature was sent to a list of research foundations, academic institutions, and corporations. The vice president of sales and his assistant were charged with the responsibility of contacting possible users of the products. Although this proved to be a satisfactory arrangement, these individuals were burdened with a major responsibility for which they did not have sufficient time. In 1974, therefore, an exclusive distributor located in the province of Ontario was selected to handle Canadian sales. Under terms of the agreement, the distributor was to take title to the goods and would be given a price discounted 20 percent from the manufacturer's domestic retail list price. The distributor chosen is a large firm that represents several Canadian and foreign manufacturers of laboratory equipment, such as that used by hospitals, academic institutions, and research foundations.

The distributor has three members on his sales staff who call on research institutions, universities, and corporations. Due to the specialized nature of the products and the somewhat limited number of potential users, the sales calls are made primarily to offer technical assistance to the user, and the sales staff often spend long hours working with researchers in their laboratories. Those on the sales staff are necessarily college graduates with some laboratory experience in biochemical research.

Until 1975, the Scientific Instruments Company sold to the Canadian distributor on the basis of sight drafts. Because experience with the distributor has been entirely satisfactory, the manufacturer now offers him open-book account. The terms offered are 2/10 net 30, FOB factory. Longer payment terms may be offered when requested by the distributor.

Distribution in Europe

Distribution in Europe is achieved through 14 exclusive distributors (merchant middlemen) located in Belgium, Denmark, Germany, France, and Great Britain. The distributors use their own sales force to call on potential customers. Sales in Europe in 1972 were $21,440, representing 4 percent of corporate sales, but by 1974 European sales jumped to $109,280, representing 16 percent of corporate sales. In 1976 Europe continued to represent the largest single market area outside the United States in terms of sales.

Gary Nelson, the corporate treasurer, recently visited several European countries to meet with the distributors there. Nelson was also interested in ascertaining the sales potential of the European market. Although he did not conduct a formal investigation of the potential European market, he was able through consultations with the company's distributors and distributors of competitors' products to estimate informally the market potential and to familiarize himself with the pricing and distribution problems in the European market.

Through his discussions with the distributors, Nelson discovered that European sales can be improved by leasing warehousing space locally to stock fast-moving items and replacement parts from the company's product line. He also was advised that his company was not well-known among European scientists; and therefore, its products do not enjoy the same "good reputation" as the products of a competing Swedish manufacturer.

Distributors in Europe are offered 30 percent trade discount and terms of 2/10 net 30. FAS vessel.

Distribution in foreign markets outside Canada and Europe

The company works with seven exclusive distributors in each of the following countries: Australia, New Zealand, South Africa, Argentina, Chile, Japan, and India. Total sales through these seven distributors in 1972 were $5,360, representing 1 percent of corporate sales; but by 1974 sales through the same distributors increased to $27,320, representing 4 percent of corporate sales; and in 1976 they jumped to $136,680, representing 6 percent of such sales. Although the manufacturer does not maintain regular contact with the seven distributors, products are shipped promptly whenever orders are received. Nelson considered it unfortunate that the company has not maintained active contact with these distributors and suspects that, therefore, the full potential of the markets is not being realized.

The company sells directly to markets that are not covered through distributors and that have a "negligible" sales potential. The manufacturer does not actively solicit orders from such markets but will ship if the buyer makes a "reasonable offer." For standardized items, the manufacturer quotes the United States retail list prices, FOB vessel. For custom-made products, such as an environmental chamber, prices are subject to negotiation and vary depending on the requirements of the buyer.

Promotion for world markets

The total promotional budget of the company is $70,000 annually, and there is no separate promotional budget for foreign markets. Advertisements are placed in scientific journals such as *Scientific American* and *Journal of Chemistry*. Because of the leadership of the United States in scientific research, it is felt that many of these journals are consulted by scientists in foreign countries. According to company policy, no advertising allowances are given to distributors abroad, but promotional literature is offered to them with the understanding that it will be passed on to the user. A mailing list has been compiled with the cooperation of distributors throughout the world, and once a year the promotional literature is mailed to present and potential users on a worldwide basis. The direct mail pieces contain information on the proper use and care of the company's products, as well as announcements of new product developments.

Since the products are technical in nature, have a high unit value, and often are made to the specifications of the purchaser, the promotional emphasis is on personal selling. It is for this reason that distributors have been carefully selected to provide the "high caliber" of personal sales effort needed. The company does not have a sales force of its own to cover foreign markets.

Physical distribution for foreign markets

Air freight is generally used to ship products abroad. Since most distributors abroad carry a limited inventory, delivery time is considered an important selling point. When delivery time is not a critical factor, however, goods may be shipped via ocean freight. Since ocean freight requires handling of the product at the docks, a freight forwarder with offices in New York City is used.

Organization for export marketing

Responsibility for export operations is divided between the vice president of sales and the company treasurer. James Mason, who is the vice president of sales, is charged with specific responsibility for the appointment of overseas distributors and maintenance of contacts with them. He also travels to foreign markets to assist distributors in improving product sales. He usually discusses unusual product features with the distributors and advises them about sales techniques that have proved successful in the United States and in other markets. Frequently Mason accompanies the distributor salespeople on their calls to prospective customers, but the company executive is aware that it is difficult to assess the effectiveness of Mason's foreign visits, except for the general goodwill that he is able to generate for the company.

Gary Nelson, the corporate treasurer, who shares the export responsibility with Mason, was assigned this responsibility because of his strong interest in foreign markets. He states that approximately 50 percent of his time is devoted to export management and the remaining to his duties as the corporate treasurer. Nelson was recently sent to Europe to contact company distributors there. Although division of export duties between Nelson and Mason is not clearly defined, generally Nelson is responsible for the supervision of credit and collections from foreign accounts, informal research of foreign markets, and documentation relative to foreign sales.

At the present time, company discussions are being held as to the proper location of export responsibility, for, in the words of Gary Nelson, "Our export business has grown so fast that we have not yet had the opportunity to adjust to it." Since exports are becoming an increasingly important part of the total operation, it is now considered likely that the company will decide to employ a person with "technical export background" to serve as export manager. If and when this happens, the export manager will probably be part of the sales department and will report to the sales manager. It is believed that appointment of such an export manager would not only help concentrate export functions under one person but would result in more effective participation in international markets.

CASE
ANALYSIS

CASE 34

**Scientific
Instruments
Company**

1. Prepare a persuasive memorandum supporting a proposal to hire an export manager.

_____

_____

_____

_____

_____

_____

_____

_____

_____

_____

_____

_____

_____

_____

_____

_____

_____

_____

_____

_____

_____

2.   What are the main arguments against hiring an export manager?

_____

_____

_____

_____

_____

_____

_____

_____

3.   What qualifications would you require of a prospective export man-
      ager for Scientific Instruments?

_____

_____

_____

_____

_____

_____

_____

_____

_____

_____

_____

4. Write a job description for the position of export manager using the following major headings as your framework.
    a. International Marketing Intelligence and Planning

_____

_____

_____

_____

_____

_____

_____

_____

b. Distribution

_____

_____

_____

_____

_____

_____

_____

_____

_____

c. Promotion

_____

_____

_____

_____

_____

_____

_____

d. Pricing

_____

_____

_____

_____

_____

_____

_____

_____

_____

5. To whom should the export manager report? What other parts of the
    organization should he or she work with on a regular basis?

_____

_____

_____

_____

_____

_____

_____

_____

PART NINE

COMPREHENSIVE CASES

CASE 35

KELLOGG RALLY CEREAL

In early 1978, Mr. A. B. Smith sat in his office in Battle Creek, Michigan, evaluating the nutritional portion of the ready-to-eat cereal market. He was particularly concerned about several trade reports he had seen recently about the success of the Quaker Oats Company's LIFE cereal commercial entitled "Mikey." The commercial was being touted as one of the best remembered commercials on the air.

Mr. Smith was also concerned about the recent trends in the ready-to-eat (RTE) cereal category such as the success of bran-type products and the declining interest in so-called natural cereals. The growth in the nutritional RTE category had been strong. Kellogg's product entries in this category, however, had not shown the same growth as the market leader, LIFE. In addition, LIFE, through the "Mikey" commercial, had strengthened its position as a "nutritional cereal the whole family will like." Kellogg's two nutritional products, Product 19 and Special K, had both been strongly positioned against the adult market.

In the early 1970s, Kellogg had successfully market tested a new product named RALLY that was directly competitive with LIFE. With the growth of the category, the established position of the present Kellogg brands in the nutritional area and the present consumer concern about sugar content in RTE cereals, Mr. Smith was reviewing Kellogg's position in the category before making a recommendation to management for 1979. Launching a new brand of RTE cereal was a major undertaking involving several million dollars. In addition, Mr. Smith was concerned about the potential cannibalization of Kellogg's Special K and Product 19, if another product were introduced.

This case was prepared by Don E. Schultz and Mark Traxler, Northwestern University.

471

Courtesy of Mike Mazzaschi/Stock, Boston

Was the "all-family" appeal communicated for LIFE through the "Mikey" commercial an area in which Kellogg was missing?

RALLY had been market tested in the early 1970s. Was that test still valid? Could the results of that test be used as a basis for a new product introduction in 1979? All of these questions and more were crossing Mr. Smith's mind as he pondered the problem.

The Kellogg Company

Kellogg Company had grown out of the Western Health Reform Institute, a nineteenth-century health clinic in Battle Creek, Michigan, affiliated with the Seventh-Day Adventist movement. Dr. John Harvey Kellogg had become head of the institute in 1876. With his younger brother Will, Kellogg became interested in whole-grain cereal products for patients at the clinic. C. W. Post, who had been a patient at the clinic, had the same idea and had developed and promoted some of the foods served at the clinic into successful products.

By 1906 Will Kellogg began producing cereal products developed at the clinic under the name of the Battle Creek Toasted Corn Flake Company. By 1922, as the company grew and the cereals were widely accepted, the name was changed to Kellogg Company.

Kellogg quickly became the market leader in RTE cereals and presently enjoys an approximate 42% share of business, followed by General Mills with 19%, General Foods Post Division with 16%, and Quaker Oats with 8%. Kellogg markets some 15 different brands of RTE cereal, including such famous names as Rice Krispies, Corn Flakes, Sugar Frosted Flakes, Fruit Loops, and Raisin Bran. Kellogg cereal sales totaled $726 million out of total corporate sales of $1.385 billion in 1976. In addition, Kellogg has expanded into other food categories, primarily through acquisition of such companies as Salada Foods, Mrs. Smith's Pie Company, Fearn International, and others.

The breakfast cereal market

In 1977, the RTE cereal industry continued its upward climb in total pound and dollar sales. RTE cereals are now the fifth fastest growing consumer product category, averaging nearly a 5% annual increase, according to the U.S. Department of Commerce. Sales for the past four years were as follows:

Year	Pounds (in billions)	Percentage change
1974	1.63	—
1975	1.69	+4
1976	1.81	+7
1977	1.85	+2

Retail sales in 1976 amounted to $1.48 billion, which is approximately 1% of all retail food store sales. Per capita consumption of RTE cereal is increasing also. Between 1972 and 1973, consumption of RTE cereals increased from six to eight pounds per person. The Cereal Institute estimates "cold cereal" consumption by age as follows:

Pounds of "cold cereal" consumed by age

Age (years)	Pounds/person/year
1–2	7.2
3–5	9.4
6–8	12.0
9–11	9.8
12–14	9.8
15–19	5.9
20–54	3.6
55 +	5.9

Since 1974, cereal prices have been steadily increasing.

RTE cereal price per pound

Year	RTE average retail price	Percentage change
1974	0.908	—
1975	0.933	+3
1976	0.951	+2
1977	1.022	+7

Consumption of RTE cereals is spread fairly evenly across the country, with nearly 80% of all persons eating them. Target group index (TGI) defines "heavy users" as those consuming six or more individual portions of RTE cereal per week. These "heavy users" comprise nearly 38% of all RTE cereal users. There is a slight variance in RTE cereal "heavy users" geographically. The Mid-Atlantic (110) and East Central (107) areas index the highest, whereas the Southeast (88) and Southwest (84) are the lowest (index average = 100). There is also a slight seasonal sales skew ranging from a high of 110 in July and September to a low of 88 in November (index average = 100).

The cereal category is broken down into seven categories by Selling-Marketing Areas, Inc. (SAMI). These categories and their approximate percentage of the total are as follows:

Category	Share (%)
Children	24
All family	46
Highly fortified	9
Bran	7
Granola	4
Variety pack	3
Other	5
Granola bars	2

TGI separates RTE cereal into three categories: presweetened, natural, and regular. Based on research data, it appears that consumers are even less discriminating, preferring to lump RTE cereals into either presweetened or regular. In spite of this generalization, consumers recognize various types of products available and generally include some five to seven "acceptable brands."

Changes in manufacturer's list prices for RTE cereals are relatively infrequent. The normal retail margin is approximately 18%.

There are few middlemen in the RTE cereal channels. Orders flow from the grocery chain buyer or food broker to the sales force to the factory. The goods are shipped to the grocer's warehouse and from there directly to the retail outlet. RTE cereals are fast-moving products with about one box purchased per family per week. Typical RTE promotion to consumers includes cents-off coupons and self-liquidating premiums. The package is used as a breakfast-time entertainment medium with interesting information or games printed on the back and side panels.

Although there are certain anticipated trade deals for new products, established brands rely more heavily on consumer advertising and promotion than promotional programs.

Because of the large number of brands marketed, there is no one dominant brand. Kellogg Corn Flakes is the largest selling brand with an approximate 7% share, followed by Cheerios with approximately 5.6%. Others range downward with most in the 1.00 to 1.5% share area.

Nutritional RTE cereals

The "nutritional" segment constitutes about 15% of the total RTE market when several all-family entries are added to the SAMI "adult highly fortified" category. The adult highly fortified brands are LIFE,

Product 19, Special K, Buc*Wheats, Golden Grahams, and Total. Other all-family RTEs that appear to be directly competitive are Cheerios, Chex (Rice, Corn, Wheat), Wheaties, Shredded Wheat, and Team. Most of the brands in this segment are long-established with few recent additions. The range in total RTE brand share are from a low of approximately 0.27% for Fortified Oat Flakes to approximately 5.6% for Cheerios. Kellogg's two entries in this category are Special K with 2.2% share and Product 19 with 1.2% share. The Special K share has been declining slightly over the past two years while Product 19 has remained steady.

The growth of the nutritional segment is much faster than the growth rate for the total RTE cereal market, as the following table demonstrates.

Percentage of pound sales increase over previous year

Year	Percentage nutritional increase	Percentage RTE increase
1974	+6	NA
1975	+13	+4
1976	+14	+7
1977	+16	+2

When new cereals are priced, prices of directly competing products are an important consideration. Typical out-of-store (OOS) pricing for brands in the competitive segment are as follows:

Brand	Size (oz)	Price
Buc*Wheats	15	$1.11
Cheerios	10	0.83
LIFE	15	0.93
Product 19	12	1.03
Special K	15	1.21
Total	12	1.05

Note that Product 19 and Total, which are in direct competition, are priced accordingly.

Because of the number of brands offered to the consumer, sales volume requires frequent assessment by grocery chain buyers of which brands to reorder. The decision is based on SAMI and Nielsen data to define the best-selling brands, the grocery's own historical sales data, and in the case of new products, the national advertising and promotional plans. New products are usually given a six-month trial period by most grocery retailers. However, gaining the necessary two-shelf facings to launch the new brand requires several decisions. It is common for the RTE cereal aisle to be set proportionately to the grocer's sales for each brand.

Sales forces in the RTE category are highly trained and motivated. Since cereal is an established category, the sales force is usually a key determinant in a successful new product introduction.

Brands in the high-nutrition segment invested an average of $6.35 million in measured media in 1977 according to Leading National Advertisers (LNA) annual summary. In 1976, investments in the directly competitive market ranged from less than $1.9 million for Buc*Wheats to over $10 million for Cheerios. LIFE expenditures in 1976 were estimated to be approximately $6.4 million compared to the Special K investment of $6.2 million and the Product 19 budget of $2.9 million. With the success of the "Mikey" commercial, LIFE was expected to increase its advertising expenditures in 1978.

As a rule of thumb, advertisers in the high-nutrition and all-family cereals invested 60% of their funds in network television, 33% in spot television, and approximately 7% in print.

The messages of the major competitors are summarized below:

Special K—an adult cereal with high protein and nutritional campaign stressing weight control and fitness. Copy focuses on the "Special K breakfast" of less than 240 calories.

Wheaties—advertising features Bruce Jenner, a current sports celebrity who included Wheaties as part of his winning diet. The brand is known as the "Breakfast of Champions."

Total—campaign stresses vitamin and nutrition content, compared with other leading cereal brands. Good taste is a secondary message to reassure the consumer.

Cheerios—a long-running family-oriented campaign which says, "Get a powerful good feeling with Cheerios."

Product 19—campaign aimed at adults focusing on good nutrition. The copy asks, "Did you forget your vitamins today?"

LIFE—uses "Mikey" (described below) as the product hero in a long-running campaign.

The "Mikey" commercial for LIFE can be summarized as follows: The commercial shows two skeptical children and a younger child,

Mikey, in a kitchen setting. Because they already know that LIFE is supposed to be "good for you"—implying that it could not possibly taste good—they use Mikey as a guinea pig to taste LIFE cereal. Mikey innocently eats it while the other two eagerly watch for his reaction. Mikey smiles. Amid shouts of "He likes it!" and "He's eating it!" the two skeptics conclude that LIFE *must* taste good if Mikey likes it.

LIFE cereal has used trial size sampling to stimulate interest in the product. The packages included three 1-oz servings of LIFE and sold for 10¢ in chain grocery outlets. Sales improved slightly as a result.

The heavy media dollars and promotional efforts described above are aimed at the primary purchasers of high-protein/high-nutrition cereals. They are profiled as women 18 to 49 for products like LIFE, Cheerios, and Wheaties, and slightly older (25–54) for Special K, Product 19, Buc*Wheats, and Total. They live in SMSAs, most have at least a high school education, with an annual household income in excess of $10,000. They are married, with three or more individuals in the household, with children ages 6 to 11 years old, according to TGI.

The product

Kellogg's new product development department describes RALLY as a delicately presweetened high-protein cereal for younger adults and children. The actual appearance is a square puffy pillow shape much like Ralston–Purina's Chex cereals. Since RALLY is a rice-based product, it stays crisper in milk than oat- or wheat-based cereals. RALLY's delicate presweetening translates into 18% sugar by volume as compared to less than 10% for nonsweetened brands. Nutritionally, RALLY has 20% of the U.S. recommended daily allowance (RDA) of protein with milk and is enriched with eight essential vitamins and iron to 25% RDA. Quaker's LIFE is the only other product with such a high protein level and light presweetening with a comparable vitamin and mineral content. RALLY contains 33% of the RDA for vitamins B_1, B_2, niacin, and iron, compared to LIFE's 25%.

In choosing a package size for RALLY, Kellogg looked at the brand's direct competitor, LIFE cereal. LIFE markets two sizes, 15-oz and 20-oz. The 15-oz box retails for 93¢. To compete with LIFE in the same price range, the largest size Kellogg can offer would be a 13-oz box at 97¢ because of a difference in cost of goods. RALLY was tested in a 7-oz box priced at 75¢ in the 1970 market test.

RALLY's test market package design showed the red Kellogg logo, a black sticker stating "HIGH PROTEIN," and the name RALLY in big black letters at the top. The bottom portion showed a bowl full of cereal. In the midsection was a set of pennants waving above the bowl as if it were a stadium.

Consumer test

The 1970 consumer panel results for RALLY among women and children were very encouraging.

	Preferred RALLY (%)	Preferred LIFE (%)	No preference (%)
General appearance	76	14	10
Shape	54	19	27
Taste	62	20	18
Texture "just right"	83	16	—

Based on the consumer test, RALLY's major advantage over LIFE appears to be that "LIFE gets soggy too soon."

RALLY was preferred three to one over LIFE by a consumer panel of children and was rated superior in taste, texture, and sweetness level. Against four leading nutritional brands (LIFE, Total, Product 19, and Special K) women showed a significant preference for RALLY. Consumers also rated RALLY as better than the cereals they were presently using.

Market test

RALLY was market tested in two Eastern cities in the early 1970s. It was positioned as an "all-family nutritional cereal with better taste" directed to children and young adults. RALLY was able to generate and maintain a sales rate equaling a 1% share of the total RTE market pound sales in these tests.

The introductory sell-in used Kellogg's own sales force to acquaint grocery clients with RALLY and offered a $0.75–$1.00 per dozen introductory case allowance to help defray warehousing and stocking expenses. The media plan included network children and prime-time programming and spot children and daytime programming for the 17-week introductory period.

Summary

In reviewing the RALLY test case, Mr. Smith was still undecided about a recommendation to introduce RALLY nationally. On the positive side, consumer response seven years ago was good. RALLY's sugar content would not stir consumer concern as with many presweetened cereals. Every day in the papers consumers read about the importance of good nutrition, and protein was certainly an important part of nutrition. And finally, RALLY seemed to overcome the consumer problem with LIFE, getting soggy in milk too soon.

There were problems to be considered, however, not the least of which was the product name. Should it still be called RALLY? Was Kellogg's target market correct during the test market—young adults and children? As a new product, could RALLY compete with LIFE in gaining both segments of the target? After 17 years, LIFE had only recently acquired a strong children's following with the "Mikey" commercial. Are the test market results still valid for a new product introduction in 1979? What about cannibalization of Kellogg's existing brands?

Finally, before giving his final recommendation to management on whether or not to introduce RALLY, Mr. Smith would have to answer such questions as: What package and pricing changes would be necessary? What improvements in the distribution system would be required? And what sort of advertising strategy and promotion should be used to make RALLY a visible competitor against LIFE and its "Mikey" commercial?

CASE ANALYSIS

CASE 35

Kellogg
RALLY
Cereal

1.   How attractive is the nutritional segment of the RTE cereal market?

_____

_____

_____

_____

_____

_____

_____

2.   Describe the competition in this segment.

_____

_____

_____

_____

_____

_____

_____

_____

_____

_____

_____

_____

_____

_____

3. What are RALLY's features and limitations compared to those of the
    competition?

_____

_____

_____

_____

_____

_____

_____

_____

_____

_____

_____

_____

_____

_____

_____

_____

_____

_____

_____

_____

_____

_____

_____

_____

4.   Assess the target market options available to Kellogg. Recommend a
      target market strategy.

_____

_____

_____

_____

_____

5.   What product changes, if any, would you recommend?

_____

_____

_____

_____

_____

_____

_____

_____

6.   Propose a pricing strategy for RALLY.

_____

_____

_____

_____

_____

_____

_____

_____

_____

_____

7.   Outline a promotion plan.

_____

_____

_____

_____

_____

_____

_____

_____

_____

_____

_____

_____

_____

_____

_____

_____

_____

_____

_____

_____

_____

8.   What recommendations can you suggest to ensure adequate distribu-
     tion?

_____

_____

_____

_____

_____

_____

_____

_____

_____

9.   What do you think Mr. Smith should do now?

_____

_____

_____

_____

_____

_____

_____

_____

_____

_____

_____

_____

_____

_____

_____

_____

_____

_____

_____

_____

CASE 36

PROMINANCE SPEAKER COMPANY

Background

The Prominance Speaker Company was begun in February 1977 by two engineers shortly after their former employer, the Bristol Speaker Company of Nashville, Tennessee, went out of business. The Bristol Speaker Company had been a nationally known supplier of loudspeakers used in radios, home entertainment systems, professional sound systems, and so forth. Speculation regarding reasons for Bristol's failure ranged from too much growth with resulting inefficient bureaucratic management practices to problems between management and the labor union.

The two engineers—Paul and Gerry—decided to establish a new operation so they could own their own business as well as maintain employment. Paul, who is in his late fifties, had been a sales engineer with Bristol and Gerry, who is in his late twenties, was a design engineer. Each man contributed capital to the new company. Some speaker-making machines were purchased from Bristol and others were designed and built by the two partners. A vacant building located about 15 miles outside of Nashville was purchased at a modest cost. This provided space for production, storage, and offices for the new company.

The owners decided to keep the company small in order to minimize their financial requirements as well as to keep overhead as low as possible. They hoped that their small size would maximize their competitiveness (the ability to turn out a reasonably priced speaker) while

This case was prepared by Professor Phillip Niffenegger, Department of Management and Marketing, College of Business and Public Affairs, Murray State University. The author wishes to acknowledge funding and technical assistance provided through a grant from the Teaching and Media Resources Center, Murray State University.

Copyright © 1985 by Houghton Mifflin Company

**Table 36–1
Annual sales of
Prominance Speaker
Company for 1977
to 1982**

Year	Total sales
1977	$ 50,000
1978	150,000
1979	250,000
1980	475,000
1981	550,000
1982*	475,000

*Projected based on orders to
June 30, 1982.

maintaining the flexibility to meet customers' requirements, thus avoiding a repeat of the problems encountered by the Bristol Speaker Company. Prominance experienced encouraging sales growth between 1977 and 1981 (see Table 36–1). Currently, however, a slowdown in consumer spending on home entertainment products together with increased competition from imported speakers is creating problems for the company.

Present situation

Prominance currently employs 13 workers. The partners would like to expand the workforce to 20 in order to fully utilize the existing plant facilities, but current demand does not justify expansion. In fact, because of a seasonable decline in demand for loudspeakers, the current workforce is only working three days each week. The raw speaker industry is fairly cyclical, with peak demand/production occurring in August, September, and October (prior to the Christmas selling season). The slowest period is May through July.

The design of loudspeakers is a combination of technology and art. Thanks to their engineering training and prior experience at Bristol, both Paul and Gerry have become quite skilled at designing speakers from the various standard parts that are desired by their customers. They see their workforce as a group of "skilled assemblers" who are quick and efficient in accurately assembling the 20 or more parts that make up a loudspeaker.

Paul's son Tim, who is in his early twenties, serves as a foreman in the plant as well as assisting Gerry in scheduling the production runs of the various speaker models. Gerry is responsible for all bookkeeping and does most of the quotes to customers. Paul also does some quotes, but his main responsibilities are operations and customer communications. All three members of the management team are willing to help out on the production line when necessary.

Paul and Gerry feel that their company's small size allows them to offer their customers greater flexibility than the larger raw speaker manufacturers in the United States and overseas. For example, Prominance can juggle its production schedules and delivery dates to suit a customer's needs. A large company may be locked into a fixed schedule months in advance. If a customer wishes to speed up or delay shipment, he need only call Paul or Gerry a few days in advance. The Prominance workforce is quite skilled in shifting from the production of one type of speaker unit to a different model. Sometimes this may be done several times during a single eight-hour production period in order to accommodate the various models and order quantities desired by Prominance customers.

As long as it is in stock, Prominance will sell any quantity (from one on up) of its standard model speakers. Special orders, however, must be ordered in at least 1,000-unit quantities. The company offers a wide range of speaker models from inexpensive units to professional quality. The price depends on the parts used. Paul and Gerry feel that their quality is high and that they offer above-average value in their products. To ensure high quality, each speaker is tested before packing and shipment. Occasional samples are taken from the production line to a special sound chamber where they are subjected to extensive tests for power handling and smoothness in frequency response.

The primary competition faced by Prominance consists of about 20 similar firms, most of which are somewhat larger than Prominance. Because of the extremely competitive nature of the business, the number of firms engaged in the manufacture and wholesaling of loudspeakers has dwindled from nearly 50 when Prominance began in 1977 to the present 20. Domestic producers have faced increased competition from imported speakers, primarily from Japan and, in the case of automotive speakers, Taiwan. Total industry sales of loudspeakers are projected to be down in 1982, because of a general economic recession in the United States. U.S. government estimates show little or no growth in the consumer electronics industry during the period between 1980 and 1981.

Major U.S. competitors include Electrovoice, Altec Lansing, JBL, and Eminance. Foreign producers include Audax (France) and Philips (Holland), but these companies represent only a minor portion of total speaker sales. The major competition comes from Japan with Pioneer and JVC Corporation being the most significant. According to Paul and Gerry, the Japanese business philosophy makes these companies extremely strong competitors. It seems that they are willing to sustain a number of years of losses in order to enter a new foreign market. Gerry reports that some Japanese firms will tolerate losses for nine years while they build their market share, as long as they make a profit in the tenth year. U.S. manufacturers, on the other hand, are often under very strong pressure to show a profit at the end of each operating year.

Gerry and Paul feel that the primary competition from the Japanese has been in the smaller-sized speakers, especially tweeters, where the labor to total cost ratio is highest. Prominance would like to concentrate its sales on the larger-sized speakers, which sell for a higher average price. Consequently, the Japanese competition has not yet made significant inroads into Prominance's sales. The prospect of increased future competition from the Japanese, however, is worrisome. One Japanese company in particular, Pioneer, has been very aggressive in the U.S. market, offering a full range of speakers. The company's liberal credit policies often allow customers to pay for orders up to three months or more after delivery. Meanwhile Prominance, with its limited financial resources and need for adequate cash flow, must receive payment within 30 days of shipment. This definitely gives Pioneer a competitive edge.

Product data

Prominance currently offers a fairly extensive line of standard model speakers. The initial 1978 catalog listed 22 standard models. To meet the requirements of individual customers, Prominance has since developed 15 other models and now offers these as additional standard models. Seven of the new models are in the automotive product line (6 in. × 9 in.), and another five consist of various sizes of speakers that have cones made out of a newly developed polypropylene (plastic) material. Figure 36–1 illustrates some models from the Prominance Speaker line. The largest selling sizes are the 10-in. and 12-in. diameter speakers (see Table 36–2).

The manufacturing procedure consists mainly of assembling the various component parts into the final loudspeaker (see Figure 36–2). A typical loudspeaker consists of approximately 20 different parts and assemblies that must fit together in fairly close tolerances. Prominance orders the cones, surrounds, spiders, baskets, and magnetic parts from outside suppliers, usually in lots of 1,000 pieces or more. These same suppliers used by Prominance provide parts for everyone in the industry. Prominance, however, does wind its own coils. This gives the company tighter control over this essential part.

As is common practice in the industry, Prominance will create a

Figure 36–1
Some typical models in the product line: (*from left to right*) **a 15-in. guitar speaker, two tweeters, and a midrange unit, a 10-in. polypropylene coned woofer, and a 6 by 9-in. automotive speaker**

Courtesy of Mark Underwood, FACULTY RESOURCE CENTER, Murray State University

Table 36–2
Breakdown of
Prominance Speaker
Company sales by size

Speaker size	Percentage of total sales
4½ in. and less	1
6 in.	2
8 in.	5
10 in.	41
12 in.	41
15 in.	5
6 by 9 in. (automotive)	5
	100

Figure 36–2
Component parts of a typical raw loudspeaker

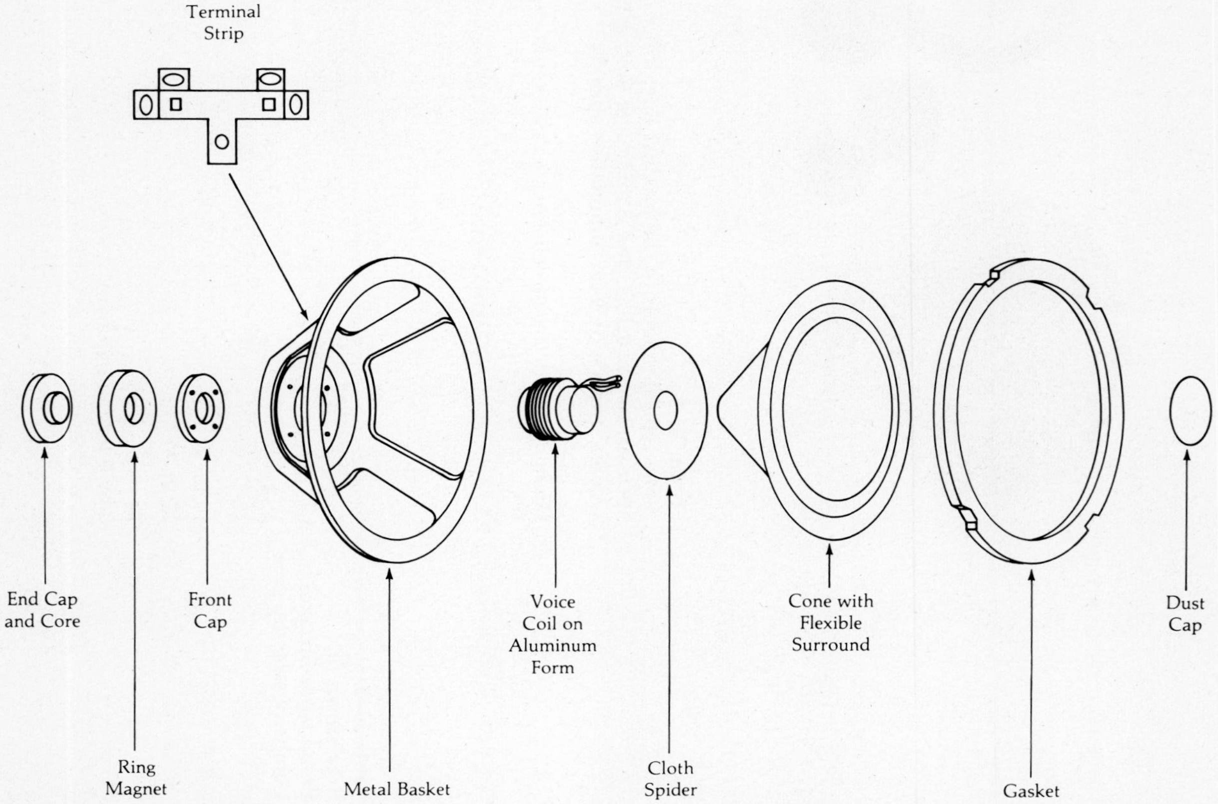

Dust Cap

Gasket

Cone with Flexible Surround

Cloth Spider

Voice Coil on Aluminum Form

Metal Basket

Terminal Strip

Front Cap

Ring Magnet

End Cap and Core

Table 36–3
Pricing structure for a
typical 10-in.
Prominance speaker

Component	Pricing (dollars)	Percentage of selling price
Parts*	$6.00	63
Labor	1.75	18
Factory overhead	.75	9
Gross margin	1.00	10
Selling price to OEM	$9.50	100

*Parts costs are reduced for quantities of over 10,000 units.

speaker to order for an individual customer. The specifications for these "made to spec" speakers may be in the form of a frequency-response curve, a written spec sheet, or, occasionally, a competitive model that Prominance is asked to duplicate.

Pricing

Pricing is basically done on a cost plus 10 percent basis. Pricing calculations for a typical 10-in. speaker are shown in Table 36–3. Quantity discounts are available, as is standard in the industry. In the case of custom-designed units, the customer will send Prominance the desired specifications and request a quote.

When the company was originally founded payment terms were cash in advance with a $100 minimum order requirement. Today the terms are 2/10, net 30 to proven customers. New customers are sent their orders COD. In both cases, the customer pays the freight.

Market analysis/ distribution

The owners of Prominance Speaker Company feel that their customers can be broken down into five basic groups:

1. Speaker manufacturers for home entertainment systems
2. Speaker manufacturers for musical instruments
3. Speaker wholesalers
4. Professional sound specialists
5. Automotive installers and retailers

The largest customer segment consists of both large and small firms that manufacture speakers for home entertainment systems. This group accounts for about 75 percent of Prominance sales. These companies buy from Prominance as well as other domestic and foreign producers of raw speakers. They either make or buy the wooden

**Figure 36–3
Parts in a typical
finished home speaker
system**

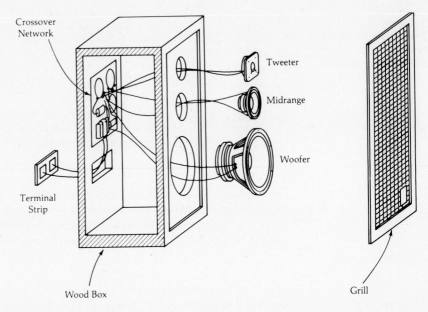

Crossover
Network

Tweeter

Midrange

Woofer

Terminal
Strip

Wood Box

Grill

enclosure box and then install the speakers and other components into a finished unit, to which they add their brand name. A typical enclosure might consist of two speakers (a woofer and a tweeter) or three speakers (woofer, midrange, and tweeter). The speakers are wired together through an electrical crossover network, which divides the audio signal and routes it to the proper speaker. Then they are mounted inside the wooden enclosure. Insulation to deaden the internal vibration is added to the inside of the cabinet. A terminal strip at the rear provides for connections to the rest of the household audio system. Application of a front grill cloth finishes the assembly (see Figure 36–3). Prices at retail for these finished speaker enclosures range from $75 to $500 per unit, depending on their size and quality.

Typically, manufacturers in this market segment approach several raw speaker manufacturers such as Prominance and ask for bids. Usually, price is the most important purchase criterion. In some cases the manufacturer will change suppliers over a difference in price of only one or two cents per unit. As a result of decreased consumer spending on home entertainment products (considered a luxury by many), this group of OEMs (original equipment manufacturers) is experiencing a rather prolonged sales slump.

The second market segment for Prominance products is manufacturers who install speakers in enclosures designed specifically for musical instruments such as electric guitars and organs. Prominance estimates that about 5 percent of its total business comes from this group. Within the instrument group are two subgroups—a quality-conscious (connoisseur) group and a value-oriented medium to lower price group. For the first group, speaker cost is a secondary consideration. The efficiency, power handling, and cosmetic appearance of the raw loudspeakers as well as the reputation of the manufacturer are more important factors. The enclosures selected and used by big-name rock groups have occasionally taken on an almost legendary product image. Unfortunately, the Prominance product is not well enough known for the company to have made much penetration into this market segment.

With the second instrument subgroup, which places a premium on good performance at a reasonable cost, Prominance has enjoyed fair sales success. Individual musicians in this group sometimes even make their own speaker enclosures in order to save costs, and then install the loudspeakers. Word of mouth has spread the good value reputation of Prominance among this group in the surrounding region. National recognition, however, is still limited. The owners feel that these two instrument groups may offer Prominance the greatest potential for future sales expansion. They are unsure, however, of how to approach these market segments.

The speaker wholesaler group consists of companies that resell the products together with general electronic components mainly through mail-order catalogs. Their customers include home hobbyists, musicians, and anyone who needs a replacement speaker. Although the majority of sales are made through the mail, some wholesalers also operate small stores where the speakers are sold at retail. These wholesalers are most concerned with price and the general reputation of the manufacturer. Sometimes a manufacturer's willingness to accept small order quantities is also a selling point to this group. Prominance estimates that about 13 percent of its business comes from the wholesaler group.

Professional sound specialists represent only a minor share (2 percent) of current sales for Prominance. This group is composed of individuals and small companies who install sound systems in auditoriums and entertainment establishments such as skating rinks and disco dance clubs. Often the owners of such establishments will perform their own installation. Dependability and good sound at a reasonable price are the most important criteria for these customers. Prominance owners feel this segment may also represent an excellent new market for their products. Because of the large number of establishments in existence and the rapid turnover of ownership of such establishments, Prominance is uncertain how best to reach this group of potential buyers.

The last market segment identified by Prominance consists of automotive installers and retailers. Automotive installers install total sound systems in cars, vans, and trucks. Retailers merely resell various sound components to consumers. For this group, performance and speaker appearance are more important than price. Prominance estimates that about 5 percent of its business comes from this segment. Competition from imported speakers made in Japan, Hong Kong, and Taiwan is becoming fairly severe in this particular market segment. The dazzling array of sophisticated appearing and sounding raw speaker units offered by overseas producers is very appealing to this group of buyers.

Personal selling and promotion

Most of the larger companies in the industry either employ their own sales forces or use the services of sales representatives who sell for a commission and carry a line of noncompeting audio products. Prominance does not currently employ either sales representatives or its own sales force. Several years ago the company used a sales representative for a trial period of a few months. Paul and Gerry were not satisfied with the representative's performance and discontinued his services. They did not feel that he secured many additional orders for the company, and some of the orders that he did accept were from customers who were slow in paying their bills. The sales representative suggested that Prominance should add a wider variety of speakers to the existing line. This would have led to increased inventory costs for the company.

Currently, new sales leads often come as the result of contacts made by Paul and Gerry when they attend annual industry trade shows. Sometimes the partners will telephone a manufacturer whom they know is using a competitive speaker and ask for permission to submit a bid for a portion of the business. Current sales come mainly from repeat orders and word of mouth advertising. Six or seven large accounts and 15 to 20 smaller occasional buyers provide the bulk of sales for the company. Occasionally a musician, audio sound specialist, or even a hobbiest will stop by the Prominance plant, and the owners will sell one or more units directly to him. However, no effort has been made to encourage this "drop-in" business.

The only previous advertising by Prominance consisted of a four-page direct mail catalog listing the original 22 standard models. The catalog was compiled by Paul and Gerry in 1978 as a means to solicit initial orders from former Bristol customers. Since then, specification sheets for new speaker models have been mailed to potential customers as a means of supplementing the catalog. Because the original catalog contains an outdated price list, current prices are given out over the phone. Two revised price sheets have also been mailed to customers. No other advertising or sales promotion activities have been attempted by the company. The owners are not aware of any trade journals in the industry in which they could advertise their products. Prominance does, however, have free listings in two industry directories—*The Thomas Register* and *The Electronic Industry Telephone Directory.*

Finances

The owners have been successful in attaining their goal of a 20 to 25 percent return on investment. They utilize an outside accounting firm to maintain their books. As the annual sales summary in Table 36–1 shows, Prominance experienced rapid sales growth from its inception through 1981. At that time the effect of the slowdown in consumer spending rippled through the industry causing the current sales slowdown for Prominance. Although the future growth rate may be somewhat slower than in the past, Paul and Gerry are optimistic that the market will eventually regain its former strength. The partners would like to attain total sales volume of $1.5 million to $2 million per year. At this level they could increase their workforce to 20 and fully utilize the existing plant capacity in order to produce a maximum return on investment.

Conclusion

Although business has been acceptable, the owners of Prominance would like to accomplish several management objectives that they feel would ensure the company's survival as a small independent enterprise in the years to come. First, they would like to use plant and labor resources more efficiently by evening out the present seasonal sales fluctuations. Paul and Gerry are unsure of the best method to accomplish this goal but are considering several possibilities. One idea is to enter the consumer market through a subsidiary company. Several other small raw speaker manufacturers have entered this market and are now manufacturing finished speaker enclosures for sale through retailers. Finished wood boxes are available, in quantities of 1,000, for as little as $10 each. The owners feel that this would provide an additional sales outlet, speed production more evenly throughout the year, and provide additional profit potential. A problem with selling the finished speakers under the Prominance name would be that current enclosure manufacturers might see Prominance as a competitor and stop ordering from the company.

A second alternative would be to use the same highly skilled assembly techniques and labor force currently used in loudspeaker manufacture to develop an additional product line. Paul and Gerry have yet to come up with such a product. A third more long-range possibility would be to export selected Prominance models to overseas markets. The owners feel that Europe represents a high potential market for the company. Paul and Gerry believe that imported speakers often enjoy an advantage over domestic speakers. Simply because they are imported gives the products a "prestige" image. Finally, the owners are concerned about the growing import threat, particularly from speakers made in Japan and Taiwan. They feel that Prominance needs a long-range strategy to cope with the import threat but they are currently uncertain about what direction to take.

CASE ANALYSIS

CASE 36

Prominance Speaker Company

1. Should Prominance concentrate its marketing effort on one or more segments of the market? Which segment(s) and why?

_____

_____

_____

_____

_____

_____

_____

_____

_____

_____

_____

_____

_____

_____

_____

_____

_____

_____

_____

_____

_____

2. Develop a promotional program based on your response to Question 1. Assume a first-year budget of $10,000.

_____

_____

_____

_____

_____

_____

_____

_____

_____

_____

_____

_____

_____

_____

_____

_____

_____

_____

_____

_____

_____

_____

_____

3. How should Prominance cope with the import threat?

_____

_____

_____

_____

_____

_____

_____

_____

4. Should Prominance attempt to export its speakers at this time? Why or why not?

_____

_____

_____

_____

_____

_____

5. What, if any, changes do you recommend in the following areas and why?

a. Product policy or strategy: _____

_____

_____

_____

_____

_____

b. Pricing policy or strategy: _____

_____

_____

_____

_____

_____

c. Distribution policy or strategy: _____

_____

_____

_____

_____

_____

6. Should Prominance enter the retail (finished enclosure) market? Why or why not?

_____

_____

_____

_____

_____

_____

_____

_____

_____

_____

_____

_____

_____

_____

_____

_____

_____

_____

_____

_____

_____

_____

_____

_____

_____

7. Identify and assess the prospects for additional products that Prominance might consider manufacturing using their present workforce.

_____

_____

_____

_____

_____

_____

_____

_____

_____

_____

_____

CASE 37

THE MILWAUKEE BLOOD CENTER

The Milwaukee Blood Center (MBC) was established in 1946 by the Junior League to meet the emerging needs for blood in the Milwaukee area. The MBC has experienced substantial growth and is now a major regional blood center. The Milwaukee Blood Center is a member of two blood banking trade associations—American Association of Blood Banks and Council of Community Blood Centers. MBC is affiliated with the Medical College of Wisconsin. For a discussion of the current state of blood donation in the U.S., see the Appendix.

In 1976, the Milwaukee Blood Center moved to a new location at the western edge of the downtown area and adjacent to Marquette University. Within several blocks of their location there are five hospitals which MBC serves. The first floor of the building was renovated for use in blood collection. Free parking is provided behind the building for donors. The MBC also makes extensive use of the five mobile units for drawing blood at business and organization sites. Furthermore, three satellite stations are utilized in suburban and neighboring city locations.

Current situation

In fiscal 1979, volunteer donors in Southeastern Wisconsin gave 91,500 units of blood to support patients' needs in the 33 hospitals that the Milwaukee Blood Center served. As Exhibit 37–1 shows,

This case was prepared by Professor Patrick E. Murphy, Marquette University, and Ron Franzmeier, Zigman-Joseph-Skeen, as a basis for class discussion rather than to illustrate either effective or ineffective handling of an administrative situation. Copyright © 1980 by Marquette University.

Exhibit 37–1
Number of volunteer blood donations, Milwaukee Blood Center, 1970–1979

During fiscal year 1979, 60,000 donors provided the 91,500 units of blood collected in the region. As demand continues to increase, the Blood Center must recruit more donors to avoid having to ask for more donations each year from the same people.

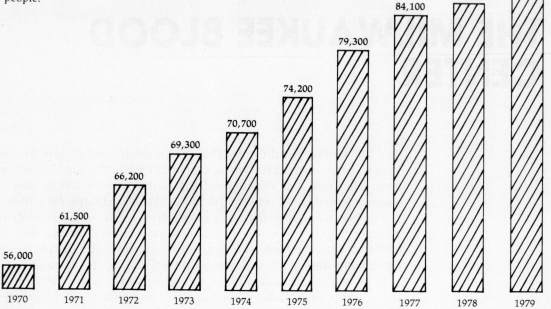

donations have increased steadily during the decade of the seventies and the 1979 total was 5,500 over the previous year.

However, local demand for blood *exceeded* local donations by 3,100 units which had to be obtained from other blood centers. The major objective of donor recruitment programs is to make this region self-sufficient.

Eighty percent of the blood collected in the region was given by members of 900 donor clubs sponsored by business, schools, churches and other civic, labor and community groups in Southeastern Wisconsin. The other 20% was drawn from individuals at MBC's central location in Milwaukee and part-time satellite stations located within the six-county area that the center serves.

These donors made it possible for the Milwaukee Blood Center to keep pace with the increasing demand for blood products in the region. Patients in the 33 hospitals served by the center required 5,400 more units of whole blood and packed red blood cells than were needed in 1978. The MBC also experienced a dramatic increase in the need for blood components.

The increased need for blood and blood components is related in part to the growing number of open heart, hip replacement and kidney transplant operations being performed. Regular transfusions of blood platelets are demanded by a growing number of patients undergoing chemotherapy for cancer.

A marketing approach

Administrators at MBC felt that the amount of blood collected from donor clubs was reaching a steady-state position. In fact, a few mobile drives had to be cancelled because of layoffs or slowdowns at local industries. Also, the demographic projections for the Southeastern Wisconsin area indicate that the area will not grow in population. Therefore, the administration felt that a program aimed at the individual donor was needed. To facilitate this process the Milwaukee Blood Center sought the services of a local marketing consulting firm.

With the assistance of the consultant, the administrators were able to relate the marketing mix elements to the process of blood donation. The product/service that they are offering is the unique satisfaction which the donor receives from the act of contributing a pint of his/her blood. This satisfaction cannot be derived from writing a check or volunteering time. The price not only represents real cost of physical discomfort of the donor, inconvenience and time lost that could be spent in other ways, but also the psychological cost of fear of the total experience. The place or distribution element is directly related to the center's location or availability of mobile units or satellite stations. Finally, promotion entails the personal selling effort engaged in by the donor recruiters and the mass media efforts. The Milwaukee Blood Center employs four full-time donor recruiters who call on industry and other donor clubs.

The mass media promotion used by the Milwaukee Blood Center took the form of Public Service Announcements. These announcements are free, but often aired late at night or at times when few people are watching or listening. Also, publicity is utilized by the Blood Center when they are experiencing a large shortage of donations. The problem with this type of promotion is that the Blood Center has no real control over the frequency with which their message reaches the target audience. Therefore, the Blood Center has relied heavily on other means of reaching prospective donors such as printed brochures, direct mail materials and telephone solicitation.

Marketing research

The consultant and administration agreed that before a marketing program could be developed for the MBC, marketing research was necessary. Specifically, they needed to know more about their market area's donation patterns and certain attitudes of thought leaders and donors toward the Blood Center.

One part of the marketing research encompassed a study of the present geographic market area. It includes six counties which comprise the Southeastern region of Wisconsin. These counties are: Milwaukee, Waukesha, Ozaukee, Washington, Racine and Kenosha. Exhibit 37–2 shows the population and donation profile of this area for fiscal 1979. One important figure in this table is the percentage of population which actually donates. It is only 3% for the Blood Center area while the national figure is between 5 and 6%. In the county-by-county breakdown, Racine and Kenosha residents are not donating at a percentage equal to their population proportion.

A second phase of the initial marketing research effort entailed a "thought leader" study. Approximately ten governmental and mass media leaders in Racine, Kenosha and Waukesha were interviewed regarding their perception of attitudes that people in their area had toward the Blood Center. Thought leaders in Milwaukee were not surveyed because the Blood Center administrators had frequent contact with them. One consistent finding was that they felt there was some reluctance of people in these cities to donate to the "Milwaukee" Blood Center. Most citizens did not realize that the Blood Center served the entire Southeastern Wisconsin region.

Research was also conducted with first-time donors. One hundred first-time donors were surveyed via telephone. They were prompted to donate by the 1979 Winter Blood Telethon which was carried by a local television station. These donors were asked why they had never donated before. Their responses are shown in Exhibit 37–3. The most frequently mentioned reason was—no one ever asked me to donate. Some of the more obvious reasons like "too busy" and "afraid to give" were designated by a much smaller percentage of donors.

Another survey was conducted at the downtown Milwaukee drawing station. Donors were asked to fill out a short questionnaire while they were being served refreshments after donating. Four hundred and sixty-two donors responded over a two-week time period. One of

Exhibit 37–2
Market—donor statistics

Region's population	1,710,000
Donors	55,000 (3.2%)
Donations needed	102,000 (6%)

Counties served by Milwaukee Blood Center
Population and donation profile

Counties	Population	% of MBC region population	Units drawn in county	% of total units drawn in MBC region
Milwaukee	982,000	57.4	56,000	61
Waukesha	276,000	16.1	15,800	17
Ozaukee	68,000	4.0	4,200	5
Washington	80,000	4.7	4,000	4
Racine	178,000	10.4	6,600	7
Kenosha	126,000	7.4	4,000	4
Other	—	—	1,400	2
Approximate region totals	1,710,000	100%	92,000	100%

the major findings of this survey was that nearly one-third of the respondents (32.4%) indicated that they would be likely to donate more often if there was a drawing station located more conveniently to their home.

Conclusion

When the consultant presented these research findings to the administration of MBC, they indicated that the consultant should develop a comprehensive marketing strategy (plan) based on these results. The administrators urged the consultants to be innovative and not to be concerned about organizational resistance to change. The only limiting factors that the administration placed on the marketing plan was that they could not afford paid television advertising. Major mass media resources for the Milwaukee area are shown in Exhibit 37–4. The Milwaukee Blood Center's Board of Directors is scheduled to meet in three weeks and the administrator wants to present the comprehensive marketing program to them at that time.

Exhibit 37–3
Reasons why people have not donated blood before

		Was a reason	Was not a reason	No answer/ don't know
a.	You thought you had a medical condition which kept you from giving.	16%	83%	1%
b.	You thought giving blood was painful.	29%	70%	1%
c.	You never knew your blood was needed.	30%	70%	0
d.	You were afraid of giving blood.	30%	70%	0
e.	You didn't know where to go to give blood.	31%	69%	0
f.	The location of the MBC was inconvenient.	22%	77%	1%
g.	No one ever asked you to donate before.	62%	37%	1%
h.	You were too busy to give blood.	37%	61%	2%

Appendix: Current status of blood donation in the United States

The blood collection system in America is going through some major changes, which may not be fully understood by the public.

Credits for donating

There used to be a national system of credits for blood donors (hence the concept of blood "banking"). If you gave a pint of blood, a credit was given to you, your family or whomever you designated to be the recipient of that credit. If you or your family needed a blood transfusion, you could draw on those credits and did not have to worry about replacing the blood. Those who had no credits for previous donations were assessed a penalty charge, called a non-replacement fee, unless they were able to find someone who would donate to replace the blood used.

Exhibit 37–4
Major mass media resources in Milwaukee area

Newspaper

	Name	Circulation	Frequency	Cost ($ per col. in.)
Milwaukee	*Journal*	329,000	Daily	13.58
	Sentinel	165,205	Daily	7.84
	Post	262,000	Weekly (suburban)	3.92
Kenosha	*Kenosha News*	31,620	Daily	4.84
	Kenosha Labor Press	21,500	Weekly	3.92
Racine	*Labor News*	16,000	Weekly	3.05
	Journal Times	40,000	Daily	4.75
Waukesha	*Freeman*	26,000	Daily	3.86

Radio

	Name	Format	Average Cost ($ per :30 spot)
Milwaukee	WTMJ	Mid Road	67.50
	WOKY	AM Rock	35.00
	WZUU	FM Rock	27.00
	WBCS	Country/West	22.00
Kenosha	WLIP	Mid Road	7.75
	WJZQ	FM Rock	6.35
Racine	WRJN	Mid Road	7.50 per spot
	WRKR	AM Rock	11.00 per spot
	WWEG	Country/West	10.00 per spot

This system of credits proved very costly to maintain and involved the transfer of paper credits rather than blood. It also seemed to place an unfair burden on the elderly and others who did not have friends or family members able to replace the blood used. For these reasons, nearly 80% of the blood centers in the country have dropped the system of credits and no longer charge a non-replacement fee. Blood is simply made available to all who need it and the only charge made is for the costs of collecting and processing it (and this is covered by most insurance programs).

Paid donors

It was very common practice at one time for donors to be paid for the blood they gave. Research has determined that the incidence of infectious hepatitis in blood from donors who have been paid is far greater than that in blood which comes from volunteer donors. As a result, most communities no longer pay donors or offer them any reward of monetary value.

Regional blood centers

At one time, many small communities had their own blood program—usually organized by the local hospital and industry leaders. Physicians have conducted research into how to use blood efficiently, and about how to separate it into various components. Today, a patient is rarely given whole blood. They receive only those components which are required.

Testing, processing and separating blood into its components required specialized staff and equipment which would be very costly to duplicate in every community. As a result, the country's blood collection system is being regionalized. Blood is being collected in small communities, but it is transported to regional blood centers where it is processed. The blood is stored at these centers, with the quantities and types of blood needed being returned to the small towns so that their supply is always adequate.

As a result of this regulation, many of the small town blood programs are now a part of larger regional programs. They are subject to new regulations and have suffered a loss of local identity.

Fewer restrictions on donors

Research has greatly improved our understanding of how disease is and is not transmitted through blood transfusions. As a result, many people who once were rejected as blood donors because of some childhood disease can now donate. At one time, the average rejection rate was 12% (i.e. 12% of the people who came in to donate were rejected as donors on the basis of their medical history). Today, only 5% of those who come in are turned away because of past illnesses.

Donors between the ages of 17 and 65 who are in good health are eligible to donate. In special circumstances individuals older or younger than those ages may be donors. A person may donate once every ten weeks (5 times per year). However, individuals who do donate in the U.S. usually do so less than once a year.

CASE ANALYSIS

CASE 37

The
Milwaukee
Blood
Center

1. What is the major problem confronting the Milwaukee Blood Center?

_____

_____

_____

_____

_____

_____

2. How has MBC segmented the market? What are promising market segments in this area?

_____

_____

_____

_____

_____

_____

_____

_____

_____

_____

_____

_____

_____

_____

3. How can the product that MBC offers be altered to better meet the
    needs of the marketplace?

_____

_____

_____

_____

_____

_____

_____

_____

4. What pricing strategies can be utilized to attract donors?

_____

_____

_____

_____

_____

_____

_____

_____

_____

5.   How might the channel of distribution be restructured to meet organizational and community goals?

_____

_____

_____

_____

_____

_____

_____

_____

_____

_____

6.   What promotional (communication) strategies might be utilized to reach current and potential donors?

_____

_____

_____

_____

_____

_____

_____

_____

_____

_____

_____

_____

_____

_____